SEX POSITIVES?

The Cultural Politics of Dissident Sexualities

GENDERS

GENDERS 25

SEX POSITIVES?

The Cultural Politics of Dissident Sexualities

Edited by Thomas Foster, Carol Siegel, and Ellen E. Berry

NEW YORK UNIVERSITY PRESS
NEW YORK AND LONDON

NEW YORK UNIVERSITY PRESS
New York and London

ISBN 0-8147-2664-X (clothbound)
ISBN 0-8147-2663-1 (paperback)

New York University Press books are printed on acid-free paper,
and their binding materials are chosen for strength and durability.

Manufactured in the United States of America

10 9 8 7 6 5 4 3 2 1

Contents

PART THREE
Dissident Sexualities: Historical Perspectives

Foreword

The essays in this volume attempt to redefine the terms of the feminist pornography debates, especially the opposition between procensorship factions and the prosex radicals or "sex positives." The legacy of these debates continues to define one of the most fundamental divisions among analysts of gender and sexuality, and these divisions often seem to lie behind the different approaches that feminist inquiry, gender studies, and queer theory take to their overlapping fields of interest.

What is the relationship between pornography debates and postmodern theories of reading and performativity? What happens to these debates when they are placed in the context of colonial or U.S. racial histories? What is the history behind today's sexual radicalism? How radical is it? On the other hand, what are the consequences of ignoring sexuality and pleasure, including their positive values, as issues for cultural criticism? These are some of the questions addressed by these essays.

The first section of this volume focuses on the recent "sex wars" in U.S. feminism and especially within lesbian culture. These essays by Nicola Pitchford, Naomi Morgenstern, and Victoria L. Smith all pose the question of what forms a feminist oppositional politics can take. The essays in the second section, by Elissa J. Rashkin, Gaurav Desai, and James Smalls, broaden the terms of the sex wars debates to include sexualized racial and colonial representations, from Chicana, African, and African American perspectives. The final section includes essays by Sander L. Gilman and Laura Frost; these authors explore a variety of historical contexts for understanding contemporary forms of sexual representation and the repression of such representations. They thereby situate the claims of both censorship proponents and sexual radicals in new ways.

PART ONE

Sex Wars: Pornography, Postmodernism, and Problems of Feminist Opposition

Reading Feminism's Pornography Conflict: Implications for Postmodernist Reading Strategies

Nicola Pitchford

BUTLER V. HER MAJESTY THE QUEEN

A Canadian Supreme Court ruling in early 1992, which paved the way for increased restrictions on pornographic and/or obscene expression, offers an instructive illustration of the stakes of recent feminist debates about the explicit representation of sexual acts. That ruling, known as the Butler case[1] (after the hapless adult-video dealer in question), has led to both domestic prosecutions and a significant increase in seizures by Canadian Customs officials of materials entering the country, primarily from the United States. The seizure of texts ranging from *Hothead Paisan* comics to works by Marguerite Duras, Oscar Wilde, Dorothy Allison, David Leavitt, Audre Lorde, Kathy Acker, *anti*porn activist Andrea Dworkin, and bell hooks—the last not for sexual obscenity but for alleged "hate speech," also open to restriction according to Customs interpretation of the Butler ruling—has provoked much alarm on this side of the border also, not only among civil libertarians but among guardians of culture such as the *New York Times*, which not long ago ran the headline "Canada's Morals Police: Serious Books at Risk?"[2]

The temporary confiscation of Dworkin's books underlines the ironies of feminist antipornography efforts better than perhaps any incident since the strange alliances of the 1986 Meese Commission on Pornography. For the Butler ruling had been, in part, based on the definition of pornography formulated by Dworkin and legal scholar Catharine MacKinnon,

3

which has shaped recent efforts at antipornography legislation not only in the United States but in Canada and in Britain.[3] MacKinnon, working with the Canadian Women's Legal Education and Action Fund (LEAF), drew on the Canadian Constitution's guarantee of equal gender rights in arguing that pornography, as "sexually explicit material that involves violence or degradation," violates women's rights by creating an environment hostile to them.[4]

The confiscations and prosecutions following the Butler case contribute a very practical angle on a number of theoretical issues surrounding pornography and censorship debates. Among these issues: the blurred line between fictional representations and real acts of hatred or discrimination; the difference between pornographic trash and "serious books"; and the apparent divergence between the interests of "women" and the interests of gays, lesbians, and people of color. This last problem is evinced by the fact that the majority of books listed in reviews of the recent seizures— works by Wilde, Allison, Leavitt, Lorde, and hooks, and Diane DiMassa's *Hothead Paisan*—primarily address gays, lesbians, and/or people of color. Owners of gay and lesbian bookstores allege that they are being "singled out" for harassment, prosecution, and fines.[5] Customs officials acknowledge this but attribute it not to direct prejudice but to the practical fact that the generally small size of shipments from gay and lesbian publishers makes them easier to examine in detail.[6]

I have begun this discussion of the antipornography movement and feminist postmodernism by reviewing the repercussions of the Butler case because all the above issues are also, I propose, questions central to postmodernism. The Butler case, and feminist debates about pornography, frame these problems from a slightly different perspective from many nonfeminist theorists of postmodernism, but if I rephrase them as (1) the textualization of reality; (2) the absorption of high culture by the terms of mass/consumer culture; and (3) the proliferation of otherness, they will start to sound very familiar to readers of postmodernist theory.

In fact, the seizure of writings by Kathy Acker under the Butler precedent, although an unhappy moment, is fortuitous for my argument for the need to articulate a feminist-postmodernist theory of how readers use and remake texts—if not for those Canadians who would have liked to read or sell her work. This incident provides a concrete illustration of the political implications of interpretation—of reading a text as pornographic versus, say, postmodernist. I have chosen to illustrate this article's model of feminist-postmodernist reading by drawing on novels by Acker and by

British writer Angela Carter (who has been memorably dubbed "the high priestess of post-graduate porn"),[7] in part because both have, on occasion, been labeled pornographers. While I believe this label is misleading—for it conflates the discrete stylistic conventions and contexts of reception of the popular genre (or range of subgenres) properly termed pornography with those of Acker's and Carter's difficult and not-exactly bestselling novels, which enjoy the legitimacy of major publishers[8]—it says a great deal about the anxieties shared by antipornography feminists and those critics who deny the possibility of progressive uses of postmodernist fiction. I also find this labelling representative of a disturbing and debilitating misunderstanding within feminism, on the part of critics of pornography, of the potential of feminist postmodernism to offer solutions to such anxieties over the status of feminist organizing in the contemporary context.

The debates among feminists over pornography that sprung up in the late 1970s, escalated in the 1980s, and continue into the 1990s, disagreements so fierce they have come to be called the "sex wars,"[9] *are* debates about postmodernism. Their subtext is the question of how feminists ought to respond to this slippery phenomenon. While Craig Owens and others have pointed out the potentially productive intersection of feminist critiques of patriarchal representation and postmodernist theories of the crisis of representation, pornography has become the site at which feminism and postmodernism diverge.[10] Antipornography feminism seeks to reject the existing regime of sexual representation entirely, seeing it as inherently masculine and therefore inimical to women's interests; postmodernism, on the other hand—at least, as I propose to outline it—maintains that cultural and political contestation is inextricably bound up with existing representations. I want to argue that antipornography feminism is on the losing side of this divergence, fundamentally misrecognizing the fact that contemporary feminism has no choice but to function in postmodern conditions.

In taking this position, I subscribe to Fredric Jameson's view of postmodernism as not merely one possible cultural option among others currently available but rather the dominant mode best corresponding to a whole contemporary economic, political, and social formation—in short, postmodernity.[11] However, whereas Jameson sees postmodernism as simply the direct *reflection* of postmodernity, my argument proposes that postmodernist forms of thought and action can also actively intervene in—or *reread*—this formation from local and specific viewpoints.

In this context, any feminist interventions in postmodernity are inevitably staged within an active and fluid circulation of representations and identities. For all their materiality, positions of "difference" (and differences of positioning) are increasingly realized within and through representation. By rejecting the existing regime of representation, antipornography feminism stands to lose an ability to conceive of the multiple differences within each gender: the differences of race, class, and sexual practice among women, but also similarly varied relations to power among men. Not only does the concept of sexual pleasure become severely constricted if one eliminates all sexual practices found in male representation; more importantly, the concept of "women" grows equally exclusive if defined solely through its opposition to a monolithic notion of hegemonic (i.e., white, straight) masculinity.

Nevertheless, the attackers of pornography do raise very important questions central to feminist theorizing—about the role of representation in shaping lived conditions and about the possibility of agency in a male-shaped system. They recognize correctly that they have hit on an immensely compelling issue for many women, able to command a wide public forum. I will argue that antiporn feminism builds on the important insight that representation is a crucial site of feminist struggle; but I am concerned that its response to this recognition takes harmful forms.

Because of the issue's power, anticensorship feminists—however tired they may get of refuting the claim that porn is the paradigmatic example of sexism and oppression in contemporary culture—have also felt compelled to talk and write prolifically about pornography (and sex) in recent years.[12] Carla Freccero exhibits some fatigue with the topic in entitling her article about it, rather optimistically, "Notes of a Post-Sex Wars Theorizer." But Freccero ends with perhaps the crucial question that must be answered before feminism in the United States and Britain can really get to that "post" position: "Feminist movement and feminist thinking have the potential to conceive action and analysis in staggeringly revolutionary terms, and there are tactical priorities: imperialism, class stratification, the conditions of the neediest women in the United States. Many of the current conflicts in feminism continue to evade these questions. Why?"[13] In this essay, I want to stage the pornography controversy yet again in order to posit an answer to that "why?" and to suggest the kind of strategy that might help feminism address and move beyond the evasions and anxieties—evasions of internal divisions of economic and racial "otherness" among women, and anxieties over the ability of representations to shape the world—that have diverted much attention from the priorities Freccero cites.

When feminist antipornography work leads (albeit unintentionally) to the blacklisting of writings by not only gay men but white lesbians and women of color—when women have to choose one identity over the other—the need for a politics based on multiple categories of otherness becomes impossible to ignore. Postmodernist approaches can offer such a politics. Postmodernism conceives of subjectivity as constructed through acts of representation and reading; feminist postmodernism suggests that readers occupy complex and multiple positions in relation to any text. A feminist postmodernist theory of readership can challenge monolithic constructions of the act of reading pornography as the duplication of male oppression and, in the process, suggest how various groups of diverse and perverse others might turn texts to their own purposes without having to resort to asking the state to intervene.[14]

Disagreements over pornography thus provide particularly useful material for evaluating the benefits of adapting postmodernist theory to feminist struggles. In this chapter, I aim to demonstrate those benefits by drawing on both historical and theoretical arguments. I will propose that antiporn feminism's theories of the material effects of representation were in part an effective response to historical conditions arising in the 1970s, fundamentally postmodern developments that resulted in the fragmentation of the women's movement and the expansion of the pornography industry. The latter factor is symptomatic of postmodernity in two ways— as an illustration of postmodern capitalism's ability simultaneously to legitimate and to exploit the new identity positions arising from liberation movements, and, in the rise of legal pornography as a topic of "serious" discussion, as an example of the breakdown of divisions between high and low culture, a breakdown feminism had itself encouraged. Feminist critiques of representation were thus a first step toward developing a feminism fitted to postmodernity.

However, I find in the rhetoric of antipornography critiques, specifically of Acker and Carter, that the tendency to treat all representations as necessarily reproducing oppressive consciousness results in a static, oppositional model of difference that leaves women without agency and threatens to erase the differences among them. I will propose that antipornography feminism arrives at this impasse because of the assumptions about pornographic reading, as ingestion and reproduction, on which it bases its generalized model of reading; the second half of my discussion develops an alternative model of the pornographic reader—one based on the use-value of texts—as the type of the postmodern reader. I will focus on the feminist-postmodernist models of reading offered by Acker's novel *Don Quixote* (1986), and Carter's *The Infernal Desire Machines of Doctor Hoffman* (1972)—especially evident in their treatment of explicit erotic representations—in order to suggest a contextual theory of how various readers might use different texts in different circumstances. Such a theory eliminates the need to see (male) representation as necessarily inimical to women; with the elimination of that binary structure, feminists need not treat internal differences among women as a threat.

PROLIFERATING IDENTITIES IN THE POSTMODERN SEXUAL MARKETPLACE: CAPITALISM CONSUMING OPPOSITION

I want to begin my argument by framing the rise of antipornography feminism as a postmodern development. Doing so allows me to situate this discourse as a response to a specific historical context, to pinpoint which of its assumptions—drawn from earlier humanistic discourses— become threatened and untenable in this new context, and to evaluate its effectiveness at rethinking those assumptions. In other words, antiporn feminism is a reaction to postmodern conditions; but the question remains as to whether it recognizes those conditions *as* postmodern, or rather attempts to reinscribe them into a humanistic frame of action. I propose the answer that while antiporn feminism effectively recognizes the increasing role of representation in shaping postmodern political conditions, it also requires a self-defeating withdrawal from the arena of representation. Such a withdrawal seems necessary because antiporn rhetoric defines feminism as an oppositional movement, and oppositionality disintegrates into diffuse and multiple categories of identity when it enters the postmodern realm of representation. Antipornography feminism fails to rethink opposition as the only model of political intervention, and therefore, I will argue, cannot offer a strategy—either of reading or of political action—fully adapted to postmodernity. I want first to establish that the threat to oppositionality inheres in postmodernity.

Second-wave feminism grew, in part, out of a political environment in the 1960s that was essentially oppositional. The now dated term *women's liberation* carries that implication, a vision of women's oppression as something entirely separate from them, from which they could be removed and set free (into some other conceptual space). Before Anglo-American feminism had had more than a few years to establish itself, however, it was faced with the loss of the oppositional model. Postmodernity challenged that opposition in two central ways: by fostering the internal fragmentation of the women's movement into further identity divisions, and by incorporating feminists' critique of the politics of representation into a general trend to foreground representation as the *only* site of interest, power, and identity-definition—thus reframing the demands of feminism as a set of desires that could be contained and addressed within an expanded representational marketplace, and positioning social transformation as a matter of commodity diversification. For instance, when women claimed the right to express and pursue their own fulfillment in sexual relationships, the pornography industry reflected that demand back to them as a call for the availability of more and better representations of female sexual pleasure. In this dual movement toward fragmentation and cooptation, any clear distinction between feminists and "society" was assailed both from within and from without.

Capitalism, far from reeling from the blows dealt it by the various countercultural movements, embraced them as new marketing opportunities, eagerly reaching out to newly articulated identity groups such as youth, blacks, and women, encouraging them to define themselves through material signifiers (such as clothing and hairstyles) and patterns of consumption (from rock concerts to drugs to vegetarianism). The opportunity to develop these new consumer markets offered a means to offset the effects of the global economic crisis of the early 1970s. But postmodern market diversification extends beyond the integration of newly existing social groups to their creation—to actively encouraging the atomization of formerly shared identities.

Geographer and cultural critic David Harvey suggests why this movement toward the subdivision of existing social groups is an especially postmodern phenomenon. Harvey sees it as a feature of deindustrializing postwar economies, systems undergoing major changes in production and consumption practices necessitated by the very success of the previous phase of Fordist modernization in much of North America, Western Europe, and Japan.[15] Fordism brought itself to a dead end in terms of both the saturation of internal markets and their constriction by the rising unemployment caused by more efficient manufacturing technologies.[16] This leads, in the new post-Fordist phase, to at least three features: increasing multinationalization as corporations seek out less-developed markets overseas and attempt to cut domestic commodity costs by moving

manufacturing plants offshore; attempts to accelerate planned obsoles-
cence, to shorten the "half-life" of commodities—including a new focus
on selling ephemeral "experiences" or images; and greatly intensified
market targeting at home, a new emphasis on market research and specialized advertising aiming to exploit every nook and cranny of the domestic
consumer base, creating new "needs" and desires and encouraging consumers to locate their identity in a variety of new lifestyle "niches." The
greater the number of highly specialized identities the market can address,
the more fully each consumer—who may identify with a number of these
subgroups—can be interpellated and "milked."

Of course, the internal divisions that threatened to undermine the
category "woman" almost as soon as it had been articulated as a political
identity were not only caused by the new configuration of capitalism.
They also owed (and owe) a great deal to a phenomenon that predates
these changes, what Donna Haraway refers to as "the worldwide development of anti-colonialist discourse, that is, discourse dissolving the
West."[17] Haraway concludes, "As Orientalism is deconstructed both politically and semiotically, the identities of the Occident destabilize, including those of its feminists."[18] While the first internal disputes in the British
and American women's movement concerned questions of sexuality
(straight versus lesbian) and, relatedly, strategy (liberal versus separatist
versus socialist), as the 1970s progressed, increasing challenges raised by
feminists of color to the construction of feminism as "white feminism"
erupted into very serious divisions over the movement's racism.[19] These
challenges certainly drew on earlier, and continuing, liberation movements of people of color. While these liberation movements are not
peculiar to postmodernity—but rather, are consistent with the liberal-
democratic tradition central to modernity[20]—they undergo alteration in
the postmodern context in that they, like feminism, can no longer function as an oppositional voice *outside* the marketplace. The potentially
anticolonialist image of a black African soldier can today crop up in a
Benetton ad, implicitly contributing an air of hip "danger" and worldli-
ness to an international corporation. (Henry A. Giroux mentions just
such a photograph in his analysis of Benetton's marketing of the *image* of
"difference.")[21]

My point here is not to argue that the formerly oppositional identities
offered by feminist, anticolonial, and racial liberation movements have
been totally coopted and neutralized by postmodern capitalism. Rather,
the location of resistance has changed. Giroux, while he reads very pessi-

mistically the transformation of "insurgent differences" into signifiers of "harmony, consensus, and fashion" for the worldly "Benetton Youth," draws the conclusion that those of us who wish to resist many aspects of postmodernity need to broaden the scope of our attention from the traditional sites of knowledge production. He admonishes, "the struggle over identity can no longer be considered seriously outside the politics of representation and the new formations of consumption."[22]

The pornography industry, which grew exponentially during the 1970s, represents precisely one such recently emerged formation where "struggle[s] over identity" take place in a context that is no longer oppositional, and where resistant identities become coopted images. The enormous surge in pornography claiming to address the "problem" of women's pleasure is perhaps the most egregious example of the cooptation of feminist rhetoric as a means to sell commodities to newly constituted consumers.[23] Following a relaxation of obscenity prosecutions in both Britain and the United States, various forms of pornography achieved new legitimacy; new forms sprung up to address wider audiences than just the traditional target group of straight males. Linda Williams cites the emergence of the feature-length X-rated movie in more-or-less legitimate movie theaters as a dramatic example of these changes. Writer Nora Ephron's much-quoted comment about the first of these movies, *Deep Throat* (1972)—"Not to have seen it seemed somehow . . . derelict"[24]— suggests just how significant were the porn industry's inroads into mainstream culture.

Some feminists saw this expansion as a direct backlash against women's struggle for equality. For instance, even anticensorship feminist Melissa Benn, in her study of attempts to ban the topless photographs of women published daily in British tabloid newspapers and known as "page threes," assumes that "It is certainly more than a co-incidence that the first Page 3 picture appeared in the *Sun* in 1970, which was also the first proper year of women's liberation in [Britain]."[25]

However, that coincidence might have broader sources and more meanings than Benn implies. I would propose a more complex model of causality, seeing the growth of the sex industry not as a simple product of backlash—that is, opposition—but in the context of general trends in postmodern capitalism: its increasing dependence on selling representations and on marketing them to as wide a range of consumers as possible. In her study *Hard Core*, Williams reads the porn industry's expansion—à la Michel Foucault—as a stage in, and product of, the increasing constitution of sex as a topic for public discourse in the twentieth century. Representations of sex have come to seem increasingly worthy of attention (or, as the academic protagonist of David Lodge's 1975 satire, *Changing Places*, puts it as he sneaks into a strip joint, "a phenomenon of cultural and sociological interest").[26] Williams traces the liberalization of US obscenity laws, arguing that the more sex was considered a controversial issue in society at large, the harder it was to demonstrate that even X-rated materials were without meaningful content or, in the Supreme Court's words, "redeeming social value." While this argument suggests that feminism's vocally framing sex as a political concern was actually one of the causes of the pornographic explosion, it also proposes that the industry's response was not necessarily hostile; Williams sees it as more an economic response than a deliberately political one. As Laura Kipnis puts it, "In social history terms we might note that *Hustler* [magazine] galumphs onto the social stage at the height of the feminist second wave, and while the usual way to phrase this relation would be the term 'backlash,' it can also be seen as a retort—even a political response—to feminist calls for reform of the male imagination."[27]

The burst of new pornography was the market's way of both pursuing and exploiting some of the issues feminism raised. Recognizing a group of consumers interested in exploring their sexuality, porn increasingly tried to address women—and not only women, but, to a certain extent, other formerly marginal sexual groups such as gays, lesbians, and practitioners of S/M, whose sexual practices had also become an object of increased public discussion thanks to the "heterogeneous event called the 'sexual revolution.' "[28]

As I will later argue that attacks on Acker and Carter illustrate, this loss of a clearly oppositional or uncontaminated subject-position for women in the area of sexuality may be what troubles antipornography feminism the most. Antiporn feminists' consternation is indicative of anxiety over the intrusion of commodity marketing into what had previously been oppositional spaces, for the pornography business proved able to draw legitimacy from feminism's insight that all representation carries political meanings. The porn makers embraced—in their own, self-interested and cynical way—calls for a rethinking of patriarchal representations of sexuality and used them to frame women not only as consumables (as images for expanded male audiences, now that female sexual pleasure was a social problem) but as consumers (as themselves a new audience "deserving of" their own sexual fantasies).[29]

Feminist organizing against pornography offered a way to reassert the foundation of feminism in the absolute difference between feminists and the mainstream of culture, and thus to reinvigorate the movement at a time when feminism was suffering on both sides of the Atlantic from a decline in measurable gains.[30] Both Ann Snitow and Andrew Ross propose that pornography initially caught on as a means of reinvigorating feminist efforts in the face of backlash partly because of the immediate emotional impact of some brutal and terrifying pornographic images, and partly because antipornography activists offered a clear moral division between men and women, in contrast to the blurring of sides and internal fragmentation that developed with postmodernity.[31]

The internal fragmentation can of course be read as a positive sign that feminism had acquired enough power and confidence, after the compulsive and impulsive push of initial actions, to begin a process of self-examination—and certainly, I do not intend to compose a narrative of its decline. However, the emergence of internal differences may also have created a desire in some (mostly white) feminists for a new agenda that all women, under the umbrella of feminism, could unequivocally share. Although in practice, campaigns against pornography have not reunified "the movement," they seemed to promise such a focus. As Snitow puts it, in the face of setbacks—and, I would add, divisions—"Antipornography theory offers relief in the form of clear moral categories: there are victims and oppressors."[32]

Antipornography feminism can thus be seen in the light of two characteristically postmodern developments—the fragmentation of the women's movement and the growth of pornography marketing—as an effort to defend a clear, oppositional model of difference against the threat of political paralysis posed by the market's diffusion and proliferation of categories of otherness—indeed, the proliferation of feminisms.

REASSERTING (POSTMODERN?) OPPOSITIONALITY—REFUSING TO (BE) CONSUME(D)

Inasmuch as antipornography feminism recognizes and addresses the major threat postmodernity poses to political opposition, it might seem a successful feminist strategy for negotiating postmodern conditions. Focusing on the one issue of pornography should enable feminism to take what is good about postmodernist thought, the view of representation as a crucial political arena, and reject what is bad—the loss of a fixed, shared identity from which to launch a critique. Pornography promises the ideal focus because sexuality is the primary site at which women enter representation—sexuality is represented as women's (whole) identity—and because the object of pornography is primarily women, a position shared in this case (albeit differently) by working women, leisured women, white women, women of color, lesbians exhibited for male voyeuristic pleasure, and so on. Attempts to rally the feminist movement around the issue of pornography therefore might appear to have the double virtue of retaining the critique of representation and preventing the cooptation of women into fragmented groups of representational consumers. These apparent advantages account for many feminists' recent privileging of pornography as the term for a wide variety of representations, not only the girlie magazines and X-rated movies that conventionally comprise the genre.

Some feminists seeking to develop a critique of pornography draw explicitly on postmodernist theories of the politics of representation, in order to be able to generalize their critique to a whole range of texts, including some which purport to be feminist. I want to analyze one critique of Acker's work that can serve as an illustration of this tendency. The work of this critic, Colleen Kennedy, suggests why antiporn feminism cannot be a fully postmodernist rhetoric, instead collapsing in self-defeat.

Writing about the implications of explicit sex scenes by Acker and novelist Catherine Texier, Kennedy deftly draws on arch-postmodernist Jean Baudrillard to develop her critique. She argues that while Acker only *simulates* pornography in her novels, simulation is "a presumably 'unreal' action whose 'effect' is identical to the 'real.' "[33] In other words, simulations, even those intended as critique or parody, cannot be distinguished from what they simulate, and Acker's fake "pornography" functions as, or *is*, pornography. The core of Kennedy's objection to Acker's work is that simulation "*cannot* be contained" (165–66); since, as Acker's pastiche strategy itself emphasizes, representations circulate in culture at large as part of a general consciousness, one author's intentions to turn them to feminist ends cannot determine how anyone will read them.

I should emphasize that Kennedy is not alone in following this apparently postmodernist line of reasoning; her argument duplicates, on a metalevel, Catharine MacKinnon's contention that pornographic simulations themselves *are* acts of sexual domination against women (although I sincerely doubt whether MacKinnon would identify herself as a postmodernist thinker).[34] In fact, Kennedy also makes that extra leap, when she equates reading one scene, in which Acker depicts a woman's lover nicking her genitals with a knife, with "witnessing the degradations of pornography," with "witnessing a woman having her vulva sliced with a knife" (181). Reading the simulation of porn equals reading porn equals standing by while real violence takes place. However, Kennedy's article is a particularly subtle example of this line of reasoning because she focuses on the dependence of representations on readers for their political import. Her trenchant critique is, in fact, aimed less at Acker and Texier—although she clearly considers their work dangerous—than at critic Robert Siegle, who sets himself up as what Kennedy scathingly calls "the 'ultrasophisticated' reader," who can explain to those more prudish readers who might be shocked by the sex in these novels why it is *really* politically subversive (Kennedy, 166). Siegle thus presumes to accomplish, and assumes that Acker can accomplish, the impossible: to contain simulation. Kennedy accurately points out that such a view of meaning as inhering in the text, waiting to be found by the good reader, completely ignores the context of a patriarchal society where men have historically had much more power than women to determine the meanings of representations.

Kennedy herself, however, then contradicts her own supposedly Baudrillardian position by implying that simulations ultimately *are* contained—by patriarchy. Far from being idiosyncratic, this move highlights the failure of much postmodern theory to follow through on the implications of the assertion that simulations do not mean inherently. Since simulations nevertheless do produce meanings somehow, this theoretical gap allows Kennedy and other antiporn feminists to assert that they do so according to a simple binary division: Simulations always speak patriarchal power, and readers will respond either by being encouraged to continue "serv[ing] unreflectively the patriarchal establishment" or by finding them "offensive" (Kennedy 171). Which camp one falls into will apparently depend on how one feels the "marked reality-effects" of such representations (171); presumably, men will feel their power validated, while women will feel victimized. One can accept representation and accept patriarchy; or one can oppose both.

Thus while antiporn feminism recognizes the importance of contestation over images as the key location of postmodern politics, its strategy to counter the threat of political paralysis posed by the postmodern dispersal and proliferation of otherness (into diverse groups of consumers) is to reaffirm a clear division between patriarchy and its feminist opponents—

those who stand at a distance from representation and refuse to consume it.

THE LOSS OF OTHERNESS AND THE LOSS OF AGENCY

I have already suggested, by referring to Canada's post-*Butler* situation, the profoundly negative consequences of this refusal of consumption or refusal to participate in the market of representations. This strategy cannot acknowledge that the material effects of pornographic (and all) representations differ according to factors other than gender. For instance, in gay male communities, and more recently and to a more limited extent among some lesbians, pornography has been instrumental in rendering visible the sexual practices central to both gay political organizing and gay oppression.[35] Some working-class women have found participating in the creation of pornography their best economic option and best route to autonomy.[36]

It stands to reason that if multiple categories of difference are created in part through the marketing of representations, to condemn that market wholesale is to lose the ability to theorize and mobilize various subject-positions—other than the two positions, inside and outside. And inasmuch as women always also participate in those categories—i.e., inasmuch as women are always white women or black women, Latinas, indigenous, and/or Asian women, and so forth—they cannot remain in the outside location. For instance, while visible, white antiporn feminists have offered cogent critiques of the racism of much pornography, they fail to address the fact that they themselves evoke and circulate a representation with racial implications, the image of women as chaste and removed from (male-imagined) sexual desire. This construction revives a discourse whose price has historically been the *increased* displacement of sexuality onto women of color.[37] And from the recent history of the American South to contemporary inner-city Britain, representations of women as innocent victims of male sexuality have resulted in the representation of black men as sexually rapacious. In addition, Laura Kipnis has pointed out that the disgust and disapproval antiporn feminists exhibit toward graphic depictions of sexual organs and acts are emblematic of a fundamentally bourgeois desire to suppress and render "other" the unruly body, an attitude that has historically functioned to support class hegemony. Her analysis of *Hustler* makes the convincing point that, seen in this light, the advent and popularity of such a magazine is emblematic less of male resistance to women's sexual and social autonomy than of a specifically class-based resentment of the middle-class values feminism is seen as embodying and enforcing. These issues can easily be lost when antiporn feminists claim that it is possible for women not to participate in the field of sexual representations.

And in addition to these areas of contestation, agency itself is cast aside. While antipornography feminism posits a location outside patriarchal ideology from which women may recognize male representations as offensive, it cannot theorize that position, how one might get there or lead other women there. For identity is created and reaffirmed through representation, and can only be redirected by interventions in the available imagery. This is not to say that identities are not also profoundly material; however, material circumstances such as poverty, hunger, health, and skin color always undergo interpretation as they intersect with cultural discourses, such that they will carry different meanings for different bodies. For example, in this country white women experience poverty differently from white men—its gender distribution is deeply intertwined with ideologies of family and marriage, and where it does exist, it carries different forms of gendered vulnerability. This is increasingly true as more and more facets of previously "private" life enter the field of commercial representation. Feminist political action depends on deploying some representation of what female identity means in a given situation, and some representation of how that meaning might be different. Agency depends on participating in representation.

The crucial question then becomes: If antipornography feminists recognize that the social place of women is primarily constructed through sexualized representations, what prevents them from intervening in those representations? Or more tendentiously, what assumptions of antipornography rhetoric preclude women's agency? These questions lead me back to antipornography critics' theories of readership, of the effects of texts on readers.

THE PORNOGRAPHIC READER AS POSTMODERN READER:
TWO MODELS

Theories of readership are a prime site at which to evaluate whether antipornography feminism offers viable strategies for addressing the context of postmodernity, for postmodern subjects are constructed through reading—that is, through interpreting and negotiating with images of themselves and others—to an unprecedented extent. And when it comes to theories of readership, pornography again offers itself as a model for postmodernism. In the textualized world of postmodernity, the model of reading long connected to pornography seems to have become a generalized norm: the text acts directly on the reader, on his (as the theory goes) material world—not so much reflecting as creating reality. Literally, the pornographic text shapes the reader's body; it also shapes his future actions, the scenarios he needs to stage in order to achieve arousal. In this way more generally in postmodernity, fictions become reality. If, for example, millions of West Coast television viewers during the early evening of a Presidential Election day hear that Candidate X is winning by a landslide, that very statement will constitute an accomplished fact. According to the classic theory of readership, this is a pornographic scenario; offered a fantasy couched as a representation of reality, we act it out.

However, in its role as a fundamental assumption of antipornography feminism, this theory of pornographic reading as a duplication of the text cannot, by definition, be generalized across society. For if all readers/viewers duplicate what they read or see, and all representations reflect patriarchal power, feminist opposition becomes impossible. The historically accepted vision of pornographic reading has always depended on the maintenance of a clear delineation between those people assumed to read pornographically and those who do not. This delineation has, again, always been part of the structural logic of bourgeois hegemony, which names the masses as the unrestrained body of society, while the role of controlled and controlling intellect belongs to the ruling elite.

Critics of pornography posit its helpless reader as someone *other*. Williams, drawing on the research of Walter Kendrick, points out that according to concerned authorities in mid-nineteenth-century England, "the person most endangered by obscenity was a young, middle-class woman, whose 'pornography' consisted of romantic novels" that might fill her head with dangerous longings.[38] In the recent debates, the primary version of that highly suggestive hypothetical person has become a lower-class male, and the dangerous longings that might fill his head after consuming pornography are assumed to be urges to rape, physically hurt, and/or objectify and disdain women.[39] I would add that given contemporary discourses of criminality, this construction of the lower-class male can also be understood to participate in racist stereotypes.[40] Whether the *actual* readers of pornography resemble these demographic profiles has been beside the point in pornography debates.

Most antipornography feminists adopt this model of the pornographic reader as automaton—and as an identifiable *someone else*—because it supports the contention that texts can produce harm yet maintains a separate, uncontaminated place for (white, genteel, female) critics of the texts' ideology. But this theory of readership makes antipornography feminism ultimately incompatible with postmodernity. For if in the post-modern context all consciousness is shaped by texts, no group of readers can hold itself apart; thus if one adopts the pornographic model of readership as direct cause and effect, no critical space can exist. Antipornography critics defy their own logic by assuming they can be immune to the effects of pornographic texts.

This contradictory theory of pornographic reading—which both denies and retains the concept of critical distance—is evident in the rhetoric of critics who condemn Acker's and Carter's novels. For example, Robert Clark begins his essay on Carter's work by asking "to what extent the fictions of Angela Carter offer their readers a knowledge of patriarchy—and therefore some possibilities of liberating consciousness—and to what extent they fall back into reinscribing patriarchal attitudes."[41] For Clark, agency cannot come from "reinscribing" existing representations; "consciousness" must remove itself to someplace elsewhere if it is to be subversive. "Knowledge of" the conditions of patriarchy clearly depends on distance in this formulation; it is something separate from those conditions, a self-contained object that can be "offer[ed]" to readers on a plate. To "fall back *into*" the conditions under examination would prevent knowledge. In his formulation, rereading society necessitates avoiding the site of pornography, for that is apparently the one location where readers have, by definition, no distance.[42] Clark therefore decries Carter's suggestion, in her book-length essay on pornography, *The Sadeian Woman*,[43] that pornography can itself be employed to critique the power imbalances in sexual relations; he asserts that "the ideological power of the form [is] infinitely greater than the power of the individual to overcome it."[44] How Clark himself, as an "individual" reader, has managed to "overcome" the "ideological power" of Carter's reproductions of pornography remains an untheorized mystery.[45]

I would agree with Clark that the reader of pornography becomes the model of readership in Carter's novels, as in Acker's. However, I believe their texts' model of readership can also account for the apparently anomalous ability of some readers (like Clark) to exercise agency within this role. While Clark assumes that the consciousness of the pornographic-automaton reader merely reproduces itself at each new encounter with a text, I think it useful to focus on the ways in which Acker's and Carter's feminist postmodernism shows that that consciousness never stops being produced; each pornographic text, and each new reading occasion, produces it slightly differently. The possibility for reshaping and redirecting desire arises in this slight, contextual difference that turns each act of reading into a retrospective *re*reading of the accumulated texts comprising subjectivity.

I am proposing a different model of the pornographic reader, as something other than a site of simple reproduction. The critical potential of Acker's and Carter's rereadings of classic pornographic scenarios comes not, as Clark suggests it would have to, from "the power of the individual" author to overcome existing textual ideology but from the force of the social (i.e., nonindividual) needs that readers bring to texts at each reading. These varied needs shape the meaning readers make of a given text; they have themselves been shaped in part by previous encounters with texts.

In the case of pornography, a range of socially acquired needs or desires will dictate how readers interact with a given pornographic text on a given occasion in order to achieve arousal. Jennifer Wicke proposes that readers of pornography engage in a "transcription of images or words so that they have effectivity within [the reader's] own fantasy universe. . . . This will often entail wholesale elimination of elements of the representation, or changing salient features within it."[46] In addition, this process of what Wicke calls "accommodation" may include the reader's identification at various times with different roles within the pornographic scenario: masculine or feminine, active or passive, giver or taker.[47] In other words, this theory of textual use suggests that through interaction with texts, readers may be able to step out of a binary relation between self and other, consumer and consumed.

Kobena Mercer proposes a theory of "ambivalence" to explain both the various positions a reader may occupy in relation to a sexual text, and the limits on such mobility. Reading his own complex reaction to Robert Mapplethorpe's eroticized portraits of black men, Mercer notes that he, as a gay black, occupies simultaneously the position of desiring spectator— "sharing the same desire to look as the author-agent of the gaze. . . the position that I said was that of the 'white male subject' "[48]—and that of aestheticized object. Yet he also qualifies Wicke's and Williams's sense of free movement, suggesting that his doubled positioning is made possible in part by the fact that both of this text's subject-positions are designed for male bodies. I would seek, in turn, to modify Mercer's emphasis on sex over other categories of identity; for instance, the deployment of the dildo in (some) lesbian sexuality, suggests to me that one's capacity to relate to the experience of erections and penetration may not be sex-dependent.[49] If viewers can identify with sexual subject-positions across race, as both Mercer and Asian American critic/artist Richard Fung suggest, might readers not also, especially when compelled by the limited availability of arousing images designed for those physically like them, identify across gender? This, while still recognizing that the need to do so may go "hand in hand with many problems of self-image and sexual identity."[50] Pornographic reading thus becomes the exemplary case of reading *not* because it inscribes woman as man's Other, but because it offers readers the possibility of shifting, contextual, and multiple relations to power—while nevertheless recognizing that the range of variation in these relations is always vexed, never freely fluid.

I want to develop this alternate model of the pornographic reader as postmodern reader step by step, illustrating each stage of my argument by drawing on Acker's or Carter's work. I will draw my examples from Acker's *Don Quixote* and Carter's *The Infernal Desire Machines of Doctor Hoffman* because these novels seem most explicitly concerned with the issues of reading, representation, and sexuality that run throughout each writer's oeuvre. Both novels can loosely be termed picaresques, each following a protagonist on a quest that takes him or her through a series of loosely connected adventures. These travelers' various encounters are primarily with existing texts—either as literal readers (in Quixote's case) or, as is the case for both Quixote and Carter's Desiderio, in the sense that the characters and scenarios they meet borrow heavily from previous narratives.

Acker's Quixote is a white, female knight who sets out, in the delirium following an abortion, to find the source of the world's wrongs and thereby to render happy heterosexual love possible. What she finds, instead, as she reads and rides through such diverse texts as memoirs of the Nixon administration, Godzilla movies, and canonical novels (rewriting all as she goes), is a long textual history of women's desire leading inexorably to abuse and suffering.

Carter's novel chronicles a war, in an unnamed Latin American nation in the second half of the twentieth century, between the central neocolonial government and a renegade physicist-cum-metaphysicist named

Hoffman, who has found a way to make the contents of the human imagination become palpable and real. Hoffman is systematically undermining the distinction between reality and fantasy by flooding the capital city with concrete manifestations of the citizens' desires, dreams, and nightmares. The narrator-hero is the cynical and alienated Desiderio, child of a white mother and an "Indian" father, an agent of the government Minister of Determination who sets out to destroy Hoffman but falls in love with the rebel's enigmatic daughter and grows ambivalent about his mission.

Premise one: Women have to read (in the broad sense of decoding) existing images of gender in order to have any identity or social location. Contrary to the position taken by antipornography feminists, Acker's and Carter's novels continually emphasize that women can't *help* participating in representation, *especially* sexual representation. In the central section of *Don Quixote*, Acker's female Quixote has to reread male texts because she finds that she—like the antiporn feminists who, in the name of separating themselves from male images, recreate a preexisting discourse of racialized, bourgeois womanhood—has no other language.

The problem Acker's Quixote engages throughout the novel is how a woman can actively love and desire in a culture with a long history of defining women as passive objects, mere receptacles of male desire. For Quixote, the ability to pursue sexual love is the key to female agency, for women have primarily been constructed in sexual terms, as beings whose significance and very essence lies in their (passive) sexual relation to men. Women like Quixote, who violate or seek to transcend that relational definition, have always been punished; the dilemma of female agency is thus: "If a woman insists she can and does love and her living isn't loveless or dead, she dies. So either a woman is dead or she dies."[51]

This patriarchal concept of woman as sexual other pervades the texts Quixote rereads in the novel's central section, "Other Texts." Her rereading of Frank Wedekind's *femme fatale*, Lulu, whom she overlays with George Bernard Shaw's Eliza Doolittle, emphasizes this entrapment in existing (male) language. Professor Schön "rescues" Lulu from the street, aghast at her class-bound inarticulateness. He tells her, "You do not know who you are because you do not know how to speak properly. . . . Your soul's language is the language of Milton and Shakespeare and the English Empire. Wouldn't you like to be able to speak properly?" Acker then adds, "(Lulu doesn't say anything)" (78). Schön makes clear that acquiring subjecthood means accepting language, which in turn means accepting class hierarchy, the valuation of male representations (Milton and Shake-speare), and the racial hierarchy of Empire; Lulu's only other option is silence. There is "speak[ing] properly" and there is not speaking at all.

If a woman is not to be silent and penniless, however, the entry into language is inherently an entry into sexuality. Schön plans to transform Lulu, by giving her language, into a fit wife for someone elevated (78). In "the language of Milton and Shakespeare," a woman's identity is through her sexuality: as wife, lover, and/or mother. The relation between Acker's Lulu and Schön underlines this construction linguistically: Schön marries Lulu, yet she calls him "Daddy"—he is the father-creator of an object defined by its relation to him sexually.

This creation, through language, of Lulu as essentially sexual leaves her in an impossible bind. While her being depends on her sexual relation to Schön, he cannot possibly return her desire, for she is an object he constructed, "brought out of nothing" (82), "a piece of shit" (88). So Lulu is doomed to suffer at the hands of a man who does not love her and whom she cannot stop loving. As she puts it, "I can not say 'No' to love to my appetite for love, and yet I must. To survive I must not love" (90). The terms of her existence and her survival contradict one another. Schön's and Lulu's (and Quixote's) world is composed only of patriarchal representations; yet Schön, in his terrified rejection of Lulu, suggests a way women might gain power without exiting representation: "What you call 'love,' if I paid any attention to it, would rip me (and this world) apart" (90). What frightens Schön is the prospect of women gaining access to representation; Lulu threatens to do this by rereading an existing discursive construction, love, from the context of the "wrong" reader. However:

Premise two: The ability to make new meanings from old representations depends on a reader's historically constructed needs. Readerly agency does not derive from women's *essential* or *biological* identity as the "wrong" readers. Such a claim would be quite compatible with antipornography theory's attempt to remove women from implication in male representations and to privilege gender over all other forms of difference. Rather, all readers occupy varying positions of "ambivalence" in relation to texts, depending on the context of reading—a context of needs and desires created in part by previous representations of each reader's identity and by the meaning or value of that identity at the present moment. There is a big difference between essentializing women's ability to misread male representations and basing a theory of subversive reading on any reader's shifting needs and experiences, which also include experiences of race, class, and sexuality, and can recontextualize a given image. Such a theory introduces the possibility of a *range* of specifically female (reading) positions that are not contained by or limited to binary representations of human heterosexuality, and not already fixed by a personal history of living out those representations.

Premise three: Readers' identities and needs—and therefore their interpretations of texts—are not established once and for all but must be continually reiterated in each new context. The mistake would be to assume that if the position from which one reads representations of gendered identity is determined by one's history, and if one's history is itself overwritten by encounters with previous representations, one always reads from an unchanging, designated gender position. However, history never stops happening; it is constantly being (re)written. The meanings that arise when a reader with established needs and images of identity meets a new text can retroactively change that reader's interpretation of previous texts, and therefore, of his or her identity. Agency results from this constant contextuality of reading, not from occupying a fixed, oppositional identity as representation's "other."

I am drawing heavily here on Judith Butler's formulation of gendered identity. Butler maintains that "what is signified as an identity is not signified at a given point in time after which it is simply there." [52] Rather, establishing one's gender "requires a performance that is *repeated*" and "'agency,' then, is to be located within the possibility of a variation on that repetition." [53] This is true, I would argue, not only of one's gender but also of one's racial identity and one's sexuality. It may be especially true of sexuality, given that the markers of this identity, sexual desire and pleasure, cannot be sustained over time but must be continually produced anew—unlike gender and race, which present the *illusion* of being consistently present. The fact of this visible discontinuity suggests again why pornographic reading may be a useful model for other forms of discursive self-construction. Not only pornographic texts but all texts produce models of desire and identity, and these models cannot stand for long; they must be continually reiterated in order to address new contexts. This reiteration leaves room for intervention.

For example, in Carter's *The Infernal Desire Machines of Doctor Hoffman*, one of the novels Robert Clark condemns, the narrator Desiderio works for a time in a traveling peep-show, a place whose sole purpose is to produce pornographic desire. The waxwork miniatures in the various viewing-machines are classic pornographic images of fragmented female bodies, their body-parts framed as food to be consumed or as sites of murderous violence, like the decapitated woman clad only in "the remains of a pair of black stockings and a ripped suspender [garter] belt of shiny black rubber" whose slashed breast hangs open "to reveal two surfaces of meat as bright and false as the plaster sirloins which hang in toy butcher's shops."[54] Carter reproduces these horrific tableaux in pornographic detail, and the language of Desiderio's descriptions emphasizes the painstaking artificiality of each detail—the very *reproduced*ness of sexual desire Clark insists upon. The wax breast "meat" is doubly distanced from real flesh by its comparison to fake (plaster) meat in a fake context, a "*toy* butcher's shop." It is not even meat hanging as advertisement in a real butcher's shop.

Desiderio describes the first image in the peep-show sequence—an image titled, appropriately, "I HAVE BEEN HERE BEFORE"—in a range of terms evoking the deliberate production of spectacle:

The legs of a woman, raised and open as if ready to admit a lover, formed a curvilinear triumphal arch. The feet were decorated with spike-heeled, black leather pumps. This anatomical section, composed of pinkish wax dimpled at the knee, did not admit the possibility of the existence of a torso. A bristling pubic growth rose to form a kind of coat of arms above the circular proscenium it contained at either side but, although the hairs had been inserted one by one in order to achieve the maximal degree of verisimilitude, the overall effect was one of stunning artifice. The dark red and purple crenellations surrounding the vagina acted as a frame for a perfectly round hole through which the viewer glimpsed the moist, luxuriant landscape of the interior. (44)

This vastly hyperbolic description associates the pornographic image with society's most elevated institutions: the viewer (who is the imagined lover) enters the woman as a conquering hero entering a "triumphal arch"; he passes under the "coat of arms" that legitimates his nobility, through "red and purple crenellations," the colors and the fortress of royalty, to survey his kingdom within.[55] The vaginal "proscenium" is the site of the elaborate staging of male power.

I read the contrast between the grotesquely pornographic emphasis on detail and Carter's exorbitantly rich language as an "attempt to achieve the maximal degree of verisimilitude" while producing an "overall effect . . . of stunning artifice." In other words, this description calls attention to the fact that desire is neither inherent nor natural; it must be artificially produced, or induced, by means of representation. Carter's language enacts the irony that all the peep-show designers' anxious efforts to attain a realistic effect only serve to highlight the manufacture of desire. This is not to say that, in my reading, this passage achieves ironic or critical distance on the construction of pornography and therefore cannot itself be read, unironically, as pornography; much pornography is couched in equally overblown language that does not appear to create a Brechtian distancing effect, and anyone who has watched a porn film knows it does not depend on an illusion of naturalness in order to do its job. However, *in the context of Carter's novel*, this foregrounding of the effort involved in producing pornographic desire becomes the key to articulating a different, postmodern model of reading. For if desire depends on constant acts of representation, it can take on different shapes in different contexts of reception.

The reappearance, later in the novel, of images from the peep-show supports not only the idea that pornographic texts produce pornographic desire but also that those texts change as they are read in new contexts. On one level, pornographic images seem to serve as predictors of future erotic encounters. While still working at the peep-show, Desiderio participates in an orgy that reminds him of a sequence of images at the show of "a girl being trampled by horses" (110). He subsequently has cause to dimly recall that image again, when his lover Albertina is gang-raped by a herd of centaurs in the magical land of Nebulous Time (180). However, the recurrence of the pornographic text in the mind of its reader, Desiderio, is *not* a simple matter of reproduction or duplication. While pornographic texts may shape or even cause readers' subsequent experiences of desire, the new, discrete context of each occasion of desire also shapes and changes the meaning of the previously read pornographic text. The new occasion becomes a rereading.

Thus the orgy, in the stables of a traveling circus, has "certain resemblances" to the trampling scene from the peep-show, including one reveler's rib being broken when a horse kicks her, but it is also "teasingly different" (110). In this event, Desiderio is positioned not as the controlling viewer who draws sexual pleasure from witnessing a woman's helplessness, as in the image, but as himself the helpless one. The woman who is his "virile mistress" at this point, a "fully phallic" lesbian who loves to shoot guns and is attracted by Desiderio's "passivity," propels him bodily into the midst of the orgy (108–9). While female, this woman is also blonde and US American, in contrast to the racially and colonially disempowered Desiderio. She is cast as the trampling animal, "reeking" with lust, "paw[ing] and claw[ing]" at our overwhelmed (but not unwilling) narrator. The consumer of pornography may reenact the image but he takes pleasure, in this new context, from occupying the role of the other.

The context of Albertina's rape again rereads the initial image, while recasting the meaning of Desiderio's helplessness. This context undoes the eroticization of both his racialized passivity and the initial position of voyeur, for he is pinned down while his lover—a brown-skinned woman—is attacked next to him. This time, when he recalls the "teasing image," he thinks of it as "a horrible thing, . . . the most graphic and haunting of memories" (180). Desiderio is not like the centaurs, those pure products of the human imagination, whose blind obedience to existing representations is figured not only by their rigid adherence to their scriptures and by the ritual rape which they undertake "grimly, as though it were their duty" (179) but by the traditional tattoos covering each one's body, their very bodies existing only to repeat conventional representations. Desiderio constantly reinterprets the pornographic representations he has seen, so that each new context of reading becomes a rewriting. By the end of the novel, he can resist acting out his most intense desire—the desire to make love to Albertina—because of the terrible meaning it would take on in context, the context of the deranged Dr. Hoffman's plan to harness their exceptional "eroto-energy" in order to take over the nation. As a (post)colonial, mixed-race subject, he already knows how supposedly "individual" sexual relationships can serve to further national conquest.

Thus even the reader of pornography—the archetypal automaton who is presumed, as Vladimir Nabokov explains in his afterword to *Lolita*, to want only endless repetition of the same clichéd images[56]—cannot make sense (i.e., use) of representations except by reading them in light of a specific context, formed in part by previous readings but also itself rewriting those previous texts. In order to be arousing, an image must become, as Desiderio puts it, "teasingly different" from the last, even if it is the same image that has served to tease and tickle in the past; it must be adapted to the present context. Which leads me to *Premise four: Reading is repetition, but no repetition is possible without revision.* (Or, one cannot step into the same river twice.) The only question remaining, then, is how revisions of existing images can be directed toward specific feminist ends.

I will read another scene from *Don Quixote* through this alternate model of readership, in order to suggest that it offers feminism the tools to address the multiple axes of difference among women that have too often seemed to paralyze feminist organizing. This scene offers an example of characters who become active readers of pornography and use pornographic representations to think their way out of the conventional heterosexual, binary view of female identity. The scene appears toward the end of Acker's novel, and is perhaps its most sexually explicit. It is based on a plagiarism of the Marquis de Sade's *Juliette*, an emblematic text in feminist pornography debates because it presents a heroine whose immense sexual pleasure and political agency are equalled only by her male-identified cruelty toward and disdain for (most) other women and the "lower" classes; antiporn critic Robin Morgan has referred to her feminist opponents as "Sade's new Juliettes."[57]

Quixote's protean sidekick Villebranche narrates this scene. In a slippage that seems to support the classic model of pornographic reading as absorption or assimilation, she begins by telling about a book she has read, whose story quickly dissolves into her own dream. However, readers familiar with Sade's text will notice that it has been changed in this dream version; all the male characters have been eliminated, so that Juliette's S/M initiation in the crypt of the girls' school chapel now takes place only among women and girls.[58]

But one need not have this extraneous knowledge in order to recognize this scene as a rereading rather than a reproduction, for it also rereads an earlier episode in Acker's novel, a complex S/M encounter between Villebranche—represented here as a dominant lesbian who dresses as a Nazi captain—and De Franville, a submissive bisexual man who masquerades as a young girl (126–41). Both scenes emphasize pleasure derived from following step-by-step a conventional narrative which must be repeated out loud: where Villebranche told De Franville, "You're going to be whipped ten times," and he responded by eagerly removing his pants (139), Juliette tells Laure, "I'm going to have to whip you badly, cunt," and Laure responds, "Oh yes, . . . whip me badly" (173). However, a significant change from the Villebranche-De Franville exchange (as from Sade's text) to the later Juliette scene—a change to which I shall return—is that both partners are now female. This new equalizing of power also draws on the earlier texts' depiction of the characters as both white and young.

This scene is useful for creating a different model of pornographic readership because it highlights the tension between repetition and revision. As the sexual action builds, Acker literally repeats each passage of dialogue from two to four times in succession on the page. One way to interpret this is as a tactic for disrupting the conventional male reader's trajectory of arousal, slowing it perhaps to a more female pace. However, it can also be read as enacting Acker's (and her characters') attempt to break out of the Nabokovian stereotype of sexual pleasure's dependence on the endless repetition of standard pornographic scenarios—to develop a new paradigm of how porn might be read and pleasure made.[59]

The repetitions end when Juliette finally confronts her own reluctance to feel pleasure and to articulate it, tracing that reluctance to her location in the patriarchal scheme of representation as the silent object of male desire. She recognizes, "I'm scared because I have or know no self. There's no *one* who can talk. My physical sensations scare me because they confront me with a self when I have no self: sexual touching makes these sensations so fierce. I'm forced to find a self when I've been trained to be nothing" (171). She finds that speaking self by using existing representations according to her (different) needs. Juliette rereads the ritualistic script of S/M, making up a narrative that she tells the others present about a girl tied to a stool. She prefaces it, "I who've been without speech speak" (172). As in the classic pornographic model, the reader's speech is a repetition of existing pornography; and as in that model, she soon acts out her storytelling with Laure. But while her acting-out is violent and painful—there is no sense here that getting to agency or pleasure can be easy—it leads to a new speech. Their sex culminates in the teacher, Delbène, interrogating the "wailing" Juliette: "Do women take no responsibility for their own actions and therefore have no speech of their own, no real or meaningful speech?" Juliette recalls her response: " 'No,' I managed to reply. 'I'm coming.' Those were my words" (175). Again echoing (and changing) the Villebranche-De Franville exchange, in which De Franville "had no intention of taking responsibility" for his masculinity, this scene ends with a borrowed pornographic scenario transformed into a "speech of [Juliette's] own," speech indicating active female sexual subjecthood.

This pleasure-claiming act of speech—perhaps readable as an ironic echo of the classic feminist moment of "coming to voice"—is significant as a first step toward agency because it demonstrates that the reader implied by dominant representations is never fully identical with real readers. Both the Sadeian text Villebranche reads in order to create this scene and the S/M script Juliette acts out within the scene are directed toward an implied male reader who finds pleasure within patriarchal, heterosexual norms; but Juliette's assertion that she has been able to find in these texts a different—active, female, lesbian—kind of pleasure suggests the multiple identifications through which readers may be able to locate themselves in a fictional scenario. Juliette is able to assume the role of the character with sexual agency because even while she has not been interpellated as male, other interpellations construct her as sexual (by definition, because she is female) and white; and dominant discourse defines "white" as "having power" and "sexual" as "having power over a woman." In other words, her lesbian pleasure is enabled by a paradoxical combination of the existing "legitimate" subject-positions or reader-positions offered by these representations. While Juliette did not create that contradiction among the identities offered her, she is able to exploit it strategically.

Juliette's reading strategy thus provides an answer to Colleen Kennedy's warning that representations cannot be contained. It suggests that representations cannot be contained because *readers* cannot be contained in the location of implied reader; the implied subject-position from which any text makes sense will always be a combination of various identities, with which not all real readers will correspond perfectly. Recognizing this, it is possible to define subject-positions that are resistant (i.e., that are not identical with representation's implied readers) without needing to be oppositional (i.e., removed from representation). The lesbian subject-position suggested here is neither a separatist "outside" space nor immune to cooptation; Sade's original text stands as a warning reminder that so-called lesbian scenes are a standard fixture of pornography meant for men's voyeuristic arousal. But writing a woman into the role of desiring, active partner need not, as Richard Walsh would have it, "succeed only in recreating the abuses of male sexual dominance, albeit with painful self-awareness."[60] Rather it can highlight the possibility, even within the confines of patriarchal representation, of articulating other models of identity by recognizing the ambivalence—"as a structure of feeling in which one's subject-position is called into question"—that representations can induce.[61]

Therefore, the wider implication of my final premise about a postmodern model of readership—that repetition entails revision—is that identity itself is always a matter of both repetition and continual revision. The political meaning of an identity—woman, lesbian, white woman, and so on—can change because each such identity participates in multiple discourses—such as sexuality, democracy, consumerism—and itself coexists with other identities in the same body. The relative power and prominence of these multiple identifications will shift according to the context.

Thus the active pornographic reader described by these four premises is, I would argue, a far more appropriate model than the automaton not only for the rereadings that compose Acker's and Carter's texts but also for generalizing to the postmodern political world. For feminism, adopting this model of readership and identity would mean that postmodernity's exacerbation of the fragmentation of the identity, "woman," by race, class, sexuality, age, nation, or body type, could itself be put to use as the source of a complex and fluid, contingent set of resistant strategies. This fragmentation, rather than being a problem to be suppressed, would become a reality to be addressed—and, in part and at times, an asset to be used. Inasmuch as white feminists remain focused on sexuality as the epicenter of social construction, we are likely to continue sweeping race and class to one side. I have, rather paradoxically, engaged with the "sex wars" at some length here in an attempt to do away with that focus. Therefore I want to conclude by being very clear about the stakes of the different models of reading I have outlined.

Adopting a postmodern model of multiply positioned readers does not simply mean accepting, relativistically, that I can read Acker and Carter as feminists, while Kennedy, Clark, or Dworkin can read them as pornographers. Likewise, the fact that Dworkin's own antipornography feminism can be read (and suppressed) as porn if the reading circumstances require it may support my position, but that position will only be useful for political struggles inasmuch as it enables readers to recognize the importance of such "reading circumstances." I hope a theory of reading as active, contextual *use* might redirect feminists' attention to the widely varying conditions (of race and class, nation, family, and so forth) under which different women negotiate with their surroundings and use literature to do so. While there may well yet be more to learn about representation from focusing on pornography, in postmodern culture the -graphies are multiplying faster than a single-issue campaign can begin to address. Geography, ethnography, and biography may offer far more fruitful sites for investigating women's power and powerlessness.

For this reason, I want to emphasize that the model of readership I have proposed to counter the conventional image of the pornographic consumer *can* and *should*, unlike that conventional image, not remain confined to pornography alone but should be generalized to diverse postmodern acts of reading (which means, to all negotiations with the postmodern world). The feminist antipornography theory of representation is not a theory for postmodernity because, in part, it is unable to extend its critique beyond the categories of gender and sexuality. Feminist strategy in postmodernity must be able to work across lines of race, class, sexuality, and even gender, inasmuch as alliances with, for instance, gay men can advance women's interests. I believe feminism can function in multiple, contingent ways without sacrificing its one defining commitment, to the economic and psychic well-being of women. The alternative is to let feminism be whittled down to an issue only concerning white, straight, middle-class women—not, I want to emphasize, that that is the intention of antiporn feminists; but in a society where the market of representations grows increasingly diverse, contributing to an increasing fragmentation of identity groups, the powers that be will use that diversity against each of us (e.g., the *Butler* seizures) if we do not use it to our advantage.

NOTES

1. I have taken the full title of the case (as cited by Leanne Katz; Carl Wilson gives a different version) as my heading for this introduction because it presents an amusing, if perhaps unfair, version of the rhetorical figures in opposition here: the (male) porno dealer versus H.M. the Queen, as ideal image of feminine justice. Her Majesty's symbolic presence as a lingering vestige of colonialism in Canada suggests to me the problems inherent in replacing male authority with a female version of the same (even a feminist version). See Leanne Katz, "Secrets of the Flesh: Censors' Helpers," Editorial, *New York Times* (4 December 1993, late ed., final): 21, ProQuest-The New York Times Ondisc 9300088522; Carl Wilson, "Northern Closure," Editorial, *Nation* (27 December 1993): 788–89.

2. On the seizures, see Sarah Lyall, "Canada's Morals Police: Serious Books at Risk?" *New York Times* (13 December 1993, late ed., final): A8, ProQuest-The New York Times Ondisc 9300091058; also Wilson, 788. Apparently, Dworkin's books *Womanhating* and *Pornography: Men Possessing Women* were released soon after seizure by "embarrassed" Customs officials. See John F. Baker, "Canada Customs a Continuing Problem for Bookstores and Distributors; Trial Postponed," *Publishers Weekly* (20 December 1993): 12, and Katz. I have been unable to find out against what group hooks's "hate speech" was presumed to be directed; see Katz, 21.

3. Julienne Dickey and Gail Chester, "Introduction," *Feminism and Censorship: The Current Debate*, ed. Chester and Dickey (Bridport, Dorset: Campaign for Press and Broadcasting Freedom-Prism Press, 1988), 3; Pratibha Parmar, "Rage and Desire: Confronting Pornography," Chester and Dickey, 119.

4. Michele Landsberg, "Canada: Antipornography Breakthrough in the Law," *Ms.* (May/June 1992): 14; "Lines in the Dirt," *Economist* (14 March 1992): 31. While MacKinnon's definition is of *pornography* as discrimination against women, the words quoted here are from the Canadian Supreme Court's definition of *obscenity*. That slippage in terminology may be what allows the ruling to extend beyond the more clearly pornographic materials (i.e., mass-cultural "trash") MacKinnon and her allies intended to more mainstream and "serious" books. I will not address the line between obscenity and pornography at any length here; for further discussion of antipornography feminists' attempts to hold the two apart, see Lisa Duggan, Nan Hunter, and Carole Vance, "False Promises: Feminist Antipornography Legislation in the US," *Women against Censorship*, ed. Varda Burstyn (Vancouver, BC: Douglas and McIntyre, 1985).

Antipornography feminists cannot be accused of wanting such widespread restrictions. Landsberg's article in *Ms.*, hailing the ruling when it was handed down, hastened to assure readers that "adult erotica, no matter how explicit, will not be considered obscene" (14). Kathleen Mahoney, the attorney who represented LEAF in the case, subsequently argued that the seizures were excessive and did not reflect the ruling's spirit; see Lyall.

5. Baker, 12.

6. Lyall, A8.

7. Amanda Sebestyen, quoted in Robin Ann Sheets, "Pornography, Fairy Tales, and Feminism: Angela Carter's 'The Bloody Chamber,' " *Forbidden History: The State, Society, and the Regulation of Sexuality in Modern Europe*, ed. John C. Fout (Chicago: University of Chicago Press, 1992), 344.

8. Jennifer Wicke, "Through a Glass Darkly: Pornography's Academic Market," *Dirty Looks: Women, Pornography, Power*, ed. Pamela Church Gibson and Roma Gibson (London: BFI, 1993), 66–68. The slippage between "pornography," as a genre, and "pornographic," as a presumed function or effect, is part of the problem facing attempts at regulation. *Any* representation of the human body can be read as pornographic, depending on context—if by pornographic, one means something like "likely to provoke arousal and/or masturbation by evoking explicit genital sexuality." Lynne Segal even proposes that representations of such unlikely but potentially suggestive objects as nuts and bolts can be put to pornographic use; see her "Does Pornography Cause Violence? The Search for Evidence," Gibson and Gibson, 15. Thus the importance of focusing on various probable contexts of reception and use, if regulators, activists, or pleasure-seekers are to judge one textual site more appropriate to their purposes than another.

For the most convincing definition of porn as a specific genre, varyingly constructed over time, see Linda Williams, *Hard Core: Power, Pleasure, and the "Frenzy of the Visible"* (Berkeley: University of California Press, 1989), 28–30. Williams backs up her general definition—representations of sexual activity "with a primary intent of arousing viewers"—with a history of various types of film and their conditions of circulation. That core definition could serve as the basis of similar concrete research into the historical construction of porn in other media, such as written porn.

9. Carla Freccero, "Notes of a Post-Sex Wars Theorizer," *Conflicts in Femi-*

nism, ed. Marianne Hirsch and Evelyn Fox Keller (New York: Routledge, 1990), 319n. Freccero attributes the term "sex wars" to B. Ruby Rich (as does Williams, *Hard Core*, 26). I understand the sex wars to include disagreements over pornography but also over some women's sexual practices that may be unrelated to porn, particularly S/M (sadism and masochism) and lesbian butch/femme roles. While these various issues have increasingly been collapsed into, or displaced onto, the question of pornography and sexual representation, I will use the term "pornography debates" more often than "sex wars" in an attempt to question the assumed slippage between texts and bodily actions. On this point, see Sheets, 335.

10. Craig Owens, "The Discourse of Others: Feminists and Postmodernism," *The Anti-Aesthetic: Essays on Postmodern Culture*, ed. Hal Foster (Seattle: Bay Press, 1983).

11. Fredric Jameson, *Postmodernism, or, the Cultural Logic of Late Capitalism* (Durham: Duke University Press, 1991).

12. Caught Looking Collective, ed., *Caught Looking: Feminism, Pornography, and Censorship* (Seattle: Real Comet Press, 1988); Ann Snitow, Christine Stansell, and Sharon Thompson, eds., *Powers of Desire: The Politics of Sexuality* (New York: Monthly Review, 1983); Carole S. Vance, ed., *Pleasure and Danger: Exploring Female Sexuality*, rev. ed. (London: Pandora-HarperCollins, 1992). See also Williams, *Hard Core*; Burstyn; Gibson and Gibson.

13. Freccero, 319.

14. Perhaps it doesn't need to be said, but I use the words "perverse" and "deviant" here in their recuperative sense not their judgmental one.

15. David Harvey, *The Condition of Postmodernity: An Enquiry into the Origins of Cultural Change* (Cambridge, MA: Blackwell, 1990). Both Stuart Hall and Henk Overbeek differ from Harvey in suggesting that Britain was an exception to the successful establishment of Fordism elsewhere in Western Europe. However, this has only made the process of deindustrialization faster and more economically disastrous in the United Kingdom. Stuart Hall, "The Toad in the Garden: Thatcherism among the Theorists," *Marxism and the Interpretation of Culture*, ed. Cary Nelson and Lawrence Grossberg (Urbana: University of Illinois Press, 1988); Henk Overbeek, *Global Capitalism and National Decline: The Thatcher Decade in Perspective* (London: Unwin Hyman, 1990).

16. Harvey, 141.

17. Donna Haraway, "A Manifesto for Cyborgs: Science, Technology, and Socialist Feminism in the 1980s," *Feminism/Postmodernism*, ed. Linda J. Nicholson (New York: Routledge, 1990), 198.

18. Haraway, 198.

19. Parmar, 123; see also Chela Sandoval, "Feminism and Racism: A Report on the 1981 National Women's Studies Association Conference," *Making Face, Making Soul, Haciendo Caras: Creative and Critical Perspectives by Women of Color*, ed. Gloria Anzaldua (San Francisco: Aunt Lute Foundation, 1990); Barbara Smith, "Toward a Black Feminist Criticism," *Feminist Criticism and Social Change: Sex, Class, and Race in Literature and Culture*, ed. Judith Newton and Deborah Rosenfelt (New York: Methuen, 1985).

20. Ernesto Laclau and Chantal Mouffe, *Hegemony and Socialist Strategy: Towards a Radical Democratic Politics* (London: Verso, 1985), 160.

21. Henry A. Giroux, "Consuming Social Change: The 'United Colors of Benetton,' " *Cultural Critique* 26 (Winter 1993–94): 20.

22. Giroux, 29, 20, 27.

23. Williams, *Hard Core*.

24. Quoted in Andrew Ross, *No Respect: Intellectuals and Popular Culture* (New York: Routledge, 1989), 172; Williams, *Hard Core*, 99.

25. Melissa Benn, "Page 3—And the Campaign against It," Chester and Dickey, 29. Lynne Segal notes that, in fact, one study did find an increase in violent imagery in *Playboy* and *Penthouse* in the early 1970s; however, violent imagery declined after 1977. She attributes this decline to "the feminist critique."

26. David Lodge, *Changing Places: A Tale of Two Campuses* (Harmondsworth, Middlesex: Penguin, 1978), 112.

27. Laura Kipnis, "(Male) Desire and (Female) Disgust: Reading *Hustler*," *Cultural Studies*, ed. Lawrence Grossberg, Cary Nelson, and Paula A. Triechler (New York: Routledge, 1992), 382.

28. Williams, *Hard Core*, 90.

29. The porn industry's various treatments of "women's pleasure" are not all equally cynical—and Kipnis's article on *Hustler* highlights the fact that some are much more openly hostile than others. See, in contrast, feminist filmmaker Candida Royalle's description of her motivations for making women-oriented "adult" films: "Porn in the USA," *Social Text* 37 (Winter 1993).

30. Anna Coote and Beatrix Campbell, *Sweet Freedom: The Struggle for Women's Liberation*, 2d ed. (Oxford: Basil Blackwell, 1987), 42, 157; Ann Snitow, "Retrenchment Versus Transformation: The Politics of the Antipornography Movement," in Burstyn, 110. Snitow records that pornography became a major issue in the US women's movement around 1977. On the emergence of pornography as a new focus of feminist energy in Britain, see Catherine Itzin, "Sex and Censorship: The Political Implications," Chester and Dickey; Sheets, 337.

31. Snitow, 112–13; Ross, 187.

32. Snitow, 113.

33. Colleen Kennedy, "Simulating Sex and Imagining Mothers," *American Literary History* 4 (1992): 165. Further references to this work will be included parenthetically in the text.

34. While I don't discuss MacKinnon's work directly here, I would refer readers to the recent controversy over Carlin Romano's review of her book *Only Words*. Romano, writing in the *Nation*, begins by imagining raping MacKinnon, in order to point to the supposed ludicrousness of her equation of fictional acts with real ones. While I agree with Romano up to a point, I find his hypothetical experiment reprehensible and think his review entirely fails to recognize the important analysis of power at the core of MacKinnon's work: that men's words frequently do have the power in our society to victimize women. Romano throws out the baby, the feminist critique of representation as having material effects, with the bathwater, a deterministic view of those effects as predictable and inevita-

ble. Carlin Romano, "Between the Motion and the Act," *Nation* (15 November 1993). In response, see Nat Hentoff, "The Public Rape of Catharine MacKinnon," *Village Voice* (4 January 1994); and the letters page for the December 27, 1993, *Nation*.

35. Michael Bronski, cited in Ross, 255.

36. Frederique Delacoste and Priscilla Alexander, eds., *Sex Work: Writings by Women in the Sex Industry* (Pittsburgh: Cleis Press, 1987). Ross and Acker give conflicting readings of what the expansion of the 1970s meant to women working in the sex industry. Ross claims that "Pornography's increasingly legitimate legal status in the marketplace over the last two decades has been accompanied by the gradual disappearance of [its most violent and misogynistic] features and a limited improvement in working conditions in the sex industry generally" (190). In an interview, however, Acker recalls from her days of acting in porn movies that when the industry "opened up," organized crime and big-time investors took over and "The ugliness and manipulation started. . . . Suddenly it was all changed and that's when I got out": Kathy Acker, "Punk Days in New York," Interview, *Fist* 1 (1988): 11. I suspect that both readings are true in different situations.

37. Jacquelyn Dowd Hall, " 'The Mind That Burns in Each Body': Women, Rape, and Racial Violence," in Snitow, Stansell, and Thompson, 333; Barbara Omolade, "Hearts of Darkness," Snitow, Stansell, and Thompson, 352; Parmar, 124.

38. Williams, *Hard Core*, 12.

39. Ross suggests that antipornography feminists reproduce "the old defense of the liberal imagination (against the brutish threat of a pervasive mass culture)" (186). I think this is an unfair simplification. Feminism has never exempted "high" culture from its critique of patriarchal ideology; indeed, feminism has contributed to the increasing breakdown of boundaries between cultural spheres. In addition, Ross implies that feminism was able simply to wipe away the conventional gendering of the mass-cultural threat as *female*, along with the denigration of femininity that entailed.

I agree, however, that there does seem to be a major shift in gendered models of mass culture, such that the perceived threat to society now represented not only by pornography but by violence on television, and so forth, is based on *masculine* behavior. Theorizing this shift is beyond the scope of my project, but I suspect it does not represent the mere flip-flop Ross suggests. The battle lines are drawn differently in postmodernity, I believe; the same conservative ideologues who call for controls on television violence also decry the degeneracy of current "high" culture.

40. Kipnis notes, however, that the resistant "underdog" male reader constructed by *Hustler* is also a white, racist male.

41. Robert Clark, "Angela Carter's Desire Machine," *Women's Studies* 14 (1987): 147.

42. See also Kennedy, 171.

43. Angela Carter, *The Sadeian Woman and the Ideology of Pornography* (New York: Pantheon, 1978; also published as *The Sadeian Woman: An Exercise in Cul-*

tural History (London: Virago, 1979). *The Sadeian Woman* has been the object of much criticism from antipornography feminists, including Andrea Dworkin and Susanne Kappeler. It is not particularly useful to my discussion here because while Carter explicitly argues in it that pornography can be turned to feminist purposes, *The Sadeian Woman* does not articulate any theory of contextual reading such as the novels offer. Carter remains very vague about the circumstances under which pornography might function as a feminist intervention.

44. Clark, 153.

45. Patricia Duncker makes a similar argument for the need to get outside previous texts in her highly critical article on Carter's collection of rewritten fairy tales, *The Bloody Chamber.* Duncker maintains that "the infernal trap inherent in the fairy tale, which fits the form to its purpose, to be the carrier of ideology, proves too complex and pervasive to avoid." For Duncker, as for Clark, there is therefore simply no way to represent heterosexual desire without reinscribing male paradigms. The "outside place," the location of true critique, that seems to be occupied in Clark's formulation by the Marxist intellectual, is in Duncker's essay implicitly occupied by the lesbian. Patricia Duncker, "Re-Imagining the Fairy Tales: Angela Carter's Bloody Chambers," *Literature and History* 10 (1984): 6.

46. Wicke, 70.

47. See Williams, *Hard Core*, 214–17.

48. Kobena Mercer, "Skin Head Sex Thing: Racial Difference and the Homo-erotic Imaginary," *How Do I Look? Queer Film and Video*, ed. Bad Object-Choices (Seattle: Bay Press, 1991), 180.

49. Susie Bright comments on the increasing use of dildos by women in heterosexual pairings, "only their lubricant knows who's playing the boy and who's playing the girl." Susie Bright, *Susie Sexpert's Lesbian Sex World* (Pittsburgh: Cleis, 1990), 137.

50. Richard Fung, "Looking for My Penis: The Eroticized Asian in Gay Video Porn," Bad Object-Choices, 154.

51. Kathy Acker, *Don Quixote: Which Was a Dream* (New York: Grove, 1986), 33. Further references to this work will be included parenthetically in the text.

52. Judith Butler, *Gender Trouble: Feminism and the Subversion of Identity* (New York: Routledge, 199), 144.

53. Butler, 140, 145.

54. Angela Carter, *The Infernal Desire Machines of Doctor Hoffman* (London: Rupert Hart-Davis, 1972; London: Penguin, 1982), 45 (page citations are to the reprint edition). Further references to this work will be included parenthetically in the text.

55. Desiderio goes on to describe the scene depicted within the "vagina," which is, in fact, a fantasy kingdom, complete with brilliant birds, exotic fruits and animals, and a mist-shrouded castle in the distance.

56. Vladimir Nabokov, "Vladimir Nabokov on a Book Entitled *Lolita*," *Lolita* (New York: Berkley Medallion, 1955), 284.

57. Quoted in Sheets, 338.

58. Richard Walsh, "The Quest for Love and the Writing of Female Desire in Kathy Acker's *Don Quixote*," *Critique* 32 (1991): 160.

59. Walsh makes a similar argument that the "trauma [of repetition] leads to sexual enlightenment" (157), but does not connect this enlightenment to representation and readership.

60. Walsh, 161.

61. Mercer, 187.

"There Is Nothing Else Like This": Sex and Citation in Pornogothic Feminism

Naomi Morgenstern

The gothic is the product of an implicit aesthetic that replaces the classic concept of nothing-in-excess with the revolutionary doctrine that nothing succeeds like excess.
—Leslie Fiedler, *Love and Death in the American Novel*

In our society, straight white males of my generation—even earnestly egalitarian straight white males—cannot easily stop themselves from feeling guilty relief that they were not born women, or gay, or black. . . . This is in part because of a calculation of the obvious socioeconomic disadvantage of being so born, but not entirely. It is also the sort of instinctive and ineffable horror which noble children used to feel at the thought of having been born to non-noble parents, even very rich non-noble parents.
—Richard Rorty, "Feminism and Pragmatism"

As soon as persons are posited, the war begins.
—Leo Bersani, "Is the Rectum a Grave?"

GENRE MIXING

With its morally superior if misguided heroine and its sexually explicit scenes of terror and persecution, Andrea Dworkin's novel *Mercy* is a "pornogothic" text. To call it so is to draw attention to its extravagant engagement with the violence of sexuality, to its joining of the conventions of pornography and gothic narrative. But it is also to frame the novel, to limit its effect, or to read its effects as limited. *Mercy* is, after all, fiction, and of a particular type: a fiction in which it is conventional to

39

represent that which is most "shocking." But if *Mercy* can be read as pornogothic fiction, it also reads as feminist testimonial. Dworkin, or "Andrea," the first person narrator, testifies to trauma, to the repeated experience of sexual violence, and to sexual violence as an experience of deadly repetition. When Andrea observes, "Everything just keeps happening," the worn-out reader must concur.[1]

As testimonial, *Mercy*'s participation in pornogothicism is, of course, qualified: a testimonial must have, the law of its genre demands that it have, a referential effect: it must appear to refer to what happened. But insofar as *Mercy* testifies, it also plays with framing, or with the idea of fiction as a mere performance or citation. That is, *Mercy* is testimonial *fiction* that always verges on being readable as *true testimony* (names, dates, ethnicity, everything matches up with the very little that one would need to know about the author's life). Yet the question of genre is more complicated than even this doubling (pornogothic and testimonial) would suggest. A review of the still limited but highly engaged and provocative criticism shows that the novel's participation in any or many genres is fraught indeed. Is *Mercy* fiction? Is it *just* fiction? Is it a political manifesto? Is it a confession?[2] *Mercy* seems to fend off classification and that has troubled its readers. If *Mercy*'s gothic performance espouses a politics of excess, this may finally be a radicalism that only literature can afford.[3]

Any reading of *Mercy* renders questions of genre and performativity inseparable. *Mercy*'s critics use Dworkin's political writing to read her fiction and suggest that one is never sure if Dworkin is actually using, or merely mentioning, the pornographic. Harriet Gilbert writes: "It could well be argued that Dworkin's novel is more—or at least *as* likely as Sade's *[Justine]* to persuade the reader that violence, power and pain are the whole of sexuality . . . and even to create the feeling that this is in some way horribly exciting."[4] But the instability of the categories "use" and "mention," their mutual implication, is also what makes a performative possible. In *How to Do Things with Words*, J. L. Austin set out to distinguish constative speech acts ("classical 'assertions,' generally considered as true or false 'descriptions' of facts") from performatives (which "allow [for] accomplishing something through speech itself"), and ended up finding performativity everywhere.[5] His mode of proceeding led him to make certain exclusions:

A performative utterance will, for example, be *in a peculiar way* hollow or void if said by an actor on the stage, or if introduced in a poem, or spoken in a soliloquy. This applies in a similar manner to any and every utterance—a sea-change in special circumstances. Language in such circumstances is in special ways—intelligibly—used not seriously, but in ways *parasitic* upon its normal use—ways which fall under the doctrine of etiolations of language. All this we are *excluding* from consideration. Our performative utterances, felicitous or not, are to be understood as issued in ordinary circumstances.[6]

What concerns me here are the kinds of utterance-acts that Austin would have excluded, or more precisely the very boundary that marks this exclusion: First, I will look at Catharine MacKinnon's theoretical writing, for MacKinnon takes on genre mixing and the problematic distinction between representations said to be only representations ("only words") and those accorded a more act-like status. In MacKinnon's account, pornography presents us with an infuriating paradox, for it at once records real acts and "nullifies the possibility of their being witnessed by the very act of displaying them as representations."[7] Second, I will examine Andrea Dworkin's fiction. *Mercy*'s destabilization of the difference between nonliterary and literary genres places it in the context of current controversies—the pornography debate, questions about the regulation of hate speech—that inquire after the relationship between representation and violence. If we do not know what kind of work *Mercy* is, how do we know what it might be said to do?[8] Writer and activist Dworkin, along with law professor Catharine MacKinnon, are the infamous theorists and would-be regulators of the pernicious effects of representation, specifically (although specificity poses its own set of problems here) pornographic representation. If representations do not reflect but constitute social reality, what is Dworkin doing in writing a certainly gothic and arguably pornographic text? Judith Butler, who has expanded upon speech-act theory's concept of the performative, argues that "a performative 'works' to the extent that *it draws on and covers over* the constitutive conventions by which it is mobilized."[9] If *Mercy* is to work, if we are to read and recognize the dreadful experience of women, it must cite and efface its relationship to the gothic and the pornographic traditions.

The politics of *Mercy*, I will argue, must be read not in where it goes (the virgin becomes the vigilante as *Mercy* heads towards the apocalypse), or not simply in where it goes, but in its gothic-effect, in Andrea Dworkin's practice of extravagance. To accuse Dworkin of excess is beside the point, or rather it is precisely the point that deserves further attention: how does *Mercy*'s excess work? If *Mercy* is a text that does something, it is also a novel that thematizes fiction's power: literature becomes a place for doing everything and anything (for example, for giving cancer to the abusive uncle). *Mercy* could be said to be engaged with a pornogothic account of performativity: words, as it turns out, can even be held responsible for the Holocaust (22). There is for Dworkin, as for MacKinnon, an almost magical or demonic aspect to the performative.[10] Fiction is also, however, the realm of futility and false promises. Andrea's very name— Andrea we are told repeatedly, means "manhood" or "courage"—makes a promise it cannot keep.

The pornographic and the gothic are genres associated with a particular force; they are both thought to have their bodily effects. Pornogothic feminism inhabits pornography and the gothic and mobilizes their power over mind and body. Richard Rorty suggests that "feminists are trying to get people to feel indifference or satisfaction where they once recoiled, and revulsion and rage where they once felt indifference or resignation."[11] Feminists are trying to get people to feel. I will read Dworkin's novel as an instance of pornogothic feminism and Catharine MacKinnon's *Only Words* as a performance bound up with a theory. With their massive gothicization of experience, MacKinnon and Dworkin aim to describe and produce the terror of an unrelentingly misogynist sex and gender system.

While MacKinnon and Dworkin have not previously been classified as writers of the "female gothic," I will argue that it is the gothic aspect of their work that is most productive and most problematic.[12] I will demonstrate that "pornogothic feminism" not only cites and uses the conventions of a pornographic version of the gothic but also subscribes to a gothic theory of history and representation. For pornogothic feminists history is not safely past, and a representation is always in danger of becoming a repetition: the event, again. MacKinnon, for example, is most compelling as a gothic theorist of language, as one who insists that language can do harm but that this injury is the harm of a hallucinatory repetition, a phantom-like return. Pornogothic feminism would seem to "choose" traumatic repetition (repetition compulsion) rather than place its faith in the "utopics of radical resignification" (a politics of subversion), yet MacKinnon and Dworkin's very choice of this kind of account, or rather their *use* of it, would suggest that repetitions can function nontraumatically.[13]

Surprisingly enough, Judith Butler, one of Catharine MacKinnon's most persistent critics, helps us to theorize the Dworkin/MacKinnon project. She writes:

One does not stand at an instrumental distance from the terms by which one experiences violation. Occupied by such terms and yet occupying them oneself risks a complicity, a repetition, a relapse into injury, but it is also the occasion to work the mobilizing power of injury, of an interpellation one never chose. Where one might understand violation as a trauma which can only induce a destructive repetition compulsion (and surely this is a powerful consequence of violation), it seems equally possible to acknowledge the force of repetition as the very condition of an affir-mative response to violation . . . the force of repetition in language may be the paradoxical condition by which a certain agency—not linked to the fiction of the ego as master of circumstance—is derived from the impossibility of choice.[14]

Butler could be offering us a rewriting of *Mercy* without the spit and venom. To call MacKinnon and Dworkin "gothic" theorists, then, is not to write them off as naive, as nontheoretical, but to begin to explore how their work engages and departs from the work of other feminists and poststructuralists.

One of the most intriguing readers of Dworkin and MacKinnon (a kindred spirit of sorts?) is Leo Bersani. Bersani argues that Dworkin and MacKinnon are right and powerful insofar as they conceptualize violence as inextricable from sexuality. They would seem to see the violence *of* and not just *in* the sexual. But if for MacKinnon and Dworkin the violence of the sexual is also always the violence of sexual difference, for Bersani gender or sexual difference is the fiction that denies a truer terror, "a nightmare of ontological obscenity."[15] If Dworkin and MacKinnon want to refuse and even prosecute the experience of femininity as injury, Bersani insists that sexuality consists of a denial and the reexperience of self-defeat. The repudiation of femininity, he suggests, repeats, or echoes, the trauma of subject formation. Bersani, Dworkin, and MacKinnon, I will argue, are theorists for whom feminism is (nearly) impossible.

SEX WORDS AND SEX

If ever there were a theorizer of "pornogothic performativity" it is Catharine MacKinnon. In *Only Words*, MacKinnon's recent collection of essays, she takes up the issue that troubles *Mercy*'s critics—what can "literary" language and/or representation be said to do? Or what distinguishes (mere) representation from that which constitutes reality?—and sets herself in a closer relationship to the very poststructuralist variety of feminism that she would seem to abhor. In attempting to specify an account of performativity, MacKinnon writes a kind of speech-act theory as a sex-act theory, a theory of the haunting sex-effect of words and/or images in the drama of embodiment. MacKinnon's theorization, as well as her own practice of extravagance—one can not but notice MacKinnon's style—it has been called "supremely rhetorical" and "rhetorically spectacular"—will facilitate my return to Dworkin's novel.[16] My concern here is with exploring the peculiar coupling of pornogothicism and feminist testimonial in what has come to be called "antisex" feminism. Do MacKinnon and Dworkin need to be warded off? Do they represent poststructuralist feminist theory's Other, its haunting doubled double?

Only Words is concerned primarily with pornography and with making the case for the constitutionality of MacKinnon and Dworkin's Minneapolis Ordinance, which was found unconstitutional in the U.S. courts.[17] MacKinnon argues that pornography needs to be thought of as a discriminatory *practice*. Current law, she asserts, in framing the pornography issue as one of free speech, leaves something out:

Pornography is essentially treated as defamation rather than as discrimination. That is, it is conceived in terms of what it says, which is imagined more or less effective or harmful as someone then acts on it, rather than in terms of what it does. Fundamentally, in this view, a form of communication cannot as such, *do* anything bad except offend. . . . Within the confines of this approach, to say that pornography is an act against women is seen as metaphorical or magical, rhetorical or unreal, a literary hyperbole or propaganda device. On the assumption that words have only a referential relation to reality, pornography is defended as only words—even when it is pictures women had to be directly used to make, even when the means of writing are women's bodies, even when a woman is destroyed in order to say it, or show it or because it was said or shown.[18]

MacKinnon makes two different arguments here. First, she argues that some forms of expression (not all?) are also acts, but then she asserts that expression works like a screen, covering over the true act that lurks behind. There is then a tension in *Only Words* between what is interestingly enough a kind of commonsense appeal to speech act theory (language is both constative and performative) and an invocation of what is extralinguistic (real women, real events).

MacKinnon and Dworkin are most often associated with the argument that says that pornography causes violence, that it makes men rape. In *Only Words*, MacKinnon stresses that she can more than make her point without needing to resort to this claim (37). So although "linear causality" is indeed one way that pornography is performative, according to Mac-

Kinnon, it is the least interesting, and indeed the least important (even some of MacKinnon's examples of "linear causality" are more complicated than one might expect).[19] Instead MacKinnon begins to argue in *Only Words* that pornography is performative because it not only represents or expresses sexual hierarchy and social reality but also effectively constitutes it: "Social inequality is substantially created and enforced — that is *done* — through words and images" (13).

In such statements, MacKinnon does not, as some contend, simply confuse words and actions but knots together different theories of the performative. Here she is arguing that language is performative in that it makes our reality. There are not real women on the one hand and representations of women on the other. MacKinnon writes, "sex in life is no less mediated than it is in art."[20] Where this theory becomes problematic is in its sense of the performative's absolute effectiveness. "Gender is what gender means," MacKinnon writes, but what gender means, for MacKinnon, would seem to be finished off and tied up. There is little sense that a making might also be an unmaking, that the excessive need to restage and restage (the boring repetitions of pornography) also signifies instability.[21]

MacKinnon also suggests that pornography is performative because it "does" its male consumer, bringing him to orgasm. Pornography has a performative dimension, according to MacKinnon, because "pornography . . . is sex" (16). Pornography acts on the body and compels it to repeat its gender assignment. The nightmare of *Only Words*, then, is the uncontrollable male body at the mercy of pornogothic discourse. MacKinnon writes: "the physical response to pornography is nearly a universal conditioned male reaction whether they like it or agree with what the materials say or not" (37). Men, as well as women, in MacKinnon's text, think, or fail to think, through the body. A performative is a performative, according to MacKinnon, because it bypasses reason, because it can do something other than it means, or because it does what it means as well as meaning it. When it comes to pornography, men are the ultimate sentimental or gothic consumers. For MacKinnon the very fact that our bodies can "act" without our consent makes men frightening and women tragic. She writes: "The forced complicity of the manipulated response of the victim's body is part of the injury and attaches both to the abusive relation and to the words that go with it" (60).

What deserves attention here is the particular way in which, for MacKinnon, sexual language is performative: "To say it is to do it, and to do it is to say it" (33). This is both a specification that MacKinnon insists upon and one that becomes quite difficult to hold on to, particularly in her discussion of harassing words. At first she argues, "The distinction that matters, in my view, is not between harassment based on race and harassment based on gender, which are often inseparable in any case, but between speech that is sex and speech that is not. Harassment that is sexual is a sex act, like pornography. Harassment that is not sexual works more through its content" (56). But then she must add, "It is amazing how few examples there are in this category, and how much of what might be simply gender or racial harassment proves on deeper examination to be sexual" (57). Sex words are sex acts when they act on the body. But when is language *not* forceful or stimulating? For MacKinnon, the answer is rarely. It is tempting to read "sexuality" as MacKinnon's name for the violence and or performativity of language, or, more accurately perhaps, for the performativity of language experienced as violence. MacKinnon asks us to consider an almost rhetorical question: when is violence not sexual?

In rejecting the reassuring distinction between sex and violence, Catharine MacKinnon arrives at a powerful critique of an earlier standard feminist account of rape:

Our problem has been to label something as rape, as sexual harassment, as pornography in the face of a suspicion that it might be intercourse, it might by ordinary sexual initiation, it might be erotic. To say that these purportedly sexual events violate us, to be against them, we call them not sexual. . . . It avoids saying that from women's point of view, intercourse, sex roles, and eroticism can be and at times are violent to us as women.[22]

To say that rape is violence not sex, MacKinnon has argued, entirely misses the problem. But this line of argumentation is precisely what makes Catharine MacKinnon and Andrea Dworkin's focus on pornography bewildering. If, as MacKinnon writes "pornography under current conditions *is* largely its own context" (108), if gender is (potentially) pornography all the time and everywhere, then why pornography as the crucial object of concern? If there were an entity to refer to with such ease would MacKinnon and Dworkin's analysis be called for? One gets the sense that pornography names something else: the unwilling participation of every gendered body in a history of violation. "Pornography," as a category, would seem to be a convenience for the pornogothic feminists and MacKinnon almost says this herself: "In pornography, there it is, in one place, all of the abuses that women had to struggle so long even to begin to articulate, all the *unspeakable* abuse: the rape, the battery, the sexual harassment, the prostitution, and the sexual abuse of children. Only in the pornography it is called something else: sex, sex, sex, sex, and sex, respectively."[23] "Pornography" would seem to name and contain the uncontainable, and unframeable: context itself. The irony here is that for MacKinnon and Dworkin the problem is not being able to frame off or frame in representations in the first place.

But *why* do sexual words "do" and thus become sex? MacKinnon writes: "I am not ultimately sure why this is the case, but it has something to do with the positioning of sex words in sexual abuse, in abuse as sex, in sex as abuse, in sex" (58). It is hard to know whether to read this "explanation" as a somewhat mesmerizing and not-so-meaningful varied repetition, or as something more. Is the argument, for example, that language use is originally associated with a traumatizing event and that thereafter the words themselves carry with them the trauma? MacKinnon goes on to argue: "It is not so much that the sexual terms reference a reality as that they reaccess and restimulate body memory of it for both aggressor and victim. The aggressor gets an erection; the victim screams and struggles and bleeds and blisters and becomes five years old. 'Being offended' is the closest the First Amendment tradition comes to grasping this effect" (59). For MacKinnon, repetition is at the heart of the matter. Language cannot be trusted to merely refer, to only represent. There is a yearning here for a doubled and untroubled origin for both language and sexuality, for "sex words . . . [and] sex." Much of the impact of MacKinnon's theory comes from the way in which it both approaches and backs away from articulating this origin as an impossibility.

To invoke MacKinnon's yearning for untroubled origins is to position her with respect to psychoanalytic debate, and more recently with respect to debate about recovered memories. MacKinnon's hostility towards psychoanalysis is explicit, as is her position on deconstruction: she writes of "a society saturated with pornography, not to mention an academy saturated with deconstruction" (7). But my concern here is not with what MacKinnon herself says about psychoanalysis (psychoanalysis as one more male practice that did not and does not believe women). In fact, MacKinnon's yearning for untroubled origins is hardly non-Freudian. I would argue instead that MacKinnon's account of trauma resembles Freud's seduction theory, although not for the reason that one might think, not because Freud once believed, and MacKinnon believes in real abuse.

In "Fantasy and the Origins of Sexuality," J. Laplanche and J.-B.

Pontalis argue that the seduction theory often gets misrepresented. That is, what gets forgotten or effaced is the fact that it is a theory and not a simple assertion of real abuse or seduction. In Freud's scheme there are at least two events: the first event consists of a child being approached by an adult in a sexual manner, but for the child, who is presexual, the event is not traumatic. The second event which occurs after puberty is even less traumatic than the first. It works, however, to invoke the earlier scene retroactively: "It is then the recall of the first scene which sets off the upsurge of sexual excitation, catching the ego in reverse, and leaving it disarmed incapable of using the normally outward-directed defenses." [24] In this account, trauma cannot be said to come either from the outside or the inside, but from an inside that is like an outside, from an incorporated "foreign body": "we may say that the whole of trauma comes *both* from within and without: from without, since sexuality reaches the subject from *the other*; from within, since it springs from this internalized exteriority." [25] While the positing of a wholly innocent child in a world of perverse adults is obviously "pure illusion," something which Freud himself was on the verge of making explicit in this period (1895–97), Laplanche and Pontalis call this illusion "myth" and suggest that "something was lost with the discarding of the seduction theory; beneath the conjunction and temporal interplay of the two 'scenes' there lay a pre-subjective structure, beyond both the strict happening and the internal imagery." [26]

I would suggest that Catharine MacKinnon, the antipsychoanalytic antiporn activist, relies on a similar theory of the subject and the event. While she argues that words and images are injurious, she does not suggest that they attack from the outside: "Pornography does not leap off the shelf and assault women. Women could, in theory, walk safely past whole warehouses full of it, quietly resting in its jackets" (15). Or again, to be more accurate, she does not say just this. Instead words and images are injurious for MacKinnon insofar as they constitute some form of repetition, a repetition that could be said to reanimate a foreign body, or that which is foreign within one's own body.

MacKinnon's theory of the particularly performative quality of sexual language would thus seem to be a theory of sexuality as trauma, or at least of sexuality as so frequently traumatizing that language gets tainted, spoiled for the rest of the time. Accounts of the difficulty of testifying to deeply disturbing events frequently include appeals to the inadequacies of language (to be traumatized is to have one's very capacity to represent be overwhelmed). But for MacKinnon the very fact that language carries sex, can so successfully be it and do it (i.e., produce its effects), leads to another type of problem: "That sexual words make sex happen, with extended effects on women, is further supported by observing what happens when victims of sexual harassment speak the abuser's words, testifying to what he said. When she says what he said, what is she *doing?*" (64).

The basic argument here is that one cannot just "mention," that one cannot protect one's speech and demand that it be only citational—or rather that this is the case when it comes to sex. MacKinnon's argument participates in the Derridian deconstruction of the use/mention hierarchy. Derrida establishes that using an expression depends on being able to merely cite it (meaning is governed by convention), and conversely every citation can rewrite the rules. For MacKinnon this has its political consequences. Her displacement of the logic of intention insists that one cannot choose simply to say what one means; words have their effects, regardless. If John Searle is worried by the fact that "use" is haunted by "mention," Catharine MacKinnon shows us what is politically at stake in the fact that "mention" is haunted by "use."[27]

MacKinnon uses her analysis of trauma and sexuality to think about Anita Hill's historic testimony before the Senate Judiciary Committee in 1991 and what compromised its effectiveness. Anita Hill, in order to testify, had to repeat what Clarence Thomas said, but the very fact that she did repeat what prospective Justice Clarence Thomas said, MacKinnon argues, undermined her credibility. Sex words are uncitable. MacKinnon says of Hill, "I felt she did not want his words in her mouth" (66). MacKinnon argues that the closer and closer Hill came to exact citation (really saying what Thomas said to her) the less plausible she became. According to MacKinnon "her" exact citation becomes "his" excitation. She writes: "There is nothing else like this. . . . Only words; but because they are sex, the speaker as well as the spoken-about is transformed into sex" (67). "There is nothing else like this." "Sexual" becomes Catharine MacKinnon's name for the unrepresentable, or the unspeakable, for traumatic repetition; sex is that which returns to haunt us. MacKinnon argues that sexuality collapses "use" and "mention," and that this is its very specific danger, but is it also precisely this danger that can do feminist work? *Only Words* begins, after all, with a peculiarly pornogothic passage. MacKinnon would seem to practice what she preaches against:

Imagine that for hundreds of years your most formative traumas, your daily suffering and pain, the abuse you live through, the terror you live with, are unspeakable—not the basis of literature. You grow up with your father holding you down and covering your mouth so another man can make a horrible searing pain between your legs. When you are older, your husband ties you to the bed and drips hot wax on your nipples and brings in other men to watch and makes you smile through it. Your doctor will not give you the drugs he has addicted you to unless you suck his penis. (3)

This passage constitutes a plea for identification. Imagine that this is you (women) and it becomes Everywoman, or imagine that this were you (men) and forever rethink your relationship to sexual politics through a conscious and conscientious, although hopefully not lascivious act of cross-gendered identification. MacKinnon issues an invitation to identify, to insert, and to locate oneself in this scene of fantasy. But the point I want to emphasize here is that no matter how true, how evidentially based, this opener strives for shock effect. The opening of *Only Words* has to work by overwhelming or fail to work for precisely this reason. The force of MacKinnon's political call comes from its fantastic similarity to the sexual force of pornography. "When she says what he says what is she *doing?*" becomes not only a question for Dworkin's *Mercy* but also a question that MacKinnon's text should ask itself.

But while a representation's bark may be its bite, there is also a strange utopian streak in MacKinnon and Dworkin's thinking. Somewhere in MacKinnon and Dworkin is the utopianism that only a paranoid theory can harbor—for maybe if "pornography" names the problem, or is a way of naming the problem, there is a solution. In other words, to call the force of words, the performative and evocative effects of language, "pornography" is to stabilize, in utopian fashion, an effect that far exceeds that of a single type of representation. A paranoid theory may be the only answer, the only way to resolve what Judith Butler has called "a fundamentally unprosecutable history."[28] While MacKinnon and Dworkin have been accused of paranoia, this would seem to be neither an unjust accusation nor a condemnation of their theory making. MacKinnon and Dworkin construct "the pornographer" and even personify pornography in order to hold someone responsible for an injury, for injuries, that would otherwise seem to get lost and be relentlessly repeated in a chain of citation.

FOREIGN BODIES

The self in *Mercy* consists of language, a set of varied and repeated sentences: "My name is Andrea. It means manhood or courage. In Europe only boys are named it. I live in the U.S.A. I was born down the street from Walt Whitman's house, on Mickle Street in Camden in 1946, after the war, after the bomb. . . . Everyone says I'm sad but I'm not sad" (29). *Mercy* is a series of monologues. We first hear the speaker at age nine, and by the novel's end she is twenty-seven.[29] And it is a catalogue of experiences of sexual violence: from child abuse, to date rape, to acquaintance rape, to abuse by the medical/juridical establishment. *Mercy*'s opening chapter explores the violence of representing sexual violation.

The narrator of "In August 1956 (Age 9)" is a child, but she already has more knowledge than the self she is narrating. She already knows, for example, the word "rape": "I wasn't raped until I was almost ten . . . I wasn't really raped, I guess, just touched a lot by a strange dark-haired man . . . and I didn't know the word rape, which is just some awful word, so it didn't hurt me because nothing happened" (5). The narrator slips into the second person ("You get asked if anything happened") which suggests a discomfort on the speaker's part that manifests itself as a form of dissociation, and also works to make the experience belong to others as well as to Andrea. Much of this opening section concerns the confrontation between the anxious adults, who want to get information from this child without telling her anything, and the desperate child, Andrea, who wants to be heard:

You get asked if anything happened and you say well yes he put his hand here and he rubbed me and he put his arm around my shoulder and he scared me and he followed me and he whispered something to me and then someone says but did anything happen . . . and then they say, thank God nothing happened. So you try to make them understand that yes something did happen honest you aren't lying and you say it again . . . you say yes something did happen. (6)

The violence of the events for the nine-year-old Andrea (a stranger sexually assaults her in an almost deserted movie theater) consists in her experiencing them as a threat to her self-ness ("[he] put his hands on my legs and rubbed me all over; my legs; *my* legs; me; my; my legs; my; my; my legs," 7). There is also a violence because there is a gap; Andrea does not understand this man's language, his sounds. It is as if he is a "foreigner," maybe even an alien being.[30] This then is the incomprehensible experience that must nevertheless be taken on, be taken in. But if this mysterious aggressor will be with Andrea forever ("even now he is right next to me," 27), the putting of this "origin" into language is at least equally a source of distress.

While the adults could be said to withhold real names from Andrea (if only Andrea knew how to name her body she would accurately describe its violation in terms we would all agree upon?), their language is also selective in what it names, what it represents: the only nameable sex act, the only act that signifies, is sexual intercourse. Either "something happened" or "nothing happened." It is the adult discourse, their fierce questions, that establish the charged significance of inside/outside ("they ask if something went inside but when you ask inside where they look away," 7). Inside/Outside becomes the novel's dominant figure, and the most crucial figure in Andrea Dworkin's work.

This original scene of violation takes place in a "theater . . . like a huge, dark castle. . . a cave of darkness," in which Andrea feels as if she is "buried alive" (25). The "dark castle" and live burial hardly need to be established as gothic motifs, yet *Mercy* would seem to repeatedly assert and deny its gothic mode. Later in the novel, a prison is described as being "not a castle or a palace or an old monastery. . . . It was cold; stone cold; just a stone cold prison outside of time, high and nasty" (135). *Mercy* denies the gothic both by asserting its own bare truthfulness ("Can't be. No one can live that way. Can't be. Isn't true. Can't be. Was. Was. . . . If I deviate I am lost; I have to be literal," 46, 231), and by paring down the gothic problematic to one of inside versus outside. Is the violation of inside by outside (in *Mercy* men are always pounding to get in) itself a figure, or the ground for all the violence that the novel refigures almost endlessly?

Recent feminist work has argued that the body, our bodies, are discursively constructed, or more precisely that there is no reference to the body that does not also produce it.[31] Dworkin, on the other hand, even as she shows that embodiment and signification cannot be thought apart, repeatedly and finally invokes the body's singular truth, a truth that no other can rival. In her texts this often happens simply and flatly (or rather, simply and extravagantly). Dworkin would seem to abandon her own theory of violence as that which cannot always be brought back to physical pain. This happens in the first chapter of *Mercy*, in which, in case we were not convinced by the heroine's "something happened," we are told repeatedly that her body actually hurts (9). *Mercy* is about *"constant, true, and perpetual pain"* that is always, in the end, bodily (321). This would seem to be an indication not only of *Mercy*'s unstable ground and desire for such stability but also of the difficulty that trauma theory must negotiate. If all traumas were initially physical (a breach of the surface, the outside coming in, the inside leaking out)—trauma means wound—what is the status of the analogy? How can a psychical trauma be like a physical trauma without being it? What is psychical injury?[32] By returning all injury to the body, I would argue that *Mercy* circumvents its own best insights. For example, it both suggests and leaves behind, gets around, the idea that the very conditions for injury (inside/integrity versus outside/force) are themselves established through an injurious process.[33]

Mercy works by collapsing. It comes off as a very self-full story of selflessness, a very egotistical account of feminine egolessness. The novel is at once all Andrea (there are no other characters) and Andrea absorbs all women. Identification has been reduced to its paranoid foundation: it is as if being or not being Andrea Dworkin were the only options for anyone. This heroine is a figure of allegorical proportions, an Everywoman without boundaries who repeatedly and madly identifies with the most spectacular of victims ("My true point of origin is Birkenau . . . where we died, my family and I. . . . Everything that matters about me begins there . . . a far back memory, back before speech or rationality or self-justification, it's way back in my mind but it's whole, it's deep down where no one can touch it or change it," 164). With little transition we go from reading about Buddhist monks, Vietnam, and self-immolation to pornography, Linda Lovelace, and Times Square ("One day the women will burn down Times Square; I've seen it in my mind; I know," 328). Andrea herself becomes a holocaust victim (*not* a survivor), one of the suicides from Massada, and a martyr to antiporn activism (at the end of section ten the heroine sets fire to herself and is consumed by the flames only to reappear in the next monologue). *Mercy* literalizes. The implicit structure of metaphor (this is like that) or identification (I am like you) dissolves. *Mercy* is maddeningly absolute.[34]

In *Mercy* she who was a victim, and who passes through a stage of exhibitory masochism ("I would have stayed there strung up against the wall my back cut open forever for him to see but he didn't see," 96), becomes in the end an avenger, and one who can, indeed, name the crime of rape. All the same, the story is not straightforwardly one of evolution or education. One cannot help feeling that the same thing keeps happening. The novel's final scene, for example, relates the academic feminist's fantasy of raping the antiporn activist (Andrea). This repetition of violence echoes pornogothic convention. Dworkin writes elsewhere of the ultimate pornogothic novel, "The Story of O," that "pornography is never big on plot."[35] But this is also the repetition, I would suggest, of the trauma victim's nonexperience, of repetition compulsion. In *Mercy* events are traumatic not because bad things are buried beneath consciousness, but because they overwhelm consciousness's ability to represent its (non)experiences to itself. The "mercy" of the title is the fact that "nobody remembers the worst" (158). *Mercy* suggests that traumatic histories are best written as gothic fictions.

Dworkin's novel is about occupied interiors, about the outside coming in and the inside being emptied out: "He pushes it in, she pushes it out, a dead spot in the brain marks the spot, there's a teeny little cemetery in her brain . . . little strokes every time there's a rape, time gone, hours or days or weeks, words gone, self gone, memory wiped out, severely impaired; I cannot remember—how do you *exist?*" (322–23). The gothic body is the body that can be violated, entered. The body that is haunted ever after. Rape produces ghosts (327). The body in *Mercy* is no *one's* body, that is no character's body, it has no particularizing traits (apart from being sexed). This at once works against the conventions of realism and pornography (realism and the pornographic both require the illusion of some specificity: blonde hair or brown) and invites identification: Joanna Russ has noted the blurriness of the heroine in the modern gothic—one is to fill in one's own features. The body is at once the ground of truth in *Mercy*—"once the body testifies you know"—and the unstable site where physical injury becomes the most extravagant of figures (133). There is a stigmata scene (162). There are kisses that turn into wounds (211). There is green acid-like blood. The body's reality is thus simultaneously what the novel insists most on and what would seem to be most in question.

Mercy's fantastic descriptions of the body swerve away from the erotic and read instead as misogynist nightmare. Wendy Steiner argues that "*[Mercy]* is to pornography what aversion therapy is to rape."[36] In Dworkin's novel the heroine's body is nothing short of repulsive:

I am a citizen of the night, with a passport, a mouth used enough, it's vulgar to say but inside it changes, the skin gets raw and red and it blisters, it gets small, tight, white blisters, liquidy blisters, it gets tough and brown, it gets leathery, it sags in loose red places and there are black-and-blue marks, and your tongue never touches the roof of your mouth, instead there's a layer of slime. (320)

It is as if there is never enough language, enough repetition, enough excess, to describe this body. *Mercy* risks becoming not only misogynist, but even humorous. If the novel draws on the élite texts in the porno-gothic tradition (Bataille, de Sade, Réage), it also participates in low gothic: the rape revenge drama, the horror film.[37]

Mercy longs after a "lost" coherence, sanctity, and wholeness, "a brilliant physical solitude with all the self spread out along the fault lines of the thighs" (314). It seems to argue that the body needs to be whole, unviolated, and perhaps unviolable, if there is to be anything like a self ("I never had a me and still don't except by forcing myself to think so," 313). *Mercy*'s obsession is quite particularly with penetration and with the violation of the body's boundaries. The very landscape is rewritten as a rape-scape. It is ultimately the fact that the wound or "gash" can be read as a figure for the feminine condition that *Mercy* cannot endure.

Mercy and *Only Words* gothicize embodiment; the body is the woman's unassimilable past always ready to take her by surprise. In both of these works the category of bodily memory is central and also paradoxical. The problem is that it is only the body that remembers, but the body cannot remember; it can only repeat or (re)embody. While *Only Words* concerns itself, then, with what language does to bodies, how language makes bodies what they are, *Mercy*'s gothic body reposes the question of femininity and its discontents in the most fantastic of forms. Pornogothic feminism articulates the undeniably conservative force of language and its thrilling power to remake and undo.

THE PHALLIC EGO AND THE REPUDIATION OF FEMININITY

While Andrea Dworkin struggles with her sense that the ego is embodied, sexed, phallicized, or lacking, Leo Bersani values precisely this: the fact that the ego is phallicized only to compensate for lack, for egolessness, for the fragility and precariousness that border self-defeat and the extraordinary ordinariness of pleasure. Bersani's "Is the Rectum a Grave?," like MacKinnon and Dworkin's work, offers an account of trauma and sexuality, and while Bersani's text is certainly not feminist, I would argue that it can offer us a prehistory for the pornogothic project. Bersani, like MacKinnon and Dworkin, suspects that the obstacle feminism faces is inseparable from embodiment itself. Indeed, "Is the Rectum a Grave?" goes some way towards accounting for Richard Rorty's "instinctive and ineffable horror," for his sense that identifying with femininity is nothing less than a gothic experience. For Bersani the repudiation of femininity may not be "bedrock," but it comes very close.[38]

"There is a big secret about sex," Bersani writes, "Most people don't like it." Catharine MacKinnon and Andrea Dworkin are not alone. "Is the Rectum a Grave?" pursues the concept of an aversion to (as opposed to a repression of) sexuality, and Bersani argues that "aversion" comes in both benign and malignant forms: "Malignant aversion has recently had an extraordinary opportunity both to express (and to expose) itself, and tragically, to demonstrate its power. I'm thinking of course of responses to AIDS—more specifically, of how a public health crisis has been treated like an unprecedented sexual threat" (198). Bersani wants to question the relationship between politics and sexuality, "the extremely obscure process by which sexual pleasure generates politics" (207). "To want sex with another man," he remarks, "is not exactly a credential for political radicalism" (205).

Bersani is skeptical about the politicization of parody. He argues, for example, that gay men who parody, or repeat, a macho style are not necessarily subversive. Or rather, insofar as they could be said to practice subversion it is not because they parody masculinity—they don't just cite it—but because their identification with the masculine ideal is a form of madness.[39] Bersani writes:

The sexist power that defines maleness in most human cultures can easily survive social revolutions; what it perhaps cannot survive is a certain way of assuming, or taking on, that power. If, as [Jeffrey] Weeks put it, gay men "gnaw at the roots of a male heterosexual identity," it is not because of the parodistic distance that they take from that identity, but rather because, from within their nearly mad identification with it, *they never cease to feel the appeal of its being violated.* (209)

This "nearly mad identification" is the loving identification with one's enemies that Bersani sees as both specific to gay male sexuality and more generally descriptive of all desire, insofar as it "combines and confuses impulses to appropriate and identify with its object" (209). But does desire confuse "having" and "being" or "being" and "being like"? For Bersani, a gay politics can be generated out of the discontinuous experience of political sympathy and fantasy, or rather out of the very discontinuity that constitutes sexual fantasy: a "yearning" towards masculinity and the passionate pleasure experienced in its defeat or violation.

While MacKinnon and Dworkin's work lacks the subtlety one associates with a calculated performance then, Bersani's concept of "mad identification" suggests that care and control, "ironic distance," is hardly the key to sexual politics. Bersani apologizes for some of MacKinnon and Dworkin's "crazy" sounding formulations, but he also appreciates their political effectiveness and appeals to their work in his effort to "understand the homophobic rage unleashed by AIDS" (213). Bersani writes: "Their [MacKinnon and Dworkin's] indictment of sex . . . has had the immensely desirable effect of publicizing, of lucidly laying out for us, the inestimable value of sex as—at least in certain of its ineradicable aspects—anticommunity, antiegalitarian, antinurturing, antiloving" (215).[40] But for Bersani, MacKinnon and Dworkin draw the wrong conclusions. They fail with their lingering desire to redeem sex, with their desire to take part in what Bersani calls its "redemptive reinvention" (215). One might consider, for example, MacKinnon's utopian flight at the end of *Only Words:* she dreams of a world in which silence would not be the site of power but would be the space of "repose," the space for thinking up, imagining, "new conversation[s]" (110). According to Bersani, "brutality" and "idealization" express the same fantasy, enact the same displacement. They are part of the same "pastoralizing project . . . designed to preserve us from a nightmare of ontological obscenity, from the prospect of a breakdown of the human itself in sexual intensities" (221). The body, argues Bersani, is our original experience of power and powerlessness; it is delusory to think of it as "belatedly contaminated by power from elsewhere" (221).

Bersani, picking up on an earlier argument of his own based on a reading of Freud's *Three Essays,* argues that sexuality is traumatic, or rather that the presexual is traumatic, for the infant is "shattered" with stimuli. The sexual is the transmutation of this trauma into masochism. The best defense, in other words, involves taking pleasure at offense, turning offense into pleasure: "Masochism," Bersani writes, "would be the psychical strategy that partially defeats a biologically dysfunctional process of maturation" (217). Bersani argues that Freud offers two accounts of sexuality: "on the one hand Freud outlines a normative sexual development that finds its natural goal in the post-Oedipal, genitally centered desire for someone of the opposite sex, while on the other hand he suggests not only the irrelevance of the object in sexuality but also, and more radically, a shattering of the psychic structures themselves that are the precondition for the very establishment of a relation to others" (217). Bersani goes on to argue that the living of the second version of sexuality (sexuality as self-shattering) as if it were the first (a desire for an object or objects) leads to the most egregious and mundane violence.[41]

What one might want to ask Bersani at this point, however, is where sexual difference enters into this account. Does it make a difference at all? Why should it make such a difference to MacKinnon and Dworkin? A Bersani-style analysis of MacKinnon and Dworkin's work would suggest, I think, that they allegorize the battle within the subject by writing the story as the battle between subjects, gendered subjects. But of course their allegorizing misapprehension is far from idiosyncratic. Nobody needed MacKinnon and Dworkin to invent masculinity and femininity, the villain and the victim, the massive gothicization of gendered experience. And even Bersani argues that misogyny is what makes a full and proud subjectivity possible. If feminism is to succeed, it is this full and proud subject (the only subject that there is?) that it must deflate.

If Bersani starts with the body, he hastens to distinguish his position from so-called essentialist thinking. The body, he insists, has its exploitable fantasmatic potential. It is this "exploitation" that Bersani labels "ideological." "Phallocentrism" names a "long and inglorious history" of such exploitation. Here is how Bersani defines the term: "Phallocentrism is . . . above all the denial of the *value* of powerlessness in both men and women. I don't mean the value of gentleness, or nonaggressiveness, or even of passivity, but rather of a more radical disintegration and humiliation of the self" (217). Pornogothic feminism, under the terms of Bersani's diagnosis, would name a decidedly phallocentric discourse. MacKinnon and Dworkin want to claim for women the privilege (of misrecognition?) that men have always had.

Bersani argues finally that sexuality is made up of two moments but that the second, self-fullness, only functions to deny the first. He writes a stunning account that rivals MacKinnon for rhetorical effect:

It is possible to think of the sexual as, precisely, moving between a hyperbolic sense of self and a loss of all consciousness of self. But sex as self-hyperbole is perhaps a repression of sex as self-abolition. It inaccurately replicates self-shattering as self-swelling, as psychic tumescence. If, as these words suggest, men are especially apt to "choose" this version of sexual pleasure, because their sexual equipment appears to invite by analogy, or at least to facilitate, the phallicizing of the ego, neither sex has exclusive rights to the practice of sex as self-hyperbole. For it is perhaps primarily *the degeneration of the sexual into a relationship that condemns sexuality to becoming a struggle for power*. As soon as persons are posited, the war begins. It is the self that swells with excitement at the idea of being on top, the self that makes of the inevitable play of thrusts and relinquishments in sex an argument for the natural authority of one sex over the other. (218)

This very dense passage suggests, among other things, that one who inhabits a male body is more likely to misread, more likely to use what he has to deny "the terrifying appeal of a loss of the ego" (220), to misrecognize the self's status in a very interested way (the name of the game is survival): "the self is a practical convenience; promoted to the status of an ethical ideal, it is a sanction for violence" (222). It is difficult, however, not to question the forceful role that the figuration plays here. Doesn't Bersani phallicize sexuality and then find that all sexuality lends itself to this phallic analogy (why should self-hyperbole become so quickly equated with "self-swelling," "psychic tumescence")? In Bersani's account heterosexuality, any positing of difference *between* the sexes, would have to be doomed, would have to be militarized if not gothicized. "Is the Rectum a Grave?" is wary of the lie (the idealization) that would have us believe that sexual *relationships* are possible, that love and sex go hand in glove. Bersani, sounding like MacKinnon ("If bottom is bottom, look across time and space, and women are who you will find there"), writes that "gay men should . . . resist being drawn into mimicking the unrelenting warfare between men and women, which nothing has ever changed" (218).[42]

THE MADNESS OF IDENTIFICATION

In searching for the source of a dangerously violent homophobia, Bersani finds not exactly the repudiation of femininity, but the repudiation of another's identification with femininity ("the . . . seductive and intolerable image of a grown man, legs high in the air, unable to refuse the suicidal ecstasy of being a woman," 212). Passionate identification with the feminine produces panic at the site of selfhood. The only way out of misogyny, it would seem, is to recognize that the self is not an ideal to fight for or to rigorously defend but a convenient and presumably pleasurable fiction. But what would it mean to experience selfhood only as a "practical convenience"? Andrea Dworkin's *Mercy* asks this question with some urgency. Isn't the self more like an emergency measure? *Mercy* dramatizes the constant effort of the self to identify with itself. It reveals the madness of identification as self-constituting and self-dispersing. Dworkin's text finds pleasure and power in multiplicity even as it would suggest that self-multiplication is (merely) posttraumatic: "And I am real; Andrea one, two, three, there's more than one, I am reliably informed; the raped; Andrea named for courage, a new incarnation of virility, in the old days called manhood and I'm what happens when it's fucked" (318).

But what makes identification mad? Perhaps the process of self-constitution is mad insofar as it fails to distinguish similarity from identity. The melancholic as paradigmatic subject: I am like you. I want you. I am where I refuse to give you up. Tellingly, MacKinnon has been accused of a similar madness, of confusing similarity with identity and even of collapsing grossly dissimilar terms.[43] MacKinnon writes, "pornography establish[es] . . . what women are said to exist *as* are seen *as*, are treated *as* . . . constructing the social reality of what a woman is," and Judith Butler asks, "through what means does the 'as' turn into an 'is,' and is this the doing of pornography, or is it the doing of the very *depiction* of pornography that MacKinnon provides?"[44] Butler cannily suggests that MacKinnon enacts what she proceeds to critique, that she claims constative status for her veiled performance. Yet MacKinnon's work, as I have been suggesting, like Butler's, is valuable for some of the ways in which it troubles this distinction: constative versus performative. While MacKinnon calls our attention to the force of sexual language, she also uses this force to effect her own political intervention.

What is most disconcerting about Dworkin and MacKinnon, finally, is that they do not parody pornography or the gothic; instead, they madly identify with these genres. And this raises questions about the position or positions of identification (of, for example, identification with the aggressor). Where does the violence come from? In a *Ms.* magazine roundtable on pornography, Dworkin describes her double vision: "It's hard to look at a picture of a woman's body," she says, "and not see it *with* the perception that her body is being exploited."[45] Pornogothic feminism describes what it is to suffer from the inability to not see, or to know when one might not see, traces of the past. For pornogothic feminism, history keeps happening, and pornography reproduces its pornographers. In this sense, pornogothic feminism offers us a very unhappy theory of the performative. Yet seeing the harm that pornography causes necessarily involves the very splitting and dissociation, the appropriation, that in turn problematizes the critique. With MacKinnon and Dworkin, it is no secret that theory produces what it also describes. Their mad identifications remind us that the space within quotation marks is no sanctuary.

NOTES

1. Andrea Dworkin, *Mercy* (New York: Four Walls Eight Windows, 1990), 156. Further references to this work will be included parenthetically in the text.

2. Wendy Steiner argues that *Mercy* forfeits a distinction between the fictional and nonfictional (Wendy Steiner, "Declaring War on Men," Review of *Mercy* by Andrea Dworkin, *New York Times Book Review* [15 Sept. 1991]: 11–12); Roz Kaveney worries that *Mercy* is dirty politics—that is, politics turned literary (Roz Kaveney, Review of *Mercy* by Andrea Dworkin, *Feminist Review* 38 [Summer 1991]: 79–85); and Harriet Gilbert is struck by the way in which *Mercy* so "carefully echoes" numerous "classic pornographic conventions" (Harriet Gilbert, "So Long As It's Not Sex and Violence: Andrea Dworkin's *Mercy*," in *Sex Exposed: Sexuality and the Pornography Debate*, ed. Lynne Segal and Mary McIntosh [New Brunswick, NJ: Rutgers University Press, 1993], 224).

3. Jacques Derrida has argued that to belong to a genre is always also not to belong. This is "the law of the law of genre. . . . It is precisely a principle of contamination, a law of impurity, a parasitical economy. In the code of set theories, if I may use it at least figuratively, I would speak of a sort of participation without belonging" (Jacques Derrida, "The Law of Genre," in *Acts of Literature*, ed. Derek Attridge [New York: Routledge, 1992], 228). He also suggests that to remark on this belonging/not belonging is what it means to be literary: "this re-mark—ever possible for every text, for every corpus of traces is absolutely necessary for and constitutive of what we call art, poetry, or literature" (229). Paul de Man's "Excuses" would also seem to suggest that difficulties in the critical receptions of *Mercy* are inevitable. De Man writes of fiction: "the radical irresponsibility of fiction is, in a way, so obvious that it seems hardly necessary to caution against its misreading. . . . [Yet] it seems to be impossible to isolate the moment in which the fiction stands free of any signification; in the very moment at which it is posited, as well as in the context that it generates, it gets at once misinterpreted into a determination which is *ipso facto* overdetermined. Yet without this moment, never allowed to exist as such, no such thing as a text is conceivable" (Paul de Man, "Excuses," in *Allegories of Reading: Figural Language in Rousseau, Nietzsche, Rilke, and Proust* [New Haven: Yale University Press, 1977], 293).

4. Gilbert, "So Long As It's Not Sex and Violence," 222.

5. The definitions of "constative" and "performative" are Derrida's para-phrases of Austin (Jacques Derrida, "Signature Event Context," in *Limited Inc.* [Evanston, IL: Northwestern University Press, 1988], 13). Jonathan Culler de-scribes what happens in the course of Austin's analysis: "Austin's analysis provides a splendid instance of the logic of supplementarity at work. Starting from the philosophical hierarchy that makes true or false statements the norm of language and treats other utterances as flawed statements or extra—supplementary—forms, Austin's investigation of the qualities of the marginal cases leads to a deconstruction and inversion of the hierarchy: the performative is not a flawed constative: rather, the constative is a special case of the performative" (Jonathan Culler, *On Deconstruction: Theory and Criticism after Structuralism* [London:

Routledge and Kegan Paul, 1983], 133). For critiques and extensions of the concept of the performative see Judith Butler's *Bodies that Matter: On the Discursive Limits of "Sex"* (New York: Routledge, 1993) and Eve Kosofsky Sedgwick's "Queer Performativity" *GLQ* 1.1 (Spring 1993): 1–16.

6. J. L. Austin, *How to Do Things with Words* (Cambridge: Harvard University Press, 1975), 22. Derrida's "Signature Event Context" is a reading of the implications of this exclusionary gesture. Derrida asks: "For ultimately, isn't it true that what Austin excludes as anomaly, exception, 'non-serious,' *citation* (on stage, in a poem, or a soliloquy) is the determined modification of a general citationality—or rather, a general iterability—without which there would not even be a 'successful' performative? . . . Would a performative utterance be possible if a citational doubling [*doublure*] did not come to split and dissociate from itself the pure singularity of the event?" (17).

7. See Frances Ferguson, "Pornography: The Theory," *Critical Inquiry* 21 (Spring 1995): 686.

8. *Mercy* has at least a doubled relationship to the performative, as both the pornogothic and testimonial have their peculiarly performative dimensions. A testimony, and particularly a testimony to trauma, produces—for the first time—what it also re-presents. Psychoanalyst Dori Laub writes, "In the process of the testimony to a trauma, as in psychoanalytic practice, in effect, you often do not want to know anything except what the patient tells you, because what is important is the situation of *discovery* of knowledge—its evolution, and its very *happening*. Knowledge in the testimony is, in other words, not simply a factual given that is reproduced and replicated by the testifier, but a genuine advent, an event in its own right" (Dori Laub, "Bearing Witness, or the Vicissitudes of Listening," in Shoshana Felman and Dori Laub, *Testimony: Crises of Witnessing in Literature, Psychoanalysis, and History* [New York: Routledge, 1992], 62).

9. Judith Butler, "Burning Acts: Injurious Speech," in *Deconstruction Is/in America*, ed. Anselm Haverkamp (New York: New York University Press), 157.

10. Peter Hamill would seem to offer one of the least recognizable descriptions of MacKinnon and Dworkin's work when he remarks "[that it] is some of the saddest writing I've ever read . . . there is no fantasy or magic" (quoted in Nadine Strossen, *Defending Pornography: Free Speech, Sex, and the Fight for Women's Rights* [New York: Scribners, 1995], 146). The "magic" in MacKinnon and Dworkin's account comes in part from treating what Austin calls a "perlocutionary" act as if it were an "illocutionary" one. In other words, while warning is an illocutionary act in Austin's terms (I warn you . . .), persuasion is a perlocutionary one. I may be able to persuade you, but no speech-act is in and of itself an act of persuasion (I can't say "I persuade you," or rather, if I said "Can't I persuade you?" I'd be pleading not persuading). This simple distinction (illocutionary vs. perlocutionary) is in turn complicated by the fact that both illocutionary and perlocutionary acts require the "proper" conditions, the right context. See Culler, *On Deconstruction*, 114.

11. Richard Rorty, "Feminism and Pragmatism," *Michigan Quarterly Review* 30.2 (Spring 1991): 233.

12. On the female gothic see Eugenia C. DeLamotte, *Perils of the Night: A*

Feminist Study of Nineteenth Century Gothic (New York: Oxford University Press, 1990); Kate Ferguson Ellis, *The Contested Castle: Gothic Novels and the Subversion of Domestic Ideology* (Urbana: University of Illinois Press, 1989); Juliann E. Fleenor, ed., *The Female Gothic* (Montreal: Eden Press, 1984); Claire Kahane, "The Gothic Mirror," in Garner, et al., eds., *The (M)other Tongue* (Ithaca: Cornell University Press, 1986), 335–51; Ellen Moers, "Female Gothic," in *Literary Women* (New York: Doubleday, 1976), 90–110; Elaine Showalter, "American Female Gothic," in *Sister's Choice: Tradition and Change in American Women's Writing* (New York: Oxford University Press, 1994), 127–44; and Anne Williams, *Art of Darkness: A Poetics of Gothic* (Chicago: The University of Chicago Press, 1995). Showalter connects the identification and theorization of the genre "female gothic" ("a genre that expresse[s] women's dark protests, fantasies, and fear") with the women's movement and the rise of feminist criticism. While the term was originally Moers's, Showalter notes its use and redefinition by a variety of critics. Moers writes, "what I mean by Female Gothic is easily defined: the work that women writers have done in the literary mode that, since the eighteenth century, we have called the Gothic. But what I mean—or anyone else means—by 'the Gothic' is not so easily stated" (90). In a recent attempt to articulate a more specific definition of this genre with its gendered forms and to explain why definition has been such a problem, Anne Williams argues that " 'the Gothic myth' . . . is the patriarchal family. . . . Gothic plots are family plots" (22). Williams's work suggests that the Gothic is both horrified by the father's power and haunted by its demise.

13. For a critique of the "utopics of radical resignification," see Butler's *Bodies That Matter,* 224.

14. Butler, *Bodies That Matter,* 123–24.

15. Leo Bersani, "Is the Rectum a Grave?" *October* 43 (Winter 1987): 221. Further references to this work will be included parenthetically in the text.

16. Stanley Fish, "Introduction: Going down the Anti-Formalist Road," in *Doing What Comes Naturally: Change, Rhetoric, and the Practice of Theory in Literary and Legal Studies* (Durham, NC: Duke Univ. Press, 1989), 1–33; and Bernard Williams, "Drawing Lines," Review of *Only Words* by Catharine A. MacKinnon, *London Review of Books* 16.9 (12 May 1994): 9–10. MacKinnon has also been accused of "play[ing] games with the English language" and of "exaggerating as magisterially and recklessly as the frippiest French intellectual" (see Ellen Willis, "Feminism, Moralism, and Pornography," in *Powers of Desire,* ed. Ann Snitow, Christine Stansell, and Sharon Thompson [New York: Monthly Review Press, 1983], 46]; and Carlin Romano, "Between the Motion and the Act," review of *Only Words* by Catherine A. MacKinnon, *The Nation* [15 November 1993]: 564).

17. For a history of MacKinnon and Dworkin's model antipornography law, see Strossen's *Defending Pornography,* particularly chapter 3. For their own explanation of the legislation, see Dworkin and MacKinnon's *Pornography and Civil Rights: A New Day for Women* (Minneapolis, MN: Organizing against Pornography, 1988).

18. Catherine A. MacKinnon, *Only Words* (Cambridge, MA: Harvard University Press, 1993), 11–12. Further references to this work will be included parenthetically in the text.

19. I would call attention here to both the wide range of activities classified as consequences (writing on bathroom walls and writing judicial opinions), and to the strange example related in MacKinnon's "Frances Biddle's Sister" in which pornography does not seem to have caused or accompanied the injury but is capable of repeating it ("Frances Biddle's Sister: Pornography, Civil Rights, and Speech," in *Feminism Unmodified: Discourses on Life and Law* [Cambridge, MA: Harvard University Press, 1987], 184).

20. MacKinnon, "Frances Biddle's Sister," 173.

21. See Wendy Brown's criticisms of MacKinnon (Review of *Feminism Unmodified: Discourses on Life and Law* by Catherine A. MacKinnon, *Political Theory* 17.3 [August 1989]: 489–92; and Judith Butler's "Burning Acts: Injurious Speech."

22. "Sex and Violence: A Perspective," in *Feminism Unmodified*, 86.

23. MacKinnon, "Frances Biddle's Sister," 171.

24. J. Laplanche and J.-B. Pontalis, "Fantasy and the Origins of Sexuality," in *Formations of Fantasy*, ed. Victor Burgin, James Donald, and Cora Kaplan (London: Methuen, 1986), 9.

25. Laplanche and Pontalis, "Fantasy and the Origins of Sexuality," 10.

26. Laplanche and Pontalis, "Fantasy and the Origins of Sexuality," 14.

27. See Jonathan Culler's discussion of John Searle's critique of Derrida on speech act theory. Searle claims that Derrida fails to understand the distinction between "use" and "mention" (Culler, *On Deconstruction*, 117–21).

28. Judith Butler, "Burning Acts: Injurious Speech," 156.

29. This is just about as long as the gothic heroine's career could be expected to last. See Joanna Russ on the profile of the heroine of the modern gothic; the heroine is always in the 19–27 age range (Joanna Russ, "Somebody's Trying to Kill Me, and I Think It's My Husband: The Modern Gothic," in *The Female Gothic*, ed. Juliann E. Fleenor [Montreal: Eden Press, 1983], 31–56). And presumably this is one of the polemical points that Dworkin is making with her repetition-with-a-difference of this convention. Dworkin's 27-year-old is decayed, war-torn, haunted, beyond victimization, as opposed to (merely) unmarriageable.

30. This is trauma as a Ferenczi-esque "Confusion of Tongues." See Sandor Ferenczi, "Confusion of Tongues between Adults and The Child: The Language of Tenderness and of Passion," in *Final Contributions to the Problems and Methods of Psycho-Analysis* (London: Hogarth Press, 1955): 156–67.

31. This is a response to an earlier version of feminist theory that opposed the terms "sex" and "gender": sex as nature, the given, and gender as culture, the site for political intervention and change. Judith Butler suggests that the body is that which gets conceded as the nonconstructed. This concession, then, is the repeat performance that produces the effect of materiality (*Bodies That Matter: On the Discursive Limits of "Sex,"* 10–11). Butler's decision to (just) cite "sex" (in her title) is worthy of its own extended analysis.

32. See Brenner's *Eight Bullets* for a doubling of trauma: trauma as departure and loss on the one hand and trauma as bodily injury on the other (Claudia Brenner with Hannah Ashley, *Eight Bullets: One Woman's Story of Surviving Anti-Gay Violence* [Ithaca, NY: Firebrand Books, 1995]). Ian Hacking and Laplanche and Pontalis offer theoretical accounts of how physical becomes psychical trauma

(Ian Hacking, *Rewriting the Soul: Multiple Personality and the Sciences of Memory* [Princeton: Princeton University Press, 1995]; and "Trauma [Psychical]" in *The Language of Psycho-Analysis*, trans. Donald Nicholson-Smith [New York: W. W. Norton, 1973], 465–66).

33. *Mercy* is also remarkable for its almost immediate politicization of trauma. This nine-year-old's experience of violation is followed fast on its heels by her accounts of several forms of social injustice. The very concept of a politicized trauma would seem to be an oxymoron. In order for an event to be experienced traumatically it needs to have a singular force, yet the politics of trauma is based on an identification with a collective. When Claudia Brenner recognizes the category "anti-gay violence" she has, in a sense, departed from her trauma. She recalls this recognition: "*This had happened to other people. I was not utterly alone*" (118). Uniqueness gets reasserted at the level of an identity category when, for example, Andrea Dworkin refuses to identify with a black male victim, or when Catherine MacKinnon both uses and refuses the analogy between women and any other group.

34. There is a limit to this madness, a scene in which Andrea disidentifies with the chained and tortured figure of Huey Newton, insisting that Newton makes the pornographic consumption of his image impossible ("the camera can't take his picture without making his statement," 243). This passage is particularly worth considering in the context of a racialized American gothic tradition. How has the tortured black body served white writers?

35. See "Woman As Victim: 'Story of O,' " in *Woman Hating* (New York: E. P. Dutton, 1974), 57. See also Harriet Gilbert's comparison of *Mercy* and de Sade's *Justine* (Gilbert, "So Long As It's Not Sex and Violence," 216–29). But do these novels suffer from lack of plotting, or from being *only* event-full?

36. Wendy Steiner, "Declaring War on Men," 11.

37. See Carol J. Clover for a description of the rape revenge film (Carol Clover, *Men, Women, and Chain Saws: Gender in the Modern Horror Film* [Princeton, NJ: Princeton University Press, 1992], 114–65). The following is an example of the kind of excess it's hard not to think of as humorous: "Sometimes a man still offers me money, I laugh, a hoarse, ugly laugh, quite mad, my throat's in ribbons, just hanging streaks of meat, you can feel it all loose, all cut loose or ripped loose in pieces as if it's kind of like pieces of steak cut to be sauteed but someone forgot and left it out so there's maggots on it and it's green, rotted out, all crawling" (291). See also the passage in which Andrea describes the pain involved in doing sit-ups ("your heart's collapsed into your stomach or your stomach into your heart and there's only a bed of pain in the middle of you that moves," 311), or the ménage à trois that follows her appendectomy (119). And who is there to rival Dworkin for the extravagant image of the self as a fetus floating in the brain's acidic blood (322–23)?

38. For the repudiation of femininity as "bedrock" see Freud's "Analysis Terminable and Interminable," 1937, vol. 23 of *The Standard Edition of the Complete Psychological Works*, 24 vols. (London: Hogarth Press, 1955), 252.

39. It is worth noting that this critique of the effectiveness of parody is a critique of parody-as-distance, as opposed to citation, and is thus pre-Butlerian.

See Judith Butler's formulations concerning parody and the performative in *Gender Trouble: Feminism and the Subversion of Identity* (New York: Routledge, 1990), and *Bodies That Matter*. See also Carole-Ann Tyler's analysis of drag which explores the difficulty of simultaneously articulating a theory of gender identity as performance and politicizing this theorization. She writes: "What passes for passing for or impersonating gender when gender is always already impersonation is symptomatic and must be analyzed" (Carole-Ann Tyler, "Boys Will Be Girls: The Politics of Gay Drag," in *Inside/Out: Lesbian Theories, Gay Theories*, ed. Diana Fuss [New York: Routledge, 1991], 54).

40. With his progay and presumably profeminist celebrations of these "anti" values, Bersani would no doubt sound just as "crazy" to MacKinnon and Dworkin as they do to him.

41. Why does Bersani's account exclude anything like a preobjective object relation, anything like the specular, the imaginary, the preoedipal? Is it Bersani or Freud whose opposition is the stark one of pre-self versus heterosexual interrelation? If Bersani is suggestive when it comes to reading heterosexual gothic, one might also consider those maternal gothic fictions which hesitate in their location of violence: is violence in such works to be found between the sexes or between the pre-sexes, between mother and child? Writers whose work includes an exploration of the violence of the preoedipal realm include Toni Morrison, Gayl Jones, Willa Cather, and Carson McCullers. In this regard, one might also examine Margaret Atwood's appropriation of the gothic form. See particularly *Bodily Harm* (1982), which also wonders about the effects of representation and the status of fantasized violence, and *Lady Oracle* (1976).

42. MacKinnon, "Frances Biddle's Sister," 167. For more on gothic narrative and trauma, see Michelle A. Massé, *In the Name of Love: Women, Masochism, and the Gothic* (Ithaca, NY: Cornell University Press, 1992). Massé argues that there is a trauma at the origin of the gothic and that it is the distinctly female trauma of being denied autonomy. Massé thinks very much like Dworkin. Bersani, on the other hand, would argue that the trauma of "prohibited identity" is the trauma of subject formation, the trauma that every subject repeats and denies. Gender and its history have a secondary relationship to the subject's initial and inevitable crisis. For feminist critiques of "Is the Rectum a Grave?" see Lynda Hart, "That Was Then, This Is Now: Ex-Changing the Phallus," *Postmodern Culture* 4.1 (September 1993); Tania Modleski, *Feminism without Women: Culture and Criticism in a "Postfeminist" Age* (New York: Routledge, 1991), 146–53; and Carole-Ann Tyler, "Boys Will Be Girls: The Politics of Gay Drag."

43. This argument gets made in a number of ways, whether by Carlin Romero, who decides to show Catharine MacKinnon that there is indeed a difference between acts and representations by writing about planning to rape her in the guise of reviewing her book, or by Nadine Strossen, arguing that it is the feminist antipornography movement that has blurred what should be a "crystal clear" distinction between "the imagined and the actual, between fantasy and reality" (Carlin Romero, "Between the Motion and the Act," 563–70; Nadine Strossen, *Defending Pornography*, 170). There are those critics who see this collapse into identity as evidence of MacKinnon's naivete and those who write of it as

wholly strategic. Bernard Williams comments that "MacKinnon deliberately enacts an indifference to almost every distinction that might be thought relevant to this subject" (10). See also Wendy Brown, Review of *Feminism Unmodified;* Judith Butler, "Burning Acts: Injurious Speech"; Frances Ferguson, "Pornography: The Theory"; and Mandy Merck for insightful commentary on MacKinnon's writing and this equation of similarity with identity (Mandy Merck, "The Fatal Attraction of *Intercourse,*" in *Perversions: Deviant Readings* [New York: Routledge, 1993]: 195–216, and "MacKinnon's Dog: Anti-Porn's Canine Conditioning," Lecture, Cornell University, May 1995). One of the ironies here is that MacKinnon herself is concerned with the status of analogy in legal argumentation. She writes, "Doing something legal about a situation that is not really like anything else is hard enough in a legal system that prides itself methodologically on reasoning by analogy ... the situation of women is *not really like anything else*" ("Frances Biddle's Sister," 166).

44. MacKinnon quoted in Butler, "Burning Acts: Injurious Speech," 173–74; Butler, "Burning Acts: Injurious Speech," 174.

45. "Where Do We Stand on Pornography? A *Ms.* Roundtable," in *Debating Sexual Correctness: Pornography, Sexual Harassment, Date Rape, and the Politics of Sexual Equality,* ed. Adele M. Stan (New York: Dell, 1995), 55 (emphasis added).

THREE

Starting from Snatch: The Seduction of Performance in Bertha Harris's *Lover*

Victoria L. Smith

> What is strangest of all is the popular conviction that a lover, and none but a lover, can forswear [her]self with impunity—a lover's vow, they say, is no vow at all. —Plato, *Symposium*

Nigel Nicholson once wrote of Virginia Woolf's *Orlando* that it was the "most charming love letter in literature"—a love letter from Woolf to Vita Sackville-West. I would like to make a claim for the second most charming love letter in literature: Bertha Harris's experimental, postmodern, fabulous, and funny novel *Lover* ([1976] 1993).[1] And though Harris's letter was not intended for me, I confess I am in love with Bertha Harris. Allow me to clarify; I have never met Bertha Harris and know her only through her writings, but the novel beckons me as lover and beloved and I am seduced. Like the besotted lover, I will make extravagant claims about the object of my affections—in this case, the novel, *Lover.* The novel as a whole is a rhetorical/theatrical performance of seduction that names into being a new identity—the lesbian "lover." It is the ultimate performative, a kind of doing by saying, as in "I do take this woman" in a marriage ceremony. And if doing by saying is ultimately an act of authority, then, in a world that seeks to erase homosexuality or to name it as simply "bad" parody of heterosexuality, Harris's performative is radical indeed.

Anticipating my second extravagant claim about *Lover,* Wayne Koestenbaum declares in a 1993 *Village Voice* article, "*Lover* is a vaudeville version of queer theory; presciently it explains everything theory has come laboriously to know since 1976."[2] Prescient indeed, and though the novel does not explain *everything* queer theory has come to know, it perhaps *performs* much of contemporary theory—often more imaginatively and humorously. The novel, in its obsession with women, the performative, performance, camp, mimicry, and in its fundamental critique of heterosexuality—and all this in 1976—stands as a "fictional" version of work by contemporary theorists such as Luce Irigaray, Teresa de Lauretis, Judith Butler, Sue-Ellen Case, and Mary Ann Doane.[3]

However, before I investigate the implications of Harris's seductive performance, I will trace the outlines of her novel. It is often hard to describe the one you love—especially if she is particularly difficult, flamboyant, and revels in disguises and verbal sleights of hand. But difficult novels, like difficult women, can be very sexy. Or they can prove too troublesome. As one reviewer, Blanche McCrary Boyd, remarked on its republication in 1993, "*Lover* is aesthetically brilliant, but I didn't like reading it, either this time or when it was originally published." She goes on to assert, "Although I prefer unnatural lust, I don't prefer unnatural fiction. I like sentences that are planed out in the service of story, not knotty with descriptiveness."[4] Harris's sentences are certainly planed, though not in "natural" ways and not in the service of a "conventional" story; she is after all attempting to create an "unnatural" creature—a "lesbian," a "lover." Harris clearly believes that her sentences should not be bound in service; that would mean that there are rules to which she must accede and that would ultimately prevent her from telling her own story. Instead, Harris uses language in the service of excess and/or love, and plays on, but beyond, normative narrative bounds.

In her foundational essay, "Sexual Indifference and Lesbian Representation," Teresa de Lauretis argues, citing Elaine Marks, "to undomesticate the female body one must dare reinscribe it in excess—as excess—in provocative counterimages sufficiently outrageous, passionate, verbally violent, and formally complex to both destroy the male discourse on love and redesign the universe."[5] Harris does just that; she uses a formally complex structure, and a passionate and sophisticated style to excess(erize) the female body and remind us that unnatural narratives and unnatural lust have a great deal in common.[6] One of the ways Harris excesserizes the female body is to provide the reader with an excess of women. The book opens with:

This one was lying strapped to a table. Covered in her juices, Samaria was being pulled through the lips of her vulva. That is how Samaria met her.

She was being pulled, yelling already, through the lips of Daisy's vulva. That is how Flynn met Daisy.

Veronica, however, came out of nowhere, and so she used to go exclusively with Veronica. They were childhood sweethearts. On February 14, 1947, Veronica gave Veronica a red heart-shaped box of candy and then they sat together in the porch swing that warmish February afternoon. Arms intertwined. Sucking on candy hearts with messages for the tongues; *Be Mine Valentine. I Love You. Thine Alone.* Like eating camellia blooms that bounced against their hair when they swung backwards. (5)

From the very outset of the novel, the reader has difficulty keeping track of the women. And indeed if one takes a risk and settles on Veronica as a stable and identifiable character, one is confounded by her lack of origin—she was not pulled from anybody—and by her doubleness—she used to go exclusively with her self.[7] This lack of origin and this duplicity are central to the novel insofar as they begin to develop a critique of women's place, and in particular the lesbian's place, in representational systems.

The text, then, moves to thwart simple identification of and with specific characters through a confusion and profusion of characters (e.g., Veronica, who came out of nowhere and used to go exclusively with herself), thus requiring the reader to perform a good deal of work to see the lesbian lover.[8] This thwarting of identification is in keeping with Harris's desire to change the formal qualities of realist fiction in order to represent lesbian difference. She writes, "Most writers of imaginative literature . . . do not understand that a lesbian form . . . is not achieved through sexual substitution. . . . My complaint lies in the fact that these individual turnabouts of heterosexual reality seem, to many, to constitute a literary expression of lesbian sensibility; and as such distract us from the apprehension of lesbian reality."[9] Here, Harris rejects a simple "inversion" of traditional heterosexual narrative form through gender substitution as representative of either a lesbian sensibility or a lesbian reality—though what this "sensibility" or "reality" may be is, of course, open to question.[10] Harris suggests that while these stories—i.e., Ramona and Juliet, rather than Romeo and Juliet—may be "good enough" in most (lesbian) readers' minds, these narratives of substitution remain simply place holders for a heterosexual matrix of "men" and "women," regardless of pronoun difference. Harris is after something different and she accomplishes this through a novel that demands an active, participatory, and unnerving defamiliarization.

Harris's narrative is "unnatural" in both form and content. It has only a minimum of plot—Flynn, protagonist of the novel, learns how to be a lover, which is a metaphysical and representational space rather than a purely physical state. In order to do this (and here I am imposing a narrative order on a text that is nonlinear and fragmented), Flynn must come to terms with the loss of her mother (to her father), leave her heterosexual marriage, and heal a mind/body split, represented by her desire to build a Brain Machine. This means she must fall in love, as a lover, all within a world where Hollywood starlets, circus performers, master forgers, and radical dykes intermingle. These bizarre narrative details do not unfold chronologically, and are interwoven with actual details from Bertha Harris's life, for example, her birth in North Carolina, her father's tap-dancing, her work as a college professor grading papers, her daughter's growing up, and so forth.

This interchange of the real with the fantastic enables the novel to function as an autobiography—the autobiography of a "lover," the object/subject that is produced as it is being written.[11] The text directly invites reading as an autobiography; in addition to the details about Harris's life, the author's name, "Bertha," is used interchangeably with the central character's name, Flynn. And, as I noted above, the novel begins with Flynn's birth: "She was being pulled, yelling already, through the lips of Daisy's vulva. That is how Flynn met Daisy" (6); it ends with Flynn's becoming a lover (206). The text also functions as a particular kind of autobiography, the kunstlerroman—a portrait of the artist as a young lesbian or rather more precisely, a portrait of the lesbian *as* artist. That is, given that the lesbian has traditionally not been represented in literature except as modeled on heterosexual forms (*The Well of Loneliness* is a representative example here), to represent the lesbian *is necessarily* to represent a fantastic creature; that is, to represent a creature created, artifice. It is not then an inversion of heterosexual form, but rather a creation of the lesbian as a new form, or as Harris says, "the lesbian *as* literature."

In addition to this unusual generic form, the characters themselves are "unnatural." According to Harris in her new introduction to the novel, the characters are "highly aestheticized . . . not intended to remind readers of actual flesh and blood"; they are also "distorted, or magnified or reduced like the stars in the Hollywood movies of the forties and fifties . . . or they are painstakingly romanticized into melodrama" (xxii). Think of it as a lesbian, literary version of Woody Allen's *Play It Again, Sam*.

Just as the characters in that play rely on wildly romantic figures (e.g., Bogart and Bergman in *Casablanca*) to help them envision their lives, so do the characters in *Lover*. In the novel's case, however, those romantic figures are more likely to be Natalie Barney and Renée Vivien in Paris in the 1920s, or the Marschallin and Octavian (a woman playing a man playing a woman) from Strauss's *Der Rosenkavalier* or, even, Brontë's Heathcliff and Cathy.

In short, the characters are not realistic but rather precipitates of romantic longing, dreams, images, and desire transmogrified into characters who perform improbable feats in a world a step removed from reality. They fall in love like us, and hurt like us, but who they imagine themselves to be in the service of love is limitless. Harris takes for granted that any "character" is always already an effect of language and embedded in a range of cultural meanings and stereotypes. And while this is true for any character in a novel, the characters in Harris's novel are aware of themselves as language effects, aware of themselves as already structured by certain rules/fantasies of heterosexual desire. For example, when Flynn loses her lover Lydia, her sister tells her, "Flynn, you have a face on you like Heathcliff yelling *Cathy Cathy*. My stomach turns" (193). Heathcliff's loss of Cathy in *Wuthering Heights* becomes a way to image Flynn's loss, while simultaneously pointing out its melodramatic excess. It is the relationship and its attendant emotions, that structure of feeling, that Flynn embodies (not, say, simply an identification with Heathcliff as male).

Another example of Harris's recourse to convention while confounding it occurs as one character decides what to wear:

It is hard to dress because she doesn't know who she will be tonight. She could be Queen Elizabeth the Second if she had time to do her hair in pin curls, if she owned something simple and fuchsia-colored, with a bolero jacket, if she had a pearl necklace. She thinks of T. S. Eliot; but her jock strap is at the laundry and her lips are too full. She wants to wear a stained trench coat and be a detective. She wants to squire this broad to a blue-plate special, and then back to her place or her place. (63)

Along with deliberately ridiculing (and loving) the Queen and Eliot and the trappings that would signify them, Harris invokes the conventions of detective fiction, both in terms of image and language. However, the last phrase, "her place or her place," twists the assumed heterosexuality of the scene, as well as the detective's presumed masculinity. Harris's novel, then, is experimental in narrative, lyrical and witty in tone, and fundamentally concerned with the action of the lover—a figure, I would contend, that uses our accustomed identificatory categories in order to subvert them and to reveal them as convention. In short, Harris uses the rules of heterosexuality to set up the figure of the lover.

Harris, however, does not simply distort traditional heterosexual and gender patterns; she also establishes criteria for becoming a lover. Becoming a lover is to stop being a woman because the lover refuses the assigned roles of the feminine—mother and/or pure body, particularly as discursively produced. For example, at one point in the novel, Flynn screams about what happened to her when she began her first period. Flynn is screaming, "They came in with a rag and a belt. They said, Now you are a woman. *I* had been exchanged for a *woman*" (102). At the very moment of Flynn's capacity to reproduce, "they" want to exchange her perceived subjectivity for what she clearly believes to be a devalued object—a woman. They have taken Flynn's "I" (or Flynn as discursively produced) and replaced it with "woman."[12] Flynn becomes object, rather than subject, in culture. Samaria, Flynn's grandmother, patiently explains to Flynn that one can battle the imposition of "woman" by becoming a lover: "The truth is I got myself back in spite of it. In spite of it, I could become a lover and could stop being a woman. What they said, *a woman.* That's why I am here, in spite of it, and not in a cage, like the rest of them, in a freak show. I am a lover, not a woman" (102–3).

For Flynn to stop being a woman and start becoming a lover, she must give up her idea of the "Brain Machine." Flynn wishes to build a device "which can (at last) irrevocably separate spirit from matter, thought from action, mind from flesh" (9). However, this classic Cartesian tearing asunder is precisely what Flynn must resist in order to become a lover. She, in fact, lives within what we might call the Great Western Brain Machine which promotes these binary oppositions. "Woman" is always already inscribed within it; lover is not. Flynn must reject an idea of the brain severed from the body as productive of truth and she must also reject the notion of the body as "so much inert matter, signifying nothing or, more specifically, signifying a profane void, the fallen state: deception, sin, the premonitional metaphorics of hell and the eternal feminine."[13] When Flynn finally falls in love, there is an amalgamation of mind and body. She becomes "like someone sick from a long illness—skin and bones to which only her beloved can give memory and intelligence and make round, like a brain" (92). Her beloved will feed her famished body with things normally belonging to the brain—like memory and intelligence. Her body is a brain, pregnant with meaning.

"CHOOSING AS IF OVER IS"

The sensibility of the novel and Harris's negotiation between fact and fiction can be illustrated by the following two instances. The first comes from Harris's introduction where she explains the production of a "gay sensibility." That practice, Harris notes, "hinges, like the arts [and like the novel *Lover*], very much on decisively choosing *as if* over *is*." She writes:

In my mid-thirties I threw a yard sale in front of my Greenwich Village building which I advertised as "The Maria Callas Memorial Yard Sale." Swarms of strangers approached, dropped some small change into my cigar box, and reverently bore away my mismatched kneesocks. No one charged me with falsifying my old clothes; everyone already knew that Maria Callas had never set foot in my socks. Together, the patrons of my "Maria Callas Memorial Yard Sale" and I were collaborating in a sort of workshop production of the gay sensibility. . . . I recall saying this to one devotee: "She was wearing those argyles the morning of the day she so tragically died in Paris. That's twenty cents, please." And he replied, "Too true. I'm going to keep them in a silver box on my coffee table." (xxiii–xxiv)

Indeed, who would charge Harris with falsifying her socks? The point here is that Harris relies upon the *sign*—here literally the sign "The Maria Callas Memorial Yard Sale"—which is already another remove from any actual Maria Callas (to say nothing of her yard sale) and already embedded in some "othered" (camp) sensibility.[14] That is, the sign holds out not only an empty promise of the real but the limitless possibilities of the unreal, foregrounding artifice and fantasy, and significantly, it is the participation in the lie/fantasy that generates the pleasure.

The second instance that indicates the sensibility of the novel comes from a case of mistaken identity. As I noted before, when I first read *Lover*, I was smitten; I wanted to know more about the "real" Bertha Harris. I began with the *Contemporary Authors* series and found, in addition to a section entitled "Personal"—which revealed that Harris was born in North Carolina in 1937—the following information:

WRITINGS: *Catching Saradove* (novel), Harcourt, 1969; *Confession of Cherubino* [sic], Harcourt, 1972; *Traveler in Eternity*, Regency Press, 1975; *Lover*, Daughters, Inc., 1976; (with Emily L. Sisley) *The Joy of Lesbian Sex*, Crown, 1977.

BIOGRAPHICAL/CRITICAL SOURCES: *New York Times Book Review*, March 9, 1969; *Nation*, May 19, 1969; Maurice Leonard, *Battling Bertha: A Biography of Bertha Harris*, Regency Press, 1975.

Now, I thought I had read all of Harris's work, but I had seen neither the novel (?) *Traveler in Eternity* nor her biography, *Battling Bertha*. There was more of her, I thought. I was delighted, but also skeptical that anyone would write a biography of a relatively obscure postmodern lesbian writer (especially back in 1975); nevertheless I went to interlibrary loan and requested the books. A few weeks later I did receive *Battling Bertha*— *Traveler in Eternity* was (fittingly) lost—and found that the biography was about a particular, *British*, Bertha Harris, or rather a peculiar, British, Bertha Harris.[15] It was the biography of, as the book jacket tells us, "the most famous figure in the controversial field of modern occultism"; indeed, Bertha Harris, spiritualist medium, had such acclaimed powers that she had been "consulted by monarchs, political leaders, generals and scientists . . . and even held a seance in a tarantula infested forest in Africa, where an ectoplasmic unicorn manifested."[16]

Harris would love this. In fact, *Battling Bertha* seemed simply like a continuation of *Lover*. It seemed entirely imaginable to me that "my" Bertha Harris (American author) was one and the same with the "other" Bertha Harris (famed British occultist), and indeed apt to go into a trance at any minute, bring back the dead, and manage to coax a woman into bed by doing it. This is partly because *Lover* asks us to believe in the transformative power of illusion—in this case that Bertha is the famed occultist—and in the powers of that agent to produce convincing illusions infinitely—e.g., ectoplasmic unicorns—and that all this energy is completely in the service of seduction. The narrator tells us "that the real action is the action of the lover; and all else is that action disguised. All else, such as sleeping, eating, forging works of art" (56). Harris is so persuasive in this assertion and her powers of illusion so strong that she induced me to believe that she had forged this biography for my entertainment, indulging and entertaining me, her lover, with her abilities. To paraphrase de Lauretis, I began to see, with Harris's help, how the universe might be realigned.

Both this case of mistaken identity and the yard sale indicate how fantasy acts as a structural and structuring principle in Harris's narrative experimentation. Both incidents underline the kind of psychic/cultural mechanics at work insofar as these incidents foreground identificatory uncertainties, performativity and the pleasures to be had in the participation in illusions. Illusions that are at once not true—these are not Maria Callas's socks, the famed British occultist is not the author Bertha Harris (nor as far as I know are either producing unicorns)—but rather fantasies that are successful.

The novel moves us into a realm based in the fantastic, or more properly based in fantasy, whether that fantasy includes camp, the supernatural, or imaginary inhabitations from the silver screen or literature. Maria Callas's garage sale and my belief in Harris as capable of producing herself as Bertha Harris, psychic, incorporate the real, reinterpret it through imagination, and return it to the real world in subversive form. Fantasy, for Harris, as it is for Teresa de Lauretis in her theory of lesbian sexuality, is a process which operates at the join of psychic and social realms. De Lauretis writes, "Foucault's term *'reverse' discourse* actually suggests something of the process by which a representation in the external world is subjectively assumed, reworked through fantasy, in the internal world and then returned to the external world resignified, rearticulated discursively and/or performatively in the subject's self-representation—in speech, gesture, costume, body stance, and so forth."[17] Perhaps Harris, in her fantastical twists of the external discourse returns rather a *"perverse" discourse* of the real, thus changing the real.

"THE WOMEN MY FATHER STOLE ME FROM"

Lest the reader think I am the only one infatuated with Bertha Harris, consider that when *Lover* was republished, the *Village Voice Literary Supplement* spent three pages and three writers to remind us of Harris's powers; the articles were grouped under the title "The Purple Reign of Bertha Harris." Dorothy Allison, author of *Bastard out of Carolina* and one of Harris's former students, began simply with, "She took my breath away" and went on to say, "When Bertha talked about literature, it was like listening to Billy Graham talk about God. Nothing was more important. Nothing was more demanding. The woman didn't lecture, she preached."[18] Like Billy Graham, Harris clearly believes in the power of the word. Wayne Koestenbaum, one of the other contributors to the *Voice*, focuses on the literary precursors and contexts of the novel and writes:

In its intolerance for the conventions of fiction, and its exclusive interest in the erotics of speaking, *Lover* is in fine company. *Lover* is indebted to and in love with the great strange queer books of the 20th century: the reader of *Lover* belongs in bed with such hoary dominatrixes as Djuna Barnes's *Nightwood* and *Ladies Alma-nack*, Virginia Woolf's *Orlando*, Jean Genet's *Our Lady of the Flowers*, and every-thing by Ronald Firbank and Gertrude Stein. *Lover* knows the handtricks of these third-sex, demimondaine works.[19]

With its radical tampering with form as a marker of radical thinking, *Lover* is rightly grouped here. We might also add more contemporary writers such as Monique Wittig, Nicole Brossard and Jeanette Winterson. Catharine Stimpson calls Harris the "American equivalent of Monique Wittig," though unfortunately Harris is much less read—much like Djuna Barnes before her.[20]

Harris herself revels in this lesbian literary lineage. For example, in an essay on lesbian society in Paris in the 1920s, "The More Profound Nationality of Their Lesbianism," Harris seeks to found a common ances-try with those women—Natalie Barney, Renée Vivien, Djuna Barnes, Romaine Brooks, and others.[21] She claims these women "as my first ancestors, the women my father stole me from."[22] In no uncertain terms is Harris godchild to a particular writer of that milieu—Djuna Barnes; this is clear from both *Lover's* intricate and obscure narrative style and Harris's own imaginary relation to Barnes. Harris writes of her obsession with, and need for, Djuna Barnes:

I was fresh out of the arms of the hotbed of lesbianism [the university Harris attended as an undergraduate] . . . and on the streets of New York: the summer of 1959. And when I was not at my $55.00 a week job I was hanging out on the corner of Patchin Place—not, under any circumstances, to catch a glimpse of e. e. cummings—but waiting for Djuna Barnes to take her afternoon walk and, with all discretion, follow her—move the way she moved, turn the way she turned, hold my head like her head. As often as I could (and with discretion) I followed her and, trailing her, received the silent messages about my past I needed and she could give; and never once during our exchange did I encroach upon her lordly solitude to give her my name. The name she made up for me was my real name; and it was the name she used, when in my fantasy, she would stop and take my hand to thank me for all the flowers I daily stuffed into her mailbox in Patchin Place and then tell me how it was to be a dyke in Paris, in the Twenties.[23]

Harris's real and imaginary communion with Barnes establishes a geneal-ogy and creates, despite and through absence and silence, a sense of the past, so that Harris "no longer saw [her]self as beginning and ending with *The Well of Loneliness*." She continues, "Like every other dyke with a book in her hand, I know that these are the women our fathers stole us from. Know thy women; know thyself; and the miracle of changeling into hero is accomplished."[24] This desire both to have a book in her hand and to know the characters and the writers of those books enables a "miracle" insofar as history grounds the production of Harris's "lover" as a discursive act.

In her rejection of a realist mode of writing like that of *The Well* and through her pursuit of a more fantastic form or baroque style like that of *Orlando* or *Nightwood*, Harris seeks to produce something not yet accounted for in literature—the concept of "lover." This category is not simply a reiteration of heterosexual norms, nor some lesbian utopia heterosexuality cannot touch, nor finally a movement toward some butch/femme parallel universe that ultimately may be recuperated back into the very oppressive structures it sought to critique.[25] Rather, this "lover" is a dizzying othering whereby Harris's "lesbian heaven" uses and abuses a heterosexual hell, a hell in which gender roles definitely confine but cannot confirm the "male" or "female" behind the mask. Harris's formal experimentation offers a way to create what Monique Wittig calls in another context, "a textual space of sexual (self-)representation."[26]

"FORGERY SANS THE ORIGINAL"

Harris's examination and production of lesbian self-representation take up issues central to contemporary feminist debates in difference theory insofar as the debates, like Harris's novel, concern women's representability and gender as performance. Harris's production of the category "lover" in particular explores the issues of mimicry, forgery, and the lack of an "original" and in part offers a method by which women's "lack" and "duplicity" can be recuperated. Let me explain via a simplified route through feminist theory. Mary Ann Doane has shown, using Joan Riviere's work on "Womanliness As a Masquerade," that "masquerade . . . constitutes an acknowledgment that it is femininity itself which is constituted as mask—on the decorated layer which conceals a non-identity."[27] Judith Butler has shown, drawing on the work of Riviere, Wittig, Newton, and others, that gender is constructed through performative acts and lacks an essence upon which to hang the mask; she asserts, "Gender is a kind of imitation for which there is no original."[28] Butler and Doane carry out similar operations; both show gender and femininity to be masquerades or "effect[s] or consequence[s] of the imitation itself."[29] Butler concludes, "compulsory heterosexual identities, those ontologically consolidated heterosexual phantasms of 'man' and 'woman,' are theatrically produced effects that posture as grounds, origins, the normative measure of the real."[30]

Harris, I suggest, anticipates the closing sections of Judith Butler's *Gender Trouble*—in particular the section on "Bodily Inscriptions, Performative Subversions"—and the subsequent reworking of the notion of "queer performativity" in *Bodies That Matter*. Butler argues that gender is a performative act, though "neither a single act nor causal process initiated by a subject and culminating in a set of fixed effects." Harris's novel effectively demonstrates that gender performativity operates at and through both theatrical and discursive levels. Harris shows us that the performance of the body as gendered seems simultaneously an act and not an act, real and artifice, in part because the historical process of its coming into being has been disguised. In the same way, I would add, power as a discursive formation, in Foucault's analysis, does not point to an originary cause and indeed is enabled by the effacement of causality and history. Harris acknowledges the idea of the effects of both femininity and of gender, and their performative natures, but goes further to formulate how that lack or blankness (i.e., the "hole" upon which the imitations are based) might be representable through the concept of "lover." That is, "lover" is a body which is constituted as a performer, as performance. Harris forces us to pay attention to the masks of gender and femininity *as* masks and consequently what those masks seem to cover.

In a sense, Harris is starting from scratch—from nothing—but in fact the nothing, as Luce Irigaray has shown, has always been occupied by woman—the "hole" in man's representational system. Harris's work is like that of Djuna Barnes, about which a critic once remarked, it "suffers from that most irritating offense of difficult writing—the mysterioso effect that hides no mystery, the locked box with nothing in it."[31] However, the "nothing" in Harris's work (as well as in Barnes) is precisely the unreadable effect in culture of a woman who might desire someone "like" herself—i.e., another woman. And so I would say Harris starts from "snatch" as well and here I mean both the vulgar sense of the word and the sense of an act of kidnapping (the invisible lesbian) from a masculine signifying system. I make this double play—"starting from scratch/ snatch"—to indicate the linguistic grounding of this "nothingness"; woman is always already a sexed subject embedded in language which has inescapable, though not predictable effects.

Harris's work takes up issues central to difference theory in her exploration of mimicry, forgery, and the lack of an "original." *Lover* foregrounds a kind of instability, making a virtue of forgery, or aliases, whether it be through the characters' constant (or rather inconstant) changing from one being to another—from movie star to temperamental artist—or the "jobs" they have—forgers of great art and forgers of history. For example, characters claim that they wrote *Hamlet, Der Rosenkavalier,* painted all the Vermeers in the Metropolitan Museum, and that *"even now"* scholarly dissertations are being written on some tanagra figurines that one of the central characters forged and planted—dissertations that "will wildly change previous conceptions of art history." The characters, then, say they are masters of illusion, magicians, con-artists capable of pulling rabbits out of nowhere, but their more profound feat, they say, is that all past art has been faked by them. In other words, history, even the tangible art objects in the Metropolitan Museum, is all a fake. Indeed, Harris's work thematizes the notion of the simulacrum, the copy without the original, and the consequences of this idea for lesbians, history and art—which in a sense for Harris are interchangeable. She pulls the reader and her characters out of "the real world" and into art and vice versa, while constantly calling attention to that movement:

And if you can't discern the difference between the original and the reproduction, then the difference does not exist: they are the same, although they take up separate blocks of time and space and may change one's idea about the course of history. "She reminds me of a character in the early fiction of a minor novelist. Indeed as far as I'm concerned, there is no difference between the two—between the living and the written—between the idea, the fantasy, and she who walks up and down upon the wooden floor, shaking it with her heavy step, above me. No matter where I turn, I find total disregard for the truth." (60)

Importantly, what we find here is that the inability to discern the difference between the original and a reproduction is fundamental to changing one's relation to history.

Lover can be read as the production of a "forgery," in its production of "lover" and a "forgery *sans* the original," as Veronica, one of the central characters in the novel, tells us. *Lover* performs a series of "roles"—gender, femininity, masculinity—that are consummated through discourse, but that point to an "emptiness" behind them. The roles themselves are contested categories, copies that lack traceable actual antecedents but that nonetheless seem to refer to a "real." For Harris, then, there is no stable origin and at any rate it can be manufactured if necessary. Harris's initial description of Flynn, the novel's protagonist, concludes by developing the connections among memory, the location of "the not original" and place of forgery: "But none of these things are Flynn. They are a lie about Flynn, or they are pictures of herself her fantasies have contrived, or they are her overworked imagination forcing memories of things that have never really happened to her. They could be an elaborate drag or a system of disguise devised by an outside agent" (9). Or, perhaps, all these things are an elaborate drag *and* devised by an outside agent. That is, Harris calls up both her own authorship (*she* is the outside agent) and the notion that the effects within the texts are generated by an agent outside of "herself"—i.e., the headless, faceless agency of cultural norms—recognized/produced within the text as drag. In short, she calls attention to her own production of the text and to its enmeshment within and resistance to compulsive/compulsory heterosexuality.

The fundamental movement in the novel subverts the need to find the one true origin and then re-present it. Instead Harris's rejection entails adoring and embracing the lack, the fault, the absence, in Luce Irigaray's terms "the hole in men's signifying economy" that signifies women in cultural representation. Harris embraces the nothing that could possibly cause "the ultimate destruction, the splintering, the break in [man's] systems of 'presence,' of 're-presentation,' and 'representation.' "[32] Harris encircles the lack and shows it to be fruitful, capable of a profusion of replicas. Harris accomplishes this gathering up of "nothing" and reproduction of it through a particular type of role-playing, one in which being is a forgery. Performativity, as Judith Butler reminds us, "is always a reiteration of a norm or set of norms, and to the extent that it acquires an act-like status in the present, it conceals or dissimulates the conventions of which it is a repetition."[33]

To grasp the importance of the replacement of the notion of "the origin," of the "true" with one of performativity depends on an understanding of what the system of representation means for women. Irigaray's intervention in Freud's texts on femininity in *Speculum of the Other Woman* points out that woman serves only as the mirror image of man and can "never reproduce her (like) self inside the/her mother, etc. She is left with a void, a lack of all representation, re-presentation and even strictly speaking of all mimesis of her desire for origin."[34] When women do try to reproduce themselves (and return to their origin) they end up as hysterics, as forgers. Irigaray sums up what happens with these hysterics:

Women's special form of neurosis would be to "mimic" a work of art, to be a *bad (copy of a) work of art*. Her neurosis would be recognized as a counterfeit or parody of an artistic process. It is transformed into an aesthetic object, but one without value, which has to be condemned because it is a *forgery*. It is neither "nature" nor an appropriate technique for re-producing nature. Artifice, lie, deception, snare— these are the kinds of judgments society confers upon the tableaux, the scenes, the dramas, the pantomimes produced by the hysteric. And if women's instincts try to command public recognition in this way, their demand and de-monstration will be met with derision, anathema, and punishment. Or at least by belittling inter-pretation, appeals to common sense or to reason. A society has the duty to ban forgeries.[35]

Truly Harris and Irigaray seem meant for each other; in fact, Harris's work is a partial answer to the problem that Irigaray identifies—the impossibility of the women's reproduction of her (like) "self." Harris and her characters become the Freudian criminal, the true hysteric and the master forger. Harris turns the "sick" hysteric into the happy forger, shifting the weight of Freud's paradigm. This particular kind of forgery is not simply a mimicry of masculine desire, but rather a step away from the masquerade because of the self-consciousness of its parody—i.e., neither "nature" nor an "appropriate" technique for re-producing nature. In effect, *Lover* becomes a kind of paradigmatic and political postmodern practice.

LOVER AS PERFORMANCE

In her introduction, Harris tells us that "*Lover* should be absorbed as though it were a theatrical performance" (xix). I agree—the novel can be read as performance. However, I would add, returning to my first claim, that the novel can be read (borrowing from speech act theory) as a *performative*—a kind of doing by saying. But elaboration and explanation are necessary: How are the notions of performance and the performative related? The performance of what? To what effect? How does the per-formative function as seduction in the context of a novel? Indeed, the natures of performance and the performative in feminist critical theory entail a complex series of interlocking notions, ranging from ideas devel-oped out of philosopher J. L. Austin's consideration of speech act theory to ideas developed out of articulations of the notions of camp, theatrical-ity, mimicry and masquerade.[36]

For Harris, seduction and performance are intimately related. To illus-trate the nature of the performative and performance in *Lover*, and the slippage between the two terms, as well as to indicate the significance of the production of the category "lover" and the novel *Lover*, as performance/performative pieces, I begin with Bertha Harris's final paragraphs in her introduction to the new edition of *Lover:*

I wrote *Lover* for Louise Fishman. The bowerbird (family *Paradisaeidae*) falls in love. Immediately, he sets about building a bower of love, a chamber or a passage made of choice twigs and grasses so elegantly made it appears architected. The bowerbird adorns the bower with *objets trouvés*, bright and shiny bits of paper and glass. When his bower is completed, the bowerbird dances in front of it. I am told that this dance is complicated, that it's so sophisticated it seems consciously choreographed. It works.

I became a bowerbird. I wrote *Lover* to seduce Louise Fishman. It worked. (lxxviii)

First and foremost, then, *Lover* is a seduction. *Lover* amasses and reveals the relations among the three connotations of *performance:* the erotic, the theatrical, and the linguistic. This erotic performance (i.e., the seduction) happens through and within the other two connotations of performance: as a theatrical performance and as a linguistic performative. Like the bowerbird that creates the bower and performs the dance, the novel *acts out* bits of shiny rhetoric (found anywhere from within snatches of *Der Rosenkavalier* to vaudeville tunes to pieces of Gertrude Stein to Harris's own elaborate and subtle sentences) and performs an intricate choreography of masquerade, where characters verbally slip into and out of some body more comfortable, say for example, performing the roles of "Natalie Barney" or a "debonair David Niven" or the "golden haired beautiful stranger." Indeed, I would argue that some persona of the author herself dons the masks of all these characters (and more) in order to seduce women, in order to become a "lover." They are the costumes of Harris's mind.

The novel, then, is not exactly a theatrical performance, or if so, it is a kind of (not in the) closet drama. Rather, it is a rhetorical performance. Consider the following passage where "Bertha" tries to persuade her lover to look more closely at her, "to *see,* be amazed":

Bertha is dazzling; is irreplaceable. . . . Meanwhile, listen to this: Bertha is a still, yellow moon reflected by troubled lake water. Bertha is the one with the dueling scar across her cheekbone, who lifts absinthe with two fingers, who sits still, as unmoved as God, while the lustful riff-raff blunders by. She is that stark dark outline high above the Cliffs of Whatever poised to leap—but too pleasured by the claptrap of her swirling cape yet to make a move. You remember her—she's the one who assassinated the Princess Royal of Transylvania and caused World War Four. Meanwhile, she dresses in white trousers and gallops her stallion through the Bois every morning and does not answer letters. At nineteen, she wore drag down to her underwear, and her neckties were raw silk and her gold monogrammed ring came down to her from her godmother. (138–39)

Here, Harris has "Bertha" speak about performing in drag; Bertha acts out famous men and women in history and literature (from Brontë's Heathcliff to Radclyffe Hall). What could be more seductive than asking us to "see" through words someone you love as Radclyffe Hall, or better as Stephen in *The Well of Loneliness*, wearing drag down to her underwear, or Natalie Barney dressing in white and riding her horse through the Bois in Paris in the 1920s? The ornate rhetorical performance persuades just as surely as the theatrical costumes of the swirling cape and the dueling scar. Her language is self-consciously "in costume" just as the characters are in costume. And importantly, Harris's language has effects—on her lover, on her reader, *as if* we had really seen her with the dueling scar and the swirling cape. That kind of speech, I would argue, enables the novel as a whole to function as a performative, a single utterance that seduces and that performs the category "lover." Thus, the successful seduction is effected through words, through the "erotics of speaking."

It is precisely as an analysis of the erotics of speaking that I will use J. L. Austin's theory of the performative. His analysis of performatives that do not work provides an especially illuminating frame through which to understand how Harris's novel works as a performative. For Austin, a performative is a specific linguistic category, an expression whose function is not to inform or to describe, but to carry out a "performance," to accomplish an act through the process of enunciation. Austin's central example of the performative are the words, "I do" (i.e., take this woman . . .) spoken in the context of a marriage ceremony, where the saying of the words accomplishes marriage. It is not unremarkable that his central example installs a legal, traditional, and heterosexual union as the foundation for a linguistic act that becomes the measure of other acts of enunciation. Austin points out that the performative is not concerned with "truth" or "falsity" in as much as the utterance is an action, but rather it can be deemed successful or unsuccessful or, in Austin's phrasing, "felicitous" or "infelicitous."

Austin divides failures into two major categories: "misfires" and "abuses." Shoshana Felman's subtle reading of Austin summarizes these categories:

Misfires result when the intended outcome of the performative utterance does not occur, *is not carried out*, owing to inappropriate circumstances: for example, because the conventional procedures to which performatives are always attached through their more or less ritual accomplishment were not respected, or were not in order. If I say, for example, "I take this woman as my lawful wedded wife" outside of the ritual ceremony, or when I am already married, the marriage is of course null and void, the act is not accomplished; it succumbs to the "infelicity" of failure; the performative utterance misfires. If on the other hand I say "I promise," but *without* the intention of keeping my promise, or in full knowledge that I will be unable to keep it, the performative act of promising is "infelicitous" because of an "abuse," not because of a misfire—it is not null and void. Indeed, whether or not I am sincere, when I utter the words "I promise" I in fact *carry out* the *act* of promising; the act succeeds, it is executed; but it may be executed in bad faith: by executing the act of promising, in such a case, I deceive my interlocutor. Although the act is "successful," then, it entails a form of failure; it is infelicitous because of my abuse.[37]

Viewing *Lover* as a performative in Austin's terms enables us to see that the novel, and the actions and words the characters carry out within the novel, partake of both major categories of "infelicity" so that they end up occupying a rather queer position. On one hand, the ritual order of heterosexuality does not recognize the homosexual insofar as conventional procedures (e.g., narrative and legal discourses) are concerned. The lesbian "lover," then, is a misfire. That is, she is null and (a) void, infelicitous because of her failure to be recognized in discourse. I mean this in the sense that it is both difficult to recognize Harris's narrative form (there are no models) or Harris's creation, "lover" (there are no models or there are *only* models). On the other hand, however, insofar as Harris seeks to deceive the reader and/or her lover, through the production of beings who are at the very least duplicitous, if not multiple (for example, Veronica as doubled or the interchangeability of Flynn and Bertha), then the lesbian lover is an abuse, successfully executing promises in order to deceive. However, this is not the result of Harris's congenital mendacity, but rather of a culture that offers nothing but bad faith in dealing with the lesbian lover. That is, to reframe this in terms of my previous argument about Irigaray's woman as forger, the culture only ever recognizes her as a "bad copy."

Lover then shows that language can succeed, perhaps seduce, even though it might be voided, or in Austin's words, a "misfire," by the rules of heterosexuality, of representation, of the law, and the like. That is, the sayings of a "lover" might succeed in one respect, but be infelicitous in terms of the rules. So we might say that the act of this sort of "lover" is, instead of felicitous (or infelicitous), a *queer* act, one that succeeds, but not within the rules. In less metaphorical terms and more practical/ actual ones, for example, because the state does not recognize homosexual unions, gays have no choice but to be lovers who must keep performing their unruly acts over and over again simply in order to be recognized as (in)felicitous.[38] Though, of course, these acts are not "voids" or "failures" altogether. Even Austin acknowledges this in his example of the "misfired" marriage ceremony: "Two final words about being void or without effect. This does not mean, of course, to say that we won't have done anything: lots of things will have been done—we will most interestingly have committed the act of bigamy—but we shall not have done the purported act, viz. marrying."[39] Of course, the act accomplished by the productive misfire of queer marriage is something other than bigamy—more like an abomination within the ritual order of heterosexuality.

I would like to make another claim about Harris's (in)felicity, her queer acts—that they call into question the rules of representation. Or as Felman suggests, "The act of failing thus opens up the space of referentiality—or of impossible reality—not because *something is missing*, but because *something else is done*, or because something else is said: the term "misfire" does not refer to an absence, but to the enactment of difference."[40] Key to understanding *Lover* is its enactment of difference. I would argue that "the something else that is done" are utterances that dissimulate or "fail" in one realm, but in fact, enact an alternate set of meanings. Take, for example, this scene near the opening of the novel, where much "impossible reality" occurs:

Then at Christmas time, Veronica's lover gives her an old silver cigarette case, with the initials *BH* engraved in one corner of the lid. Her lover gives her a second present, and this is an ivory and tortoise-shell cigarette holder. . . . She stuffs the case with Balkan Sobranies, then flips it open again and holds it open in her left hand like a little book. She stretches her arm toward Jenny, offering the open case. *See garette, my dair?* she leers. The waiter passes the hot hor d'oeuvres. In the lobby of the Algonquin Hotel, Veronica is a man in a 1939 Twentieth Century Fox movie. She is David Niven in a pin-striped suit and a pencil-line mustache. She leans across the table and leers, "*See garette, my dair?* Don't be nervous. Trust me. Soon I shall reveal all!" (6)

Harris locates her characters performing an act of seduction or at least an act of romantic intrigue—connoting eloquence, wealth, sophistication, and wit (the Algonquin). This scene becomes a microcosm of the way the novel works as a whole. On the most literal and "truthful" levels, Veronica is not David Niven, sometimes Veronica is not even Veronica (sometimes she is Bertha, sometimes Flynn); it is not 1939 and they are not at the Algonquin Hotel. The situating of this act also calls up a specific history and a kind of glamour; the cigarette holder and silver case bring up the rich and famous of lesbian lore—from Una Troubridge to Tallulah Bankhead. A mystery is also designated by the situation—"soon I will reveal all" and announces an essential aspect of the performative, "trust me." That is, I make you a promise to be trustworthy. What we have set up here with all these richly evocative details is a grounding in the past, in Hollywood illusion; it is not a deception but a way to understand what will unfold. We will be witness to a theatrical performance that calls out to us as readers and addresses us as "my dair."

Actions that, if performed in a heterosexual context would be "misfires" and "abuses" meant to deceive, then become, in the context of *Lover*, perfectly "queer" acts—successful, neither true nor false, and freighted with other meaning (of the meaning of otherness). *Lover* is concerned with seduction by misfire and abuse, seduction by "as if," and through these concerns, Harris calls attention to what is missing, what is written out and unwritten in terms of the law. And even though her utterances are "infelicitous," they succeed; the lover revels in the pleasure of the feast of language. *Lover* uses language as a field of enjoyment, not meant to inform, but rather to perform. Finally, Harris's *Lover*, like the trickster figure, subverts the uniqueness of the performative act in order not to ruin the performance of language but its authority.

The importance of the performative is that it illustrates something more general about the nature of language itself: the impossibility of the separation between body and language. Felman states, "through the new concept of 'language *act*' [Austin] explodes both the opposition and the separation between matter (or body) and language: matter, like the act, *without being reducible to language*, is no longer entirely separable from it, either."[41] The novel *Lover* as a performative also partakes of that explosion between body and language. That is, the novel creates through its linguistic act a different kind of "body," the body of the "lover." This is significant in that this creation is a different conceptual field/desiring subject, neither man nor woman, but lover. Thus if language has effects, if "as if" creates reality, then *Lover* itself begins to create a new category, a lover, in the world.

LOVER—AN INTERPELLATION

I read *Lover* as a productive self-fashioning and so a sort of autobiography, and autobiography is itself a kind of performative. According to Paul de Man, though autobiography seems to depend on the actual and verifiable, in fact the "distinction between fiction and autobiography is not an either/ or polarity but . . . it is undecidable."[42] He suggests that while we assume that life *produces* the autobiography, we can equally maintain "that the autobiographical project may itself produce and determine the life."[43] Harris implicitly invokes the form of that which is itself contestable as a generic category and contestable as to whether it depicts "life" or "art." A true/false dichotomy is again rejected in favor of something more subtle— the successful or unsuccessful.

However, *Lover* is not the autobiography of Harris exactly, or of a certain lover; rather it is a discursive/operatic act that calls attention to the notion of performativity and to what it might mean to be a lover, as opposed to, say, a woman. Both the novel *Lover*, and the "thing," lover, are the performance of categories that are themselves undecidable, like autobiography. The one line from her novel that Harris calls attention to in her introduction is this: "That a thing, if performed, is its own duplicate" (xx). The performing creates the original; this inheres in the title of the novel—one who loves, which is ultimately what Flynn learns to be/ do.[44] The notion that the doing creates is especially important when we consider that the "thing" being performed might not exist within a representational system designed to deem inadmissible any desire between women.

Importantly, the word lover as the body/object performatively brought into being has a host of meanings. The Oxford English Dictionary (OED) offers these meanings: friend and well-wisher (now rare); one who loves spiritually; one who is in love with, or who is enamored of a person of the opposite sex; one who loves illicitly; a form of address. Implicit within the matrix of the word itself is a set of roles and rules, which Harris constantly exposes and undermines because she calls up two quite different registers. On one hand, within a heterosexual register, the meaning of lover usually devolves into sexual partner (sometimes illicit). Whereas, in a gay register, lover is a standard form by which one names his or her same sex partner, but always illicit vis-à-vis dominant culture. I would suggest, then, in opposition to the OED's heterosexualized array of meanings, that in a gay register, "lover" offers us many meanings at once—friend, sexual partner, spiritual lover, and so on. The word *lover* in a gay register, then, possesses a kind of double consciousness, foregrounding contiguities and multiplicities. That is, the word works to encompass many of the received meanings at once, even though some of them may seem to be mutually exclusive.

I read *Lover* as an autobiography of sorts, as a performative of the category *lover*, of a not yet defined subject, but one can also think of the title of the novel as the OED suggests, as an address. It is an interpellation, a naming into being of an object heretofore unaccounted for. To cite somebody as a lover is a kind of performative act that designates an actor, someone who loves, but also an interpellation that doubles back on itself. That is, naming the other as lover would in conventional binary paradigms place the addresser in the category of "beloved"—a sort of passive object. Yet in fact, naming someone as your lover is an active movement, a taking hold of subjectivity. But again, when someone is named as a lover ("so-and-so is my lover"), it is for the purpose of designating her as object (of my affection).

It seems then that the word *lover* entails both an active and a passive meaning—being the subject who loves and being the subject of another. As the novel ends, the narrator sums up what has been shown and done:

This is true love; and its course runs true, though not smooth. All that really happened is that the lover won the beloved, and became the beloved; and the nature of all kinds of rapture, including this, is that it must clothe itself in disguise—the god in swan's feathers, the mother in sheaves of wheat; the act of love a magic-lantern show, a proliferation of forgeries; which, taken all in all, seem real enough. There is no ending that is, eventually, not happy. (207–8)

The modest phrase, "all that really happened" understates the significance of what *Lover* has done. For the lover to win the beloved (and the reader) and change roles to beloved—for the lover to be at all—signals a successful seduction, an infinitely complex and felicitous speech act. Coupled with this act is the illusion of the act, the god in swan's feathers, an act of love that becomes hand shadows on the wall, but that nevertheless convinces and works, no matter how monstrous or strange. I have aimed to take Harris's felicitous "strangeness," her "private" love letter and to show its public persuasiveness, indeed perhaps to persuade the reader also to fall in love with the subject and object of my affection.

NOTES

I would like to thank the members of my writing groups in Santa Cruz and at Miami University, especially Yvonne Keller and Julia Erhart. I am also grateful to Tom Foster and the members of the editorial board at *Genders*.

1. First published by Daughters Inc., in 1976, *Lover* has been out of print for more than fifteen years. Only with *Lover's* republication in Karla Jay's series, "The Cutting Edge: Lesbian Life and Literature," do we once again have access to this text. Bertha Harris, *Lover* (New York: New York University Press, [1976] 1993). All references to this work will be included parenthetically in the text.

2. Wayne Koestenbaum, "The Purple Reign of Bertha Harris: Excess Story," *Voice Literary Supplement* (October 1993): 18.

3. It seems hardly accidental that Harris's *Lover* (1976) was produced around the same time as Esther Newton's *Mother Camp* (1972), Gayle Rubin's "The Traffic in Women: Notes toward a Political Economy of Sex" (1975), and Luce Irigaray's *Speculum de l'autre femme* (published in France in 1974). These works have had an enormous impact on the field of queer/gender/feminist/lesbian/ sexual difference studies. I use these inelegant slashes to indicate the contested nature of these terms—that is, who claims them, whom they serve, and in what contexts. Harris's work seems to me to have more affinity with the latter three terms than the former two, though her connection with gay male camp is quite marked. However, part of my argument is that Harris performs transgressive movements across boundaries—including ones between theoretical positions. The "trouble" generated by the meeting of "queer" theory and feminism (as well as these other terms) is the subject of a complex and lengthy debate; see the double issue of *differences* devoted to this topic, especially the conversation/inter- view between Braidotti and Butler. Rosi Braidotti, "Feminism by Any Other Name: Interview with Judith Butler," *differences: A Journal of Feminist Cultural Studies* 6.2–3 (Summer-Fall 1994): 27–61.

4. Blanche McCrary Boyd, "The Purple Reign of Bertha Harris: Bitter Har- vest," *Voice Literary Supplement* (October 1993): 19.

5. Teresa de Lauretis, "Sexual Indifference and Lesbian Representation," *The- atre Journal* 40.2 (May 1988): 165.

6. Harris also "frames" her novel uniquely, by beginning in three different ways. Following the title page, Harris offers a hand-drawn, mock genealogical table. It is mock insofar as it is circular and convoluted; there are no men in the chart and it is difficult to determine who is descended from whom. All that one can be sure of is that the names Bertha and Flynn occupy the center and all other names flow from that center. Following that chart, Harris gives a synopsis of Strauss's *Der Rosenkavalier*. Finally, Harris begins her novel (that is, the actual text as opposed to the genealogical chart or *Der Rosenkavalier*) by prefacing each of the forty-six episodes of her novel (except for the episodes that include men) with a few short sentences in italics that recount the stories of various mythic women (a sort of lives of women saints and martyrs) who in some way reject traditional

gender roles and "compulsive"/compulsory heterosexuality, from Saint Dorothea to Faith and her sisters.

7. The name Veronica is hardly incidental; for Veronica, master of illusion (in the novel), comes from the Latin "verum," meaning true and "iconicus" meaning image, likeness; indeed "Veronica" is the "true" image of the author embodied in the fiction. The name Veronica also plays on the idea of the veil and St. Veronica. As Veronica's grandmother, Samaria, tells us, "Like the veil. Veronica's veil took the face on itself and afterwards no one could tell which was the real face and which was the face on the veil" (58).

8. For a more extended and general delineation of a similar mechanism for seeing the invisible, the off-screen and what it might mean for a lesbian thwarting of the "constant reproduction of heterosexuality," see Marilyn Frye, *The Politics of Reality: Essays in Feminist Theory* (Trumansburg, NY: The Crossing Press, 1983), 172.

9. Bertha Harris, "What We Mean to Say: Notes toward Defining the Nature of Lesbian Literature," *Heresies* 3 (Fall 1977): 6.

10. Harris has written only a few pieces about what might constitute this sensibility. See the somewhat bitter and ironic exchange between Harris and Irena Klepfisz (and Joanna Russ's engaging and level-headed letter following the exchange) in *Sinister Wisdom*. Irena Klepfisz, "Criticism: Form and Function in Lesbian Literature," *Sinister Wisdom* 9 (Spring 1979): 27–30. Here, Harris produces an amusing and sarcastic rebuttal to those writers and critics she believes are unable to see the "monstrosity" of what she calls "the lesbian as literature" (25). Bertha Harris, "Melancholia, and Why It Feels So Good . . . ," *Sinister Wisdom* 9 (Spring 1979): 24–26.

11. For an excellent discussion of the autobiographical function, especially in relation to the lesbian subject, see Leigh Gilmore's account of *The Autobiography of Alice B. Toklas*, where she focuses on "how Stein writes an autobiography profoundly concerned with visibility, with what can and cannot be seen and why, as a way to explore the contradictory codes of lesbian and autobiographical (self-) representation." Leigh Gilmore, *Autobiographics: A Feminist Theory of Women's Self-Representation* (Ithaca: Cornell University Press, 1994), 200.

12. Monique Wittig's idea that lesbians are not women is an obvious reference point here. Wittig answers succinctly the question that Freud kept knocking his head against: What is a woman? She writes, "Frankly it is a problem that lesbians do not have because of a change of perspective, and it would be incorrect to say that lesbians associate, make love, live with women, for 'woman' has meaning only in heterosexual systems of thought and heterosexual economic systems. Lesbians are not women." See Monique Wittig, "The Straight Mind," *Feminist Issues* 1.1 (1980): 110. Rosi Braidotti calls Wittig's move here a "willful self-naming" and finds Wittig's rejection of the term "woman" an inadequate strategy for an "exit from the prison-house of phallocentric language." See Rosi Braidotti, "Feminism," 51. Harris takes a more complex approach than Wittig; Harris renames the world but is not blind to the pain and loss that accompany her entry into the signifying order. This is evident in her relation to language and in her analysis of

the loss of the mother. Though I do not have space here to pursue the complexities of Harris's maternal imaginary, suffice it to say, in order to become a lover, she must reject the idea that it is natural for daughters to lose (figurally and mythically, at the very least) their mothers in the cycle of reproduction and heterosexuality. Harris shows us this in literal terms; she writes, "For seven years, she [her mother] let me sleep in bed beside her. But then one morning the footsteps in the corridor *were his*. He was back from World War II, and I had to run and hide" (38).

13. Judith Butler, *Gender Trouble: Feminism and the Subversion of Identity* (New York and London: Routledge, 1990), 129.

14. See "The Callas Cult" for an acute reading of the significance of Maria Callas for gay (male) subculture in Wayne Koestenbaum, *The Queen's Throat: Opera, Homosexuality, and the Mystery of Desire* (New York: Poseidon Press, 1993), 134–53.

15. *Traveler in Eternity* was, as the reader might have surmised, by the British Bertha Harris.

16. Maurice Leonard, *Battling Bertha: The Biography of Bertha Harris* (London: Regency Press, 1975).

17. Teresa de Lauretis, *The Practice of Love: Lesbian Sexuality and Perverse Desire* (Bloomington and Indianapolis: Indiana University Press, 1994), 308.

18. Dorothy Allison, "The Purple Reign of Bertha Harris: The Passion," *Voice Literary Supplement* (October 1993): 19.

19. Koestenbaum, "Purple," 18.

20. Of course, a number of people have recognized Harris's abilities. For example, Joanna Russ, author of *The Female Man*, refers to *Lover* as "the best Lesbian novel I've ever read and possibly the best novel of the last thirty years" in "Letter to the Editors," *Sinister Wisdom* 10 (Summer 1979): 54. In the editor's introduction to the new edition of *Lover*, Karla Jay remarks, "when I queried the board of 'The Cutting Edge' series about which books they thought worthy of reprinting, Bertha Harris's *Lover* was the title most often named" (xv). See also Catharine Stimpson, "Zero Degree Deviancy: The Lesbian Novel in English," in *Writing and Sexual Difference*, ed. Elizabeth Abel (Chicago: University of Chicago Press, 1982), 243–60. Despite these critics, however, Harris's work has remained in relative obscurity—due in part to the combination of her allusive style and the demise of Daughters Press. Additionally her work was called, in the 1970s, "politically incorrect" by some lesbian feminists (perhaps because of its relative inaccessibility)—long before the term came into vogue; see Russ.

21. Harris remarks that even obtaining information about these women was difficult during the late 1950s and early 1960s, when she first began her search. For example, in order to read the works of Djuna Barnes, Harris tells of "prevaricating my way into the New York Public Library rare book room (my phony ID proclaimed me Dr. Valerie von Trilling, Cambridge; I wore a dumpy tweed skirt, a starched white shirt, black necktie." See Bertha Harris, "The More Profound Nationality of Their Lesbianism: Lesbian Society in Paris in the 1920s," in *Amazon Expedition: A Lesbian Feminist Anthology*, ed. Phyllis Birkby, Bertha Harris,

Jill Johnston, Esther Newton, and Jane O'Wyatt (New York: Times Change Press, 1973), 78. Harris's article is an attempt to provide some sense of lesbian history and community by naming names and providing facts about lesbian society in the 1920s.

22. Ibid., 79.

23. Ibid., 77.

24. Ibid., 79.

25. I do not mean to imply that butch/femme is always recuperable by dominant culture. See Lynda Hart's insightful discussion of a Split Britches theatrical production entitled *Anniversary Waltz*, where Lois Weaver and Peggy Shaw tell the story of their ten-year lesbian relationship. Hart charts the audience's reception (lesbian and heterosexual) to this deconstructive performance, as well as the critical assessments and arguments that follow. Lynda Hart and Peggy Phelan, eds., *Acting Out: Feminist Performances* (Ann Arbor: University of Michigan Press, 1993).

26. Monique Wittig, "Point of View: Universal or Particular?," *Feminist Issues* 3.2 (1983): 64.

27. Mary Ann Doane, "Film and the Masquerade: Theorizing the Female Spectator," *Screen* 23 (1982): 81.

28. Judith Butler, "Imitation and Gender Insubordination," in *Inside/Out: Lesbian Theories, Gay Theories*, ed. Diana Fuss (New York: Routledge, 1991), 21.

29. Ibid.

30. Ibid.

31. Anne B. Dalton, " 'This Is Obscene': Female Voyeurism, Sexual Abuse, and Maternal Power in *The Dove*," *The Review of Contemporary Fiction* 13.3 (Fall 1993): 117.

32. Luce Irigaray, *Speculum of the Other Woman*, trans. Gillian C. Gill (Ithaca: Cornell University Press, 1985), 50.

33. Butler, *Bodies*, 12.

34. Irigaray, 42.

35. Irigaray, 125, emphasis original.

36. Eve Sedgwick makes a similar point: " 'Performative' at the present moment carries the authority of two quite different discourses, that of the theater on the one hand, of speech-act theory on the other. . . . 'Performativity' is already quite a queer category, then—maybe not so surprising if we consider the tenuousness of its ontological ground, the fact that it begins its intellectual career all but repudiated in advance by its originator, the British philosopher J. L. Austin, who introduces the term in the first of his 1955 Harvard lectures (later published as *How to Do Things with Words*) only to disown it somewhere around the eighth. He disowns or dismantles 'performativity,' that is, as the name of a distinctive category or field of utterances (that might be opposed to the 'constative'); and indeed the use that deconstruction has had of 'performativity' begins with the recognition of it as a property common to all utterance." Eve Kosofsky Sedgwick, "Queer Performativity: Henry James's *Art of the Novel*," *GLQ: Journal of Gay and Lesbian Studies* 1.1 (1993): 2.

37. Shoshana Felman, *The Literary Speech Act: Don Juan with J. L. Austin, or Seduction in Two Languages*, trans. Catherine Porter (Ithaca, NY: Cornell University Press, 1983), 16, note 2.

38. I owe parts of this formulation to Julia Erhart.

39. J. L. Austin, *How To Do Things with Words*, 2d ed. (Cambridge: Harvard University Press, 1975), 17.

40. Ibid., 84.

41. Ibid., 147, emphasis original.

42. Paul de Man, "Autobiography As De-Facement," *Modern Language Notes* 94 (1979): 921.

43. Ibid., 920.

44. This works on a microcosmic level in the text as well. For example, the epigraph that precedes the text of the novel, but follows the synopsis of Strauss's *Der Rosenkavalier*, reads: "To save herself from marriage, Lucy gouged out her own eyes; but Agatha appeared to her and declared, 'Thou art light.' " I read this epigraph as Harris's way of accomplishing two things: first, alerting us to an alternate way of seeing, turning a blind eye, as it were, to heterosexuality, yet still in part propelled or influenced by it; second, Harris accomplishes this alternate way of seeing through the power of the word—a magical world is produced in a sentence. Agatha (Greek for good) names Lucy into being by pronouncing to her (and indeed asking her to assume) the meaning of her own name; "Lucy" means light.

PART TWO

Queer Nations: Colonialism, Race, and Sexuality

Historic Image/Self Image: Re-Viewing *Chicana*

Elissa J. Rashkin

In 1979 Sylvia Morales directed a film inspired by activist Anna Nieto Gómez's slide show *Historic Images of the Chicana*, a union organizing vehicle which traced the history of the Chicano people from pre-Columbian times to the present from a woman-centered perspective. First entitled *Bread and Roses*, then renamed *Chicana*, Morales's film brought stock images to life with a mobile camera, narration by actress Carmen Zapata, an expressive soundtrack, and original live footage. A recognized watershed in the history of Chicano cinema,[1] *Chicana* would seem to be a textbook example of 1970s feminist "herstory," the practice of countering gaps and absences in dominant male-centered history with accounts of the experiences of both ordinary and exceptional women. Chicana intellectuals, seeking to recover a history they felt had been denied them, joined other feminists of that era in developing and perpetuating this approach to the past; Cotera's *Diosa y Hembra* and Mirandé and Enríquez's *La Chicana* stand as two pioneering examples.[2]

Although initially compelling, "herstory" has since been criticized for not adequately addressing the power relations underlying knowledge production itself.[3] Many feminists in the 1990s, influenced by recent trends in critical theory, would argue that the oppressive, patriarchal nature of dominant history lies less in its factual omissions than in its very claim to authority, its monopoly over interpretation such that its constructs are taken to be the truth, "what really happened." From this perspective, the liberation of women and other oppressed groups requires more than positive images from the past; it requires changes in the discourse itself.

A project like *Chicana*, intended to upgrade the image of Chicanas by including the "story of women" in Chicano history,[4] and based on chronologically ordered conventional images (archival photographs and classic paintings, most originally male-authored), seems more reformist than revolutionary.

On closer examination, however, *Chicana* is more than a litany of Chicana and Mexicana achievements and oppressions. In fact, it shares concerns expressed by the most innovative of contemporary feminist thinkers: like Gloria Anzaldúa, it focuses on the act of "haciendo caras," on women's use of masks, dissimulation, and masquerade; with Cherríe Moraga, it rethinks notions of female treachery, reclaiming the sexual legacy of betrayal; and like Norma Alarcón and other poststructuralist-influenced feminists, it centers on the importance of mythic archetypes in Mexican and Chicano culture and attempts to deconstruct and demystify these archetypes.[5] Morales saw Chicanas as caught in the crossroads — and the crossfire — of competing discourses: Anglo/liberal feminism, Marxism, male-centered nationalism, and hegemonic views of U.S. and Mexican history. Her response was to select what was useful from these discourses, and construct a narrative of women's historical experience using counterhegemonic techniques of parody and bricolage. *Chicana* is pieced together from preexisting texts, which it alters and selects to create new meanings.

Chicana may have been intended as a relatively straightforward presentation of facts, yet its narrative strategies make its critique far more complex; its montage style, deploying canonical images to serve feminist ends, initiates a game of interpretation that calls conventional historiography into question. Although many of its segments can be seen as boldly revisionist, its critique of history as a patriarchal apparatus is particularly apparent in its presentation of a figure whose historical existence is inseparable from her mythic status: Malintzin Tenepal, the translator, advisor, and captive mistress of the conquistador Hernán Cortés. The importance of Malintzin, or La Malinche as she is most often called, for the formation and continuation of Mexican and Chicano identity — personal as well as social and national — has been attested to by such writers as Octavio Paz, Carlos Fuentes, and Rosario Castellanos, as well as by the visual artists whose graphic depictions of the Conquest (see below) have been almost as influential as written accounts.

The image or idea of Malinche has appeared in hegemonic ideology in service to national and nationalist projects; yet it has also been appropriated and refigured as a challenge to those projects. *Chicana*'s interpretation of Malintzin continues and extends this trajectory; using a privileged medium to which few Chicanas have had access, Morales and her collaborators do more than amend the historical record; they also challenge male-produced notions of what it means to be Chicano.

MYTHS OF ORIGIN: WOMEN IN *THE LABYRINTH OF SOLITUDE*

In an essay evaluating Chicana historiography, Rosaura Sánchez complained that "works tracing Chicana roots in Mexican history need not postulate direct links between us and La Malinche or Sor Juana Inés de la Cruz. References to Aztec goddesses similarly prove absolutely nothing. . . . Chicana historians need fewer myths and more historical analysis."[6] Yet constructs of identity in Mexican and Chicano culture in general and in the Chicano political movement in particular have been deeply rooted in myths of origin, including those of Malinche, the Virgin of Guadalupe, and the goddess Coatlicue. It is because these myths impact upon women's lived experience that they have figured prominently in the Chicana feminist struggle. The reasons for the feminist use of these myths can best be understood by looking at the myths themselves as they circulated during the period of the Chicano political movement, out of whose strengths and weaknesses Chicana feminism emerged.[7]

Although ideas about Malintzin could be traced from the time of the Conquest, the point of departure for Chicanas recounting her story has most often been Octavio Paz, the writer who explicitly defined the Mexican people as "sons of La Malinche," or more pointedly, "hijos de la chingada."[8] In *The Labyrinth of Solitude* (1950), a meditation on the psychology of Mexican society, Paz repudiated idealized Spanish and indigenous pasts alike, and argued for the centrality of cultural mestizaje, or hybridity. He also attempted to analyze gender divisions in modern Mexico, and in his discussion of La Malinche, merged the question of national origin (Mexicans as offspring of the Conquest itself rather than of one side or the other) with that of sexuality, figured strongly in terms of hierarchy and violence.

For Paz, Malintzin was La Chingada, the fucked one, "the mother forcibly opened, violated or deceived."[9] Although he characterizes her relationship with Cortés as a "betrayal" on her part (87), he mainly portrays her as the victim of a double violation, raped both as a symbol of pre-Hispanic Mexico *and* as a woman. While the first rape defines a

crucial historical moment (the Conquest), the second is constantly reen-
acted in gender relations to the present day.

Paz's primary interest, not surprisingly, was in analyzing what it means
to be the product of a founding rape—that is, what it means to Mexican
men. How Mexican women were meant to incorporate this understanding
of their heritage is a nonquestion, since Paz's text closes off the possibility
of women escaping the plight of Malintzin herself. Malintzin, as La
Chingada, "loses her name; she is no one; she disappears into nothingness.
She *is* Nothingness. And yet she is the cruel incarnation of the feminine
condition" (86). Similarly, women in general are seen as instruments of
either individual male desires or patriarchal social values. While Paz
seems to lament this situation (considering it evidence of male dysfunc-
tion), many of *Labyrinth*'s passages strongly suggest its inevitability:
woman is always passive, thus always already chingada.

In his effort to demonstrate that "open versus closed" is the fundamental binarism underlying Mexican society, with the fear of vulnerability
leading to the exaggerated closedness he associates with machismo, Paz
links women's subjugation to an openness which is both socially constructed and biological—or rather, just as in many psychoanalytic accounts of castration and female lack, his analysis of a symbolic status
frequently slides into an unexamined biological determinism. Woman, he
writes, "is submissive and open by nature. But through a compensation
mechanism that is easily explained, her natural frailty is made a virtue and
the myth of the 'long suffering Mexican woman' is created" (38). Paz
leaves no room for female agency, for: "in effect, every woman—even
when she gives herself willingly—is torn open by the man, is the chingada" (80). The only way for woman to transcend her "unfortunate
anatomical openness" is through suffering—the stoic suffering of the
Virgin Mary herself. Although La Virgen and Malintzin are often seen as
opposed models of femininity (literally madonna and whore), Paz argues
that both are characterized primarily by their passivity.

Further aspects of Paz's account of La Malinche are worth noting.
First, Paz ignores her role as translator and adviser in order to base his
argument on sexuality. By doing so, and by treating Malinche's complex
relationship to the Spaniards solely in terms of rape, Paz maintains binary
oppositions that her other roles would seem to complicate. Yet at the
same time he characterizes her as a traitor, associated with the "mala
mujer" (bad woman) who is, almost by definition, aggressively active.
This dual characterization is contradictory, and in order to resolve it, Paz

falls back on biological determinism; if female activity is limited to the transmission of cultural values *in which she does not believe*, the source of her betrayal and that of her victimization must be the same: a "taint" that "resides in her sex" (85). The image Paz finally offers of Malinche and by extension of all women is that of someone who at the moment of being raped is labeled *vendida*—a disquieting example indeed, for which the Christian promise of redemption through suffering provides little consolation.

At the time *The Labyrinth of Solitude* was written, feminism was already taking issue with Paz-style models of female passivity; Rosario Castellanos, who would later write the poem "Malinche" addressing Malintzin's original betrayal by her family when she was sold into slavery, was then dissecting the paradox of female creative agency in her master's thesis, "Sobre cultura femenina." [10] Yet in 1950, Mexican women had not yet won the right (which they would be granted in 1953) to vote in federal elections; they were legally considered subordinate to men within marriage and the family until the Civil Code was reformed in 1974. In the Mexico of the 1950s, women were literally considered a separate, inferior class of persons.

Paz's disavowal of female agency was thus in keeping with the prevailing views of his time. But by the late 1960s, feminism in Mexico as elsewhere had called the passive model of womanhood into question. The class- and gender-conscious Castellanos, for example, spoke to Mexico's cultural complexity, a complexity overlooked by male authors seeking a distinguishing national identity, or "mexicanidad." With hindsight, the border-straddling Chicano/a, like Castellano's figurative "border crossers," can be seen as troubling this search for a unified notion of Mexican identity; Paz's "pachuco," after all, represented a puzzled if poetic outsider's view of the U.S. Latino experience. Yet Paz's analysis of an existential crisis of lineage was taken up by many Chicano thinkers, for whom his attempt "to explain the failure and nonrevolutionary status of the revolts of 1910 in terms of indigenous/Hispanic duality" resonated with their own experience of a similar Anglo-Mexican dichotomy. [11]

Because of his overwhelming influence, angry criticisms of Paz appeared regularly in Chicana feminist writings of the 1970s. For example, in a 1975 essay entitled "Identidad," Marta Cotera accused Paz of using "poetic license" to insult women: "Poets can do anything they want to, including calling you the things they called you, and calling me the same thing." [12] Cotera held Paz responsible for encouraging men to use the example of Malinche as "a club for us, to keep us down."[13] Although her basic objection—that historical accounts of the Conquest locate Malintzin's actions within a wider rebellion against the Aztec rulers—ignores the fact that Paz's essay is specifically about myth and its effects rather than historical truth, it is nonetheless a significant strategic move that is echoed in the work of many of her contemporaries. This feminist response to Paz (or rather, to his influence on what he calls "the living flesh of the present") must be seen as part of the political context from which the film *Chicana* emerged.

VISUAL HISTORY: FROM MURAL TO SCREEN

Before discussing this response, however, I would like to turn to the sources whose influence *Chicana* manifests most directly: the Mexican murals out of which the film's Conquest sequence is composed. The original paintings, while diverse in style, strongly resemble *The Labyrinth of Solitude* in their historical vision; they do not glorify the conqueror, but neither do they settle for a facile indigenism. Instead, they represent the Conquest in its full horror and violence, from a formal perspective of stark modernism that cites (in order to transform) both European classical painting and pre-Cortesian traditions of representation. The confrontation is thus often depicted in aesthetic as well as literal terms.

Often the murals are fully developed narratives, their stories proceeding temporally as well as spatially across the sides of buildings or between different walls and surfaces. The very use of these paintings in *Chicana* must be seen not simply as a means of illustration, but as citation of works that already contain their own versions of the events the filmmakers sought to narrate. This is especially true considering that the paintings by Rivera, Siqueiros, and Orozco are among the artists' most famous and would likely be familiar images to many members of *Chicana*'s audience.

How are women represented in these paintings? With the important exception of Orozco's *Cortés y la Malinche*, the answer is hardly at all, in the "active" foregrounds. The main portions of the murals often show meetings between Spanish and indigenous leaders, or focus on individual male heroes and villains such as Cuauhtémoc and Cortés. Indian women populate the background as anonymous, frequently faceless victims, sometimes veiled, more often nude and distorted, often desexualized but sometimes, as in certain works by Siqueiros, feminized to the point of fetishism.

Just as in Paz, the idea of rape as a constitutive metaphor for the Conquest looms large: the phallic swords of the conquistadors are represented piercing and slicing open the sprawled bodies of the naked, inert victims. Although the latter are not exclusively women, all are shown as androgynous to feminine, in contrast to the masculine potency of the conquistadors. To be Indian and/or female in these paintings is to be nothing except a naked, open, featureless body, whereas the conqueror's features—and emphatically "closed" armor—are rendered in detail, highlighting his power.

Again, the conflation of biological sex with a historical status of victimization poses problems that a feminist project like *Chicana* will have to confront. On the one hand, there is little doubt that indigenous people, male and female, were violently oppressed by the invading Spaniards, and that the muralists were simply utilizing their artistic skills to convey in the most direct, visceral way possible the brutality of the situation, the violence which at that point had not often been acknowledged as the collective past of the Americas. On the other hand, the use of a chingón/chingada opposition as a visual strategy somewhat begs the question of historical authenticity. For the muralists were artists in the conventional sense, well versed in European traditions of painting and participants in international modernist movements such as Cubism. It was in this role as artists (rather than as cultural activists) that in their nonmural work they painted extremely conventional nudes. In the tradition of nude painting from which even these radical artists did not depart, women are typically rendered as anonymous bodies, supposedly "pure form" but nonetheless emphatically gendered. The models' faces are often obscured or turned away from the viewer. Their "lack," or what Paz called "anatomical openness," is put on display, refigured as the object of ambivalent (fetishistic) contemplation.

In the representation of women and/or Indians in the Conquest murals and paintings, this tradition is by no means left behind, in spite of the historical and narrative context into which the nude figures are placed. In the works of Siqueiros, for example, female victims are eroticized, adorned with ample flesh and enormous round breasts that are incongruous with their presumed condition of privation. Even more prevalent than these sexualized images are those of idealized maternity; Orozco's veiled, weeping mothers, for instance, adhere to the model of the Virgin of Guadalupe, the woman redeemed by fidelity and suffering but always powerless. Much as in Paz's *Labyrinth*, there is in the murals a visible

confusion between women as historical victims in the specific circumstances of the Conquest, and woman as a passive object within a universal-
ist tradition of patriarchal representation.

It is important to emphasize that both the muralists and writers such
as Paz were modernists in the sense of breaking with traditional, especially
religious orthodoxies; that they were not interested in promulgating the
ideology of Catholicism, but rather worked "to wrest contemporary consciousness away from religious cosmologies."[14] Yet despite their modern,
secular, and often radical underpinnings, their work did little to change
the Catholic equation of woman with mother (or whore). "Paradoxically,"
Alarcón writes, referring to Labyrinth, "Paz has displaced the myth of
Guadalupe, not with history, but with a neomyth, a reversal properly
secularized yet unaware of its misogynistic residue."[15] The values associated with Malinche and Guadalupe persisted within a Mexican/Chicano
culture that was neither homogenous in its thinking nor unified around
the church, so that when Chicana feminists chose to address these two
female figures in their own work, they were responding both to the
traditional beliefs that shaped their upbringing *and* to the cultural movements and texts that constituted their heritage as artists and intellectuals.
As Alarcón rightly argues, the "residue" of misogyny has proved to be in
many ways more resilient than the structures and institutions that give it
specific shape. Although Malinche and Guadalupe are perceived as mothers of their people, their legends originated and persist in social formations that already equated womanhood with passivity, considered female
nonmaternal activity to be treacherous, and associated suffering with
virtue.

What is immediately striking about *Chicana* is its attempt to break
from this pervasive active/passive opposition and, using existent male-
authored texts, to put forth a different vision of female agency.[16] Although
the narrative virulently criticizes the suppression of Aztec and other
indigenous female deities and the emergence of the Virgin as a model of
female virtue and submission, little is said that directly contradicts the
modernist interpretation of events. The bulk of the critique comes from
judicious selection, juxtaposition, framing, and camera movement; in contrast to the narration, which presents interpretations as if they were
verifiable facts (albeit with a healthy layer of humor and irony), the
strategy of formal composition does not create a new story but literally
revises the ambivalent images that already exist, making the work of
cultural negotiation visible.

Even in the film's prologue, it is made clear that *Chicana*'s relation to its visual sources will not be an uncritical one, since the figure of a whore, the personification of bourgeois decadence in Orozco's *Catharsis*, is denounced as a traditional stereotype. In the Conquest sequence, the technique of isolating female figures from the larger paintings is used less for denunciation than for emphatic recentering. Ignoring the central, foregrounded images of the paintings, Morales's camera seeks out the images of women relegated by their creators to the margins, and makes them the focus of each shot. Whereas so many of the women in the original murals appear to be faceless (and almost formless), *Chicana* subverts this anonymity by magnifying the impact of the female faces that do exist, often at the expense of the centrality of the male protagonist.

For example, while several sections of Siqueiros's *The Torture of Cuauhtémoc* (including an almost full shot) are shown in the Conquest montage, the figure of the young Aztec emperor is given little attention and filmed only from a distance. Instead, the small figure of a mutilated woman

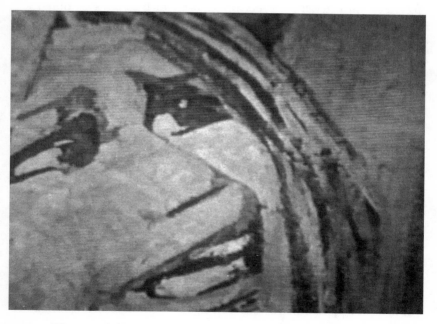

FIG. 4.1 The cry of the conquered: *Chicana*'s take on *The Torture of Cuauhtémoc*. Still from *Chicana* by Elissa Rashkin and Jim Clinefelter, reproduced with the permission of Sylvia Morales.

standing off to the left becomes the principal actor; her face is shown several times in close-up, and "her" voice, in the form of an anguished wail, dominates the soundtrack. Intercut with the image and sound of a fierce dog, her bleeding arms, tortured eyes and open mouth take on a resonance beyond that suggested by the painting as a whole; in other words, her suffering is not that of an anonymous victim but of a human being whose torture and mutilation is as momentous and tragic as that of Cuauhtémoc himself.

Perhaps this image attracted Morales for the reason that in it, Siqueiros depicted the female body wounded *by* the conqueror rather than the body *as* a wound created by/in the act of conquest, like the bodies lying at the feet of Orozco's *Cortés and Victory*. The former feels, responds to, protests and potentially rebels against her suffering, whereas the latter, like La Chingada, does not exist apart from her/its suffering. Clearly both remain victims, for there is no honest way to depict the events of 1519–21 without showing indigenous men and women as victims. What is at stake is the ideological analysis of victimization: whether passivity and objectification (literally, the person reduced to the status of thing) are represented as conditions imposed on the (potentially rebellious) body or as functions of the body, specifically of the "taint that resides in her sex." Clearly the feminists of the 1970s felt that if the limitations placed on women could be shown to be external, the myths that identify women with weakness and passivity would collapse, allowing women to fully become actors and subjects of their own history.

It is useful to compare *Chicana* with the film it most resembles in terms of editing structure, the Teatro Campesino's 1969 production of *I Am Joaquín*, based on the poem by Rodolfo Gonzales and directed by Luis Valdez.[17] The two films use the same murals to tell the story of the Conquest, but whereas *Chicana* excerpts from the murals in order to revise their interpretations, *Joaquín* preserves the values of the original paintings. Thus there are fewer close-ups in the 1969 film, and more pans across large sections of the murals. Figures such as Cortés and Cuauhtémoc retain their phallic centrality, and the Conquest is portrayed as a struggle between men, as it is in the original poem. In fact, in contrast to Paz, Gonzales's poem posits the Chicano as the result of a dialectical synthesis of opposed patriarchal forces, accomplished through violence rather than procreation: "I am Aztec prince and Christian Christ." The myths of maternal origin are conspicuously elided; however, they are brought in at the visual level both by images of women as mothers, and most interestingly, by the use of Orozco's *Cortés y la Malinche*. This painting itself is extremely ambiguous. It depicts the couple alone without the more familiar signifiers of the Conquest, naked and isolated, appearing as innocent and as guilty as Adam and Eve. They are posed seated and holding hands. Yet lest the scene seem overly tranquil, it is disturbed by the presence at their feet of the impersonal but accusing body of an Indian, lying in front of what seems to be an open grave. Although this third figure goes unnamed, he is an important reminder of the violence that defines the union of the other two—which is also complicated by Cortés's authoritative gesture of holding Malinche back, perhaps from this corpse. *Joaquín* nearly elides this third figure (although the motif of violence is amply brought out elsewhere) in order to develop the theme of mestizaje. To this end, Valdez presents the painting in four shots:

1. Close-up of Cortés's face as his racial identification is given.

2. Close-up of Malinche's face, identified verbally as Indian.

3. Two-shot at waist level, showing their clasped hands as well as their stomachs, thighs and genital areas, suggesting their procreative union, corresponding to the word "mestizo"; then cut during the phrase "we're all God's children" to:

4. Their feet, where a glimpse of the prostrate body adds the note of irony needed to return the concept of mestizaje to the overall theme of violent synthesis.

Malinche here seems to be complicit in the oppression of "God's children," but is also celebrated as a mother of her people. She is not counted among the victims of the invasion (let alone of her enslavement prior to Cortés's arrival); she is simply the transmitter of a cultural lineage from which she—*Joaquín* does not bother to tell us—is excluded.

In *Chicana*, the same mural completes a longer sequence on Malinche that also borrows images from another painting, *Los Señores de Tlaxcala Welcome Cortés and La Malinche*, by Desiderio Hernández Xochitiotzin.[18] Here, however, a historical context is provided for Malinche's actions,[19] first of all by the description of unrest and oppression under the Aztecs, and secondly, by her introduction as one of the female slaves that were actually given to the Spaniards. While this crucial aspect of her background is clearly articulated by both Bernal Díaz del Castillo and by Cortés himself,[20] it had to be "forgotten" in order for the myth of her betrayal and/or rape to succeed. A slave, in the first instance, can hardly be a traitor when she herself has been betrayed and treated as an object of exchange, while for her to negotiate for her freedom and for power means that she is more than a passive victim. Obviously this information causes problems for those who would idealize the pre-Cortesian world, but it also undermines the "neomyth" of mestizaje, if the result for women is the fusion of two systems of oppression, if both "Aztec prince and Christian Christ" make Malinche their slave and scapegoat.

Chicana moves from a colonial-era image of the twenty virgins to a close-up of Malintzin herself. Only after this shot establishes Malintzin as the subject of the narration do we get the longer shot showing her in her mediating role between the two male leaders. She is presented as "taking bold action" to change her subjugated condition. The act of symbolic appropriation is implicit: "The Spaniards called her Doña Marina," we are told, as a cut from a second close-up of her face brings us to Orozco's painting, here conveying very different sentiments than in *Joaquín*, "the Indians, La Malinche." The camera zooms out to a two-shot of the couple, as "she becomes the symbol of a ravaged Mexico, for the overthrow of the Aztec rulers does not bring freedom." The camera pans down Malintzin's and Cortés's bodies to the corpse at their feet. The ambivalence of the painting is fully exploited. Malintzin's troubled expression and the patriarchal gesture of Cortés holding her back just as his foot holds down the body are amplified via juxtaposition with the previous images, making it clear that the sexual union of Spaniard and Indian does not lead to "una raza cósmica" but to apocalyptic destruction. This is emphasized by the final dissolve from *Cortés y la Malinche* to Orozco's later *Cortés and Victory*, showing the triumph of the conqueror's violent tactics. His victory is posited as a betrayal *of*, not *by*, Malintzin Tenepal.

Whereas other sources emphasize Malintzin's sexual connection with Cortés, Morales focuses on her role as interpreter. She depicts the indigenous woman's actions as voluntary on one level, yet fundamentally coerced—not "simply" because she was a woman and therefore an object to be used by men but because she was a slave (and in fact had been sold into slavery by her own family). While not glorified, her assumption of the role of interpreter is transformed from an act of betrayal to one of resistance, albeit one that turns out to be misguided, since she herself is betrayed and defeated along with the rest of her people, former masters and slaves alike.

The point is not that this interpretation of Malinche is more (or less)

FIG. 4.2 Malinche as mediator . . . Still from *Chicana* by Elissa Rashkin and Jim Clinefelter, reproduced with the permission of Sylvia Morales.

correct than any previous one. Indeed, the "detournement" (the term used by the French situationists to describe their practice of plagiarizing images from popular culture and filling them with new words, captions and meanings seems appropriate to describe the use of images in this film) or "against the grain" manipulation of historical paintings insures that the question of representation, rather than that of truth, remains primary. As Alarcón points out, "our disquisitions truly take place over [Malintzin's] corpse and have no clue as to her own words, but instead refer to the chroniclers who themselves were not free of self-interest, motive, and intention."[21] Thus what Alarcón says of a mid-1970s essay by Adelaida R. del Castillo is also true of *Chicana*: that it "is not so much reconstructing Malintzin's own historical moment as [it] is using her both to counter contemporary masculine discourse and to project a newer sense of a female self, a speaking subject with a thoroughly modern view of historical consciousness."[22] In contrast to the binary models found in male-authored texts from *The Labyrinth of Solitude* to *I Am Joaquín*, Malin-

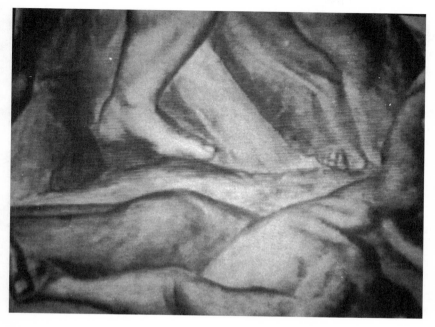

FIG. 4.3–4.5 . . . and as mother of a "ravished Mexico" in Orozco's *Cortés y la Malinche.* Still from *Chicana* by Elissa Rashkin and Jim Clinefelter, reproduced with the permission of Sylvia Morales.

tzin as resurrected by Morales teaches us that there are no simple answers to the problems of history.

FROM MALINTZIN TO CHICANA FEMINISM:
A LONG LINE OF VENDIDAS

The engagement with history as a discourse of power that *Chicana* manifests in its sequence on La Malinche is reinforced and intensified throughout the film, most acutely in its treatment of historical figures that were not only "women worthies" but also women whose achievements depended on a certain amount of subterfuge and guile. Indeed, masquerade is a potent subtext of *Chicana:* in an episode about the cultural ascent of the Virgin of Guadalupe, a European image of the Virgin gives way to a brown-skinned indigenous representation, which in turn gives way to today's omnipresent Guadalupe icon. Yet undermining the myth of racial

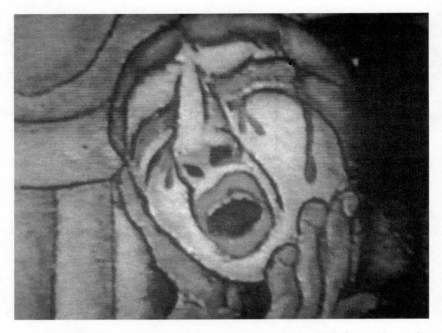

FIG. 4.6 "Making faces": female identity as masquerade. Still from *Chicana* by Elissa Rashkin and Jim Clinefelter, reproduced with the permission of Sylvia Morales.

and spiritual fusion that this icon represents, Morales then cuts to Diego Rivera's idyllic *Creation*, within which she zooms into and isolates the figure of a woman wearing a distorted mask. This odd sequence draws attention to the distortion required to impose Christian submissiveness onto the powerful and voracious indigenous goddesses that the Virgin replaced. The mask also suggests the pain underlying women's enforced complicity.

Gloria Anzaldúa, in her introduction to *Making Face, Making Soul/ Haciendo caras*, writes about the double-edged nature of masquerade. On the one hand, the face is where emotion is expressed; on the other, the face is "the surface of the body most inscribed by social structures, marked with instructions on how to be *mujer, macho*, working class, Chicana." When what one feels or is comes into conflict with one's social environment, one is forced to assume a mask, "to acquire the ability, like a chameleon, to change color when the dangers are many and the options few." However, stripping off such masks is not simply an act of revelation of a preexisting self, but one of active construction. The conscious construction of one's own identity can be seen as "making faces," a liberating form of masquerade.[23] These multivalent meanings are present in Morales's invocation of the masked woman at a foundational moment in the construction of gendered Mexican identity.

The mask of Christianity is not the last that women assume over the course of the film. Sor Juana Inés de la Cruz will submit her strong intellect to the judgment of secular and religious authorities, burning her books in a symbolic fire that is one of only two live action shots in the film's central section. The other shows (in extreme close-up) the teapot of Estefana Cabazos of Brownsville, Texas, who retaliates against Yankee settlers for the loss of her lands by shooting intruders and doling out poison at her infamous tea parties. A sequence on the 1910–20 Revolution draws on photographic evidence of women who dressed in male attire to fight for their cause, sometimes attaining high military rank.

In each of these segments, the film implicitly questions the meaning of betrayal; while Malinche and Sor Juana are betrayed by an oppressive patriarchal society, many other women betray the rules of that society out of commitment to a higher cause. Since these "betrayals" of gender ideology occur within national struggles (Independence, Revolution) and serve the most cherished ideals of *mexicanidad*, they must be seen as heroic. Yet, as the extremely emphatic use of live footage and the narrator's playful tone underline, they are carried out by what Cherríe Moraga might describe as "a long line of vendidas." Although the Chicana activists celebrated at the end of the film no longer resort to such audacious subterfuge, their feminism is clearly the product of many centuries of struggle, a genealogy that begins in Malintzin's effort to extract gain from her precarious, oppressed position.

MALINCHE REBORN

Morales's vindication of Malinche was, of course, not an isolated act in the context of the Chicana feminism of the era.[24] In her essay "Traduttora, Traditora," Alarcón portrays the compulsion felt by feminists to explore and appropriate the history of La Malinche, at a time when Chicano Studies textbooks were publicizing the views of Paz and Fuentes, when neoindigenism, synthetic perspectives like *I Am Joaquín*, and the popular Catholic iconography centered around the Virgin of Guadalupe were all putting forth a view of women as passive objects of history, and when women who diverged from the ideal of the nurturing mother were likely to be stigmatized as "malinchistas." Perhaps only by unpacking the myth of woman as traitor to her people could Chicanas comfortably reconcile feminist goals with the cultural nationalism they had developed in their political struggle. Cotera, for example, complained of women's exclusion from many arenas of decisionmaking, and explained how the suggestion that a certain woman was a feminist was enough to discredit her in the eyes of the movement.[25] In contrast, she felt that feminism was a basic aspect of her identity:

I disagree with those who think feminism is not inherent to all of us. For reasons of oppression you may have subverted your feminism so much that it can't come out, but it's there. People ask "when did you turn feminist?" You can tell them the first time you turned feminist was when you compared "pipis."[26]

In the 1980s, feminists continued to focus on Malintzin, not so much any more to disprove the myths but increasingly to try and understand their effects as myths on the consciousness (and unconscious) of the Chicano people. Moraga, for example, returns to the sexual aspects of Malinche in *Loving in the War Years: lo que nunca pasó por sus labios.* She does not use historical data to explain Malinche's actions but instead appropriates her act of treachery as a fable of deviant, antipatriarchal sexuality. As a lesbian and a daughter of a white father and Chicana mother, Moraga identifies with Malintzin's vilified status; she concludes that Malinche *did,* in a sense, betray her people when she chose to align herself with the white men, but that this betrayal shows the limits inherent in patriarchal definitions of sexuality and femininity. Thus she proclaims, "I come from a long line of vendidas."[27]

Anzaldúa also expresses an identification with La Malinche, writing in *Borderlands/La Frontera: The New Mestiza,* "Not me sold out my people but they me."[28] Although Anzaldúa's self-conscious embrace of myth as the domain of mobile subjectivity led her away from the historicist tendencies dominant in 1970s feminism, her approach to Malintzin is still one of "setting the record straight." Yet a few pages prior to that discussion, she poignantly displays her personal stake in the discourse of malinchismo, or female treachery—a discourse she is inevitably dragged into as a woman who refuses conventional roles. She recounts a dialogue in which she is asked by concerned relatives when she is going to marry. Her response is that if she marries, it won't be with a man. She adds: "*Se quedan calladitas. Sí, soy hija de la Chingada.* I've always been her daughter. *No 'tés chingando."*[29]

Both Moraga and Anzaldúa see in Malinche the need to challenge all aspects of their heritage and present environment, not only the Spanish or the Anglo but also the aspects of Indian, Mestizo and Chicano culture that oppress women. A radical response to Paz comes through in Anzaldúa's statement:

As long as woman is put down, the Indian and the Black in all of us is put down. The struggle of the *mestiza* is above all a feminist one. As long as *los hombres* think they have to *chingar mujeres* and each other to be men, as long as men are taught that they are superior and therefore culturally favored over *la mujer,* as long as to be a *vieja* is a thing of derision, there can be no real healing of our psyches.[30]

For Anzaldúa, mestizaje need not be only a reminder of past violence but creates the conditions of possibility for new, nonoppressive forms of consciousness. Moraga, in her most recent book, *The Last Generation,* has continued this line of thought, exploring the "breakdown of the bicultural mind" ("We are Malinche's children and the new Malinches of the 21st century") and radically rewriting Chicano nationalism in her call for a "Queer Aztlán."[31]

Taking a somewhat different approach, Alarcón focuses on the issue of language and on the idea that translation itself threatens any worldview founded on unitary notions of self, culture, and authenticity.[32] Taking up aspects of Paz that earlier feminists chose to ignore, she finds considerable irony in the fact that Malintzin, blessed with the double-edged gift of language, effects transformations on the utterances of others but leaves no record of her own. For Alarcón, the legacy of Malintzin may not be illegitimate paternity (which, she points out, is far more threatening to sons than to daughters) so much as a certain illegitimacy of language that undermines discourses of authenticity and fractures traditional (e.g., religious) ways of understanding and interpreting the world.

In the texts surrounding the production of *Chicana,* there is little indication of the ambiguity inherent in historical representation, nor of the potential treachery implied by translating/transforming the texts of others. Morales's interviews at the time emphasized the economic constraints imposed upon her shoestring-budget film, and subsequent commentators tended to assume that the use of found images was purely practical, ignoring the elements of choice and selection inherent in such a project.[33] Yet it is possible to read the use of the murals as a subversive

FIG. 4.7 "Subversive acts of translation": Siqueiros's *Nueva Democracia* as figure for Chicana liberation in *Chicana*. Still from *Chicana* by Elissa Rashkin and Jim Clinefelter, reproduced with the permission of Sylvia Morales.

act of translation: one which exceeds the boundaries of positivist discourse claiming to arrive at historical truth, and begins to reflect self-consciously on the politics of representation.

In this regard, *Chicana* resembles the work of visual artists such as Yolanda López and Ester Hernández, who take the symbol of the Virgin of Guadalupe and infuse it with a modern, feminist sensibility. In several paintings from the late 1970s, López removes the placid saint from her aura of rays and fills the latter with images of herself and other women in active poses, while Hernández shows the no-longer passive virgin mother executing a karate kick.[34] These images are more than playful updates of the icon, for in moving her from a state of passivity to one of activity, the artists question the values represented by La Virgen and imposed on women as a whole. Along with poets such as Moraga and Anzaldúa, they best illustrate Alarcón's claim that "it is through a revision of tradition and self that culture can be radically reinvented."[35]

While feminist historians have raised valuable questions about the events and ideological consequences of the past, poets and artists have had greater freedom to explore the ambiguity and multiple meanings found in or implied by mythic and historical narratives. The layering of images found in Chicana art, from the abuela-as-Virgin in López's paintings to the fragmentation and juxtaposition of Conquest murals in *Chicana*, suggest a deferral of absolute truth, a willingness to preserve traditional images while at the same time freeing them from their oppressive baggage, not without the judicious application of humor and irony. This strategy would seem to be essential in coming to terms with the Conquest, and especially with La Malinche. For if she can be said to be the foremother of modern-day feminists, it is not because of her status as victim, traitor, mother of the mestizo race, or feminist prototype but rather because the ambiguity which surrounds her, as well as her own contradictions, stand as a metaphor for what it means to be both Chicano and female (especially feminist and/or lesbian), when this dual status is experienced as conflict. While Malintzin's act of translation proved most dangerous to herself, ending ironically in her own silence, modern feminists utilize tactics of translation and revision to question the fate of Malintzin, and that of all women who have been silenced, in order to move towards a more positive future.

NOTES

The author wishes to thank Sylvia Morales for sharing information and reflections on the production and reception of *Chicana*. An earlier version of this essay won third place in the Society for Cinema Studies' Student Writing Contest. *Chicana* is available from Women Make Movies, 462 Broadway, Suite 500 C, New York, NY 10013.

1. Chon Noriega, "Between a Weapon and a Formula: Chicano Cinema and Its Contexts," in *Chicanos and Film: Essays on Chicano Representation and Resistance*, ed. Noriega (New York and London: Garland, 1992), 175.

2. Jorge Klor de Alva, "Chicana History and Historical Significance: Some Theoretical Considerations," in *Between Borders: Essays on Mexicana/Chicana History*, ed. Adelaida R. Del Castillo (Encino, CA: Floricanto, 1990).

3. Ibid., 67. See also Norma Alarcón, "Traduttora, Traditora: A Paradigmatic Figure of Chicana Feminism," *Cultural Critique* 13 (Fall 1989): 86–87.

4. Sylvia Morales, "Filming a Chicana Documentary" (1979), in *Chicanos and Film*, 341.

5. Gloria Anzaldúa, "Haciendo caras, una entrada," in *Making Face, Making Soul/Haciendo caras: Creative and Critical Perspectives by Women of Color*, ed. Anzal-

dúa (San Francisco: Aunt Lute, 1990): xv-xxviii; Cherríe Moraga, *Loving in the War Years: lo que nunca pasó por sus labios* (Boston: South End, 1983), and *The Last Generation* (Boston: South End, 1993); Alarcón, "Traduttora, Traditora."

6. Rosaura Sánchez, "The History of Chicana: Proposal for a Materialist Perspective," in *Between Borders*, 13.

7. Alma M. Garcia, "The Development of Chicana Feminist Discourse, 1970–1980," in *Unequal Sisters: A Multicultural Reader in U.S. Women's History*, ed. Ellen Carol Du Bois and Vicki L. Ruiz (New York and London: Routledge, 1990), 418.

8. Alarcón, 63.

9. Octavio Paz, *The Labyrinth of Solitude* (New York: Grove, 1985), 79. Further references to this work will be included parenthetically in the text.

10. Rosario Castellanos, "Sobre cultura femenina" (Mexico: Ediciones de America, Revista Antologica, 1950); "Malinche," in *A Rosario Castellanos Reader*, ed. Maureen Ahern (Austin: University of Texas Press, 1988), 96.

11. Rosaura Sánchez, quoted in Rosa Linda Fregoso, *The Bronze Screen: Chicana and Chicano Film Culture* (Minneapolis: University of Minnesota Press, 1993), 6.

12. Marta Cotera, "Identidad," in *The Chicana Feminist* (Austin, TX: Information Systems Development, 1977), 28.

13. Ibid., 30.

14. Alarcón, 66.

15. Ibid., 65.

16. Morales says that at the time of *Chicana's* release, her choice of sources was criticized by some self-identified feminists; these critics, who overlooked her subversive deployment of male-authored images, felt she should have used Frida Kahlo instead—a suggestion she found absurd. (Personal communication, 2 August 1995.)

17. Since the first version of this essay was written in 1992, Fregoso has published a similar comparison of *Chicana* and *I Am Joaquin* in *The Bronze Screen* (14–18). Fregoso argues that the differences between the films are not reducible to their gender emphases but are symptomatic of changes and conflicts unfolding within the Chicano movement during the 1970s, specifically the emergence of Chicana feminism. While I agree with Fregoso's analysis, I hope in the present essay to draw attention to the different *uses* the two films make of similar or identical images, given that (as she points out) Morales and Valdez faced similar practical and financial constraints.

18. This artist is not identified in *Chicana's* credits, but photos taken at the government palace in Tlaxcala match the images from the film. Thanks to Peter Rashkin for providing this evidence.

19. Albeit a somewhat inaccurate one: Malinche was not given to the Spaniards in Tlaxcala, as the film's narrator states, but earlier, in the southern Mayan region which is now Tabasco. She was a Nahuatl-speaking woman who had been sold by her family to a Mayan lord, who later gave her to Cortés.

20. Bernal Díaz del Castillo, *The Discovery and Conquest of Mexico* (New York:

Farrar, Straus and Giroux, 1956), 67; Hernán Cortés, *Conquest: Dispatches of Cortés from the New World* (New York: Grosset and Dunlap, 1962), 209.

21. Alarcón, 74.

22. Ibid., 75.

23. Anzaldúa, "Haciendo caras," xv–xvi.

24. In Siqueiros's *Cuauhtémoc Reborn,* the martyred Aztec emperor returns, on horseback and wearing the armor of the conquistador. In reclaiming agency for Malinche, feminism performs a similar imaginary vindication.

25. Cotera, 31.

26. Ibid., 26.

27. Moraga, *Loving in the War Years,* 117.

28. Gloria Anzaldúa, *Borderlands/La Frontera: The New Mestiza* (San Francisco: Spinsters/Aunt Lute, 1987), 21.

29. Ibid., 17.

30. Ibid., 84.

31. Moraga, "The Breakdown of the Bicultural Mind" and "Queer Aztlán: The Re-Formation of Chicano Tribe," in *The Last Generation,* 112–31 and 145–74.

32. Alarcón, 68.

33. For example, Jesús Salvador Trevino wrote, "The use of familiar murals and other art work by Mexican masters has been criticized by some as being merely a 'copying' of existing works. This criticism may not appreciate the fact that Chicano filmmakers are usually working under financial limitation far greater than that of a typical industry film." "Form and Technique in Chicano Cinema," in *Chicano Cinema,* ed. Gary D. Keller (Binghamton, NY: Bilingual Press, 1985), 112; see also Fregoso, 15.

34. Hernández's *La virgen de Guadalupe Defendiendo los Derechos de los Xicanos* (1975) and Lopez's *Portrait of the Artist as the Virgin of Guadalupe, Margaret F. Stewart: Our Lady of Guadalupe,* and *Victoria F. Franco: Our Lady of Guadalupe* (all 1978) are reproduced in *Chicano Art: Resistance and Affirmation 1965–1985* (Los Angeles: Wight Art Gallery/UCLA, 1991).

35. Alarcón, 71.

FIVE

Out in Africa

Gaurav Desai

At one point in Wole Soyinka's novel *The Interpreters*, the African-American homosexual[1] Joe Golder, who incidentally also happens to be a historian of Africa, attempts to discuss indigenous African homosexuality with the Nigerian journalist Sagoe:

> "Do you think I know nothing of your Emirs and their little boys? You forget history is my subject. And what about those exclusive coteries in Lagos?"
> Sagoe gesture[s] defeat. "You seem better informed than I am. But if you don't mind I'll persist in my delusion."[2]

In this brief encounter, Soyinka dramatizes the hitherto dominant narrative of attempts at discussing alternative African sexualities. Typically an "outside"[3] observer, with motivations which are probably too overdetermined to be clearly delineated, ventures into the vexed territory of studying alternative sexualities in a given culture; typically, again, an "insider" says "Leave us alone. We are not interested in talking about these things and it's really none of your business." An impasse—suspicious of the historically ethnocentric renderings of non-Western sexualities as "primitive," the "insider" prefers to draw attention away from any nonnormative sexual practices; at the risk of not being offensive, at the risk of not being unethical, the "outsider" exits. Some necessary questions continue to remain unasked.

In this troubled exchange however, it is not entirely clear where the moral high ground lies. Just as Western feminism finds itself in a "nervous condition" vis-à-vis its negotiations with non-Western practices such as incision and clitoridectomy,[4] an antihomophobic politics finds itself unable to open up gay-affirmative spaces without running the risk of being culturally insensitive. And yet, if no "culture" is so monolithic, so homogeneous, as to be fully recuperable within a singular sexual, aesthetic, economic, moral, or epistemic order, if "culture," that is, always exceeds the limits it seeks to set for itself, then what divides the "culturally sensitive" from the "culturally insensitive?" Could sensitivity to the needs and desires of *some* subjects mean risking insensitivity to the needs and desires of others? If so, to which subjects and voices must such a politics pay heed?

By drawing on a variety of texts—some literary, some historical, some anthropological—I want, in this chapter, to join hands with those African(ist)s[5] who are interested in opening up a space for considerations of African sexual practices in all their fluid forms. In particular I am interested in the ways in which literary works interpellate issues of sexual normativity and transgression. I open with the general problematics surrounding scholarship on nonnormative African sexualities and show the discursive continuities in the arguments from colonial to postcolonial times.[6] I then proceed to read Bessie Head's short novel *Maru* against the grain of existing scholarship, which insists on reading it as a traditional heterosexual romance. I suggest that my alternative reading of the novel is enabled by, and hopefully in its own small way contributes to, the work of those who are currently struggling to open up the discourses of alternative African sexualities both within and without the continent. I follow the seminal work of Chris Dunton whose essay " 'Whetyin be Dat?' The Treatment of Homosexuality in African Literature" remains the single most comprehensive treatment of the subject to date, and the more recent work of Rhonda Cobham on the integral relationship between sexual and national identities in the writings of Nuruddin Farah.[7] While Cobham's work, in its critical interrogation of the construction of masculinity is most directly relevant to my own reading of *Maru*, my interest in Dunton's essay is rooted in the larger question of the conditions of possibility of literary interpretations.

Through critical readings of a variety of African literary texts written since the 1950s, Dunton argues in his essay that with few exceptions, African writers tend to present homosexuality monothematically. Homosexuality is, in these texts "almost invariably attributed to the detrimental impact made on Africa by the West" and consequently "the function that it plays in the text's larger thematic and narrative design is restricted and predictable."[8] While Dunton's argument is indeed confirmed by the numerous critical readings of these texts written since the 1960s, the issue of *where* the blindness lies—on the part of the authors or on the part of the critics—is one that needs greater scrutiny. If, as reader-response theorists would have us believe, texts are as much the product of the interpretive practices of readers as they are the product of authorial intentions, then could the supposedly monothematic treatment be a product not of authorial agency but rather of the critic's interpretive limitations?

Consider the case of Joe Golder. Joe, the professor of African history with whom we began this essay, has consistently been read in the critical literature as Soyinka's emblem of everything that is wrong with a Western-based, romanticized Afrocentricity. This critical reading emphasizes Joe's alienation from his Nigerian colleagues who read him as a doubly foreign person—not only is he an American but also one who engages in sexual practices unknown (at least so far as these interpreters are concerned) in indigenous Nigerian society.[9] Joe Golder becomes in this reading an impotent (because homosexual) character who can only poach upon African subjects (such as the young boy Noah)and be the cause of destruction. Read in this manner, the character of Joe Golder confirms Chris Dunton's thesis: he is presented as no more than a scaffold for the larger narrative thematic so that consistent with the dominant theme of the novel, this particular "interpreter," much like his Nigerian counterparts, is unable to be a productive force in the newly independent society. Like philosophers, Joe and his friends can interpret the world but cannot change it. Yet, is there a different Joe Golder in this text who remains to be heard? A Joe Golder who is not predictably lecherous and filled with vice?

In one episode in the novel, the young boy Noah jumps off a balcony to his death, the narrative suggesting that his death is caused by Joe's sexual advances. The unfortunate incident is read by most critics as Soyinka's last straw in his rebuke of Golder. Thus Derek Wright writes "(Noah) is subsequently left at the *mercy* of the *neurotic* American quadroon Joe Golder, whose attraction to blackness is *more sexual than racial* and whose *inevitable* homosexual advances result in the boy's death."[10] Let us note immediately that the supposed *inevitability* of sexual desire and a forthcoming solicitation when a homosexual man finds himself in the company of a young boy speaks more perhaps to the critic's interpretive assumptions and cultural imaginary than to the actual unfolding of the narrative. For there is sufficient reason to believe that Golder doesn't quite understand why the boy jumps to his own death especially since he has assured him that he would not touch or harm him.

What is clear in the narrative, and what is rarely addressed by critics, is the double-bind that Joe consistently finds himself in—on the one hand, he *does* want people to know about his sexual preferences and to be proud of his homosexual identity (as is evident in the exchange with Sagoe), and yet on the other, he hopes that he is not reduced to *just* being a desiring and lecherous body by society, read by his friends, that is, as a foreign parasite whose sole purpose is to prey upon the Nigerian men. Read from Joe's point of view, his implication in Noah's death is less a product of his direct actions than it is of his perceived identity. Much like the famous Marabar Cave scene in Forster's *Passage to India*, the victimization is more the effect of a larger social imaginary than of an actual sexual offense. If to the British, Aziz can be read as no other than the emblem of a desiring Muslim India, then to the Nigerian interpreters, Joe Golder too emerges as a dangerously desiring body. But while Aziz, by the end of Forster's novel and in most literary criticism, is exonerated of his alleged crime, Golder remains to this day in the criticism of this text, the homosexual—and therefore—the accused.

Herein, then, lies Joe Golder's tragedy—attempting to escape both the homophobia within the African American community at home and the insistent hypersexuality ascribed to the black man by the larger predominantly white American society, Joe finds that in Africa too he is no more than a sexual body. Yet, if the possibility of this reading is left open by the narrative, it is one that few critics have pursued. Instead, the critics *replay* the textual tragedy in their own criticism. So, for instance, in Wright's reading, Joe emerges as an odd man, a "neurotic" whose identification with the black race for what it's worth, is "more sexual than racial."

While a more detailed reading of Joe Golder is best left for another occasion, I want to reiterate that it is precisely in addressing his simultaneous negotiations of racial and sexual identities that Soyinka presents Golder as a profoundly sympathetic character. Golder is an individual who has had to claim actively at least two identities which continually threaten to escape him—he is at once a light-skinned black man capable of "passing" as a white man and a homosexual capable of passing as straight. His choice not to pass—his choice to reaffirm at once two identities not only at odds with the hegemonic order of things but also, more importantly, at odds with one another—is a choice that must sober even the most unsympathetic of readers. Furthermore, Joe's decision to study African history and his move to Nigeria, despite its potentially romanticizing implications, is presented by Soyinka as his continual attempt to negotiate the different demands placed upon his identities. Like DuBois, Joe has continually been confronted with a "double consciousness, (the) sense of always looking at one's self through the eyes of others, of measuring one's soul by the tape of a world that looks on in amused contempt and pity."[11] He comes to Africa hoping to erase at least one if not both of these sources of difference. He fails.

It is significant in this context that Soyinka presents us a Joe armed with a copy of James Baldwin's *Another Country*. For here is the suggestion that Golder is not some singular oddity but one with a legacy. Just as Baldwin, a gay black man, felt unable to find a home in the United States and thus sought Paris, Golder too seeks to find a different home in Nigeria. In this new African context, however, Joe Golder is unable to connect either emotionally or physically and remains desperately lonely. Golder then, is a character full of pathos if not tragedy, living through the experience of a transcendental homelessness, of belonging nowhere. To heighten this sense of pathos, towards the end of the novel, Soyinka has Joe Golder sing "Sometimes I Feel Like a Motherless Child," a song whose performance profoundly increases the sense of alienation already being felt by the other Nigerian protagonists. It is important to note that Soyinka's choice of this song is not innocent but draws upon the very same James Baldwin who has affected Joe's life. In his *Notes of a Native Son*, Baldwin, reflecting upon the distance between the African and the African American writes:

[The African American] begins to conjecture how much he has gained and lost during his long sojourn in the American republic. The African before him has endured privation, injustice, medieval cruelty; but the African has not yet endured the utter alienation of himself from his people and his past. His mother did not sing "Sometimes I Feel Like a Motherless Child" and he has not, all his life long, ached for the acceptance in a culture which pronounced straight hair and white skin the only acceptable beauty.[12]

Soyinka's tragic vision then, appropriates this song from the African American tradition to now include the predicament of a postcolonial nation-state in Africa. Rather than providing a supportive and inviting space for the alienated African American, the postcolonial nation-state too joins hands in the tragic condition.

THE EMERGENCE OF A DISCOURSE

I have focused on the character of Joe Golder not so much in the interests of promoting him to a heroic type but instead to ask a basic question in the history of literary interpretations. If indeed Joe can be read in a sympathetic manner today (indeed, if as some of my students suggest he could not be read as anything *but* tragic), then how do we account for the fact that he has never so far been read as such? The answer, I suggest, has less to do with any intentional malice on the part of critics than with the nature of critical discourse itself and the contingencies of its production. Simply put, just as literary genres have their histories, so does the genre of criticism, and critical discourses like any other have rules of exclusion and inclusion. Until these rules, both internal as well as external to the discourse, realign themselves to open up different conditions of possibilities, certain kinds of claims remain unthought, or if at all thought, remain unintelligible and unallowable within the dominant discourse.[13] Or, as Michel Foucault puts it, for a claim to be considered true, it must first be "within the truth."[14] What causes realignments within the field of discursive legitimacy are a multiplicity of factors—some relatively external to the discourse, such as political revolutions, others relatively internal to it, such as sheer boredom with existing models of explanation on the part of participants. Most often, of course, the various contingencies work together to form new conditions of possibility and new intellectual configurations. Thus, with the simultaneous growth of gay and lesbian political activism in Africa, and the emergence of gay and lesbian studies as legitimate foci for scholarly research, we find ourselves today in the midst of such a process vis-à-vis the discourse of African sexuality. As such the times are both politically and intellectually exciting.

In addressing the limits and the stakes involved in this newly emergent discursive field it is important to note the complicated issue of the relationship between anticolonial politics, gay-lesbian liberation, and the politics of feminism. If we are embarked on a space-clearing project, the desire to keep it antihomophobic, feminist, and anticolonial at the same time is one which I share and uphold, but it is important to state that the specific lines of alliance between these three nodes will for now have to remain undetermined. While one may expect to find a continuity between certain political positions, such as between feminism and antihomophobia for instance (since both share the project of being critical of patriarchy), these continuities are not natural but rather contingently forged. And if such forging is to take shape in the threshold of a colonial landscape, it is always susceptible to the overdeterminations of "race" and "nation."

Take for instance, the seminal work of Ifi Amadiume on the changing construction of gender in Nnobi society. In her work, Amadiume shows how the institution of woman-to-woman marriages in precolonial Nnobi society suggests that there existed in this society a certain fluidity in the gender-sex system so that biological sex did not necessarily determine social gender. Amadiume's compelling insight is that the relative reification and indeed "naturalization" of sex-gender roles which one observes in more contemporary times among the Nnobi was not a precolonial legacy but rather a direct consequence of British colonial practices aimed at regulating the possible gender options available for Nnobi women. In other words, by drawing on a precolonial social institution in which women could marry other women and play the social role of husbands, Amadiume shows that things were not always as they seem today in Nnobi society. Gender roles were not easily tied to biological sex and individual women did indeed have social possibilities that they have no more. So far, her argument is an important historical corrective to those who tend to either essentialize women or to essentialize patriarchy. But the force of Amadiume's argument is lost in her consideration of sexual practices. For having demonstrated gender-mobility in precolonial society, Amadiume proceeds to insist that the phenomenon of woman marriages should not be misread as any kind of institutionalized lesbianism. Such a reading, which Amadiume suggests has been carried on primarily by black lesbians in the West, can only result from the interpreter's "wishes and fantasies" and ultimately reveal nothing more than her "ethnocentrism." Furthermore, she suggests that such a reading would be "shocking and offensive to Nnobi women"[15] for whom lesbianism remains a foreign practice.

While Amadiume's cautionary remarks are indeed ones that any reader must pay heed to, the precise *argument* made in their defense remains elusive—for surely while Amadiume is probably correct in suggesting that contemporary Nnobi women would find any hints of lesbianism "offensive,"[16] her own greatest insight that colonial practices severely disturbed precolonial *gender* possibilities resulting in a different normatization of gender roles may also *potentially* lend itself to sexual practices. In other words, could it be that just as British colonialism radically changed the gender possibilities available to women, it may also have instituted and regulated sexual practices so that "offense" at the thought of lesbianism may be precisely the ideological mark of such intervention? Or to put it differently, can we be reasonably sure that through a historical change in which gender seems to have transformed so much, sexuality could have gone unaffected? *We cannot yet be sure*—more research would have to be done to answer this question, and indeed it may well turn out that Amadiume is right in suggesting that sexual practices were always resolutely heterosexual among the Nnobi.[17] But to silence the question through accusations of ethnocentrism and offense seems an unfortunate way to deal with an uncomfortable question. An unquestionable and unquestioning nativism is no satisfactory response to even the most pervasive ethnocentrism.

My point in singling out Amadiume's work is to show how even the most sophisticated feminists and the most engaging critics of patriarchy can nevertheless lend themselves to a theoretical silence or even downright hostility when issues of homosexuality are raised. But this hostility we must note is, at least in our case, not unconnected to the complex problematics of cultural difference and race which are always informing such accounts. For if Amadiume's anger is directed towards black lesbians primarily in the West who it would seem bring their false desires to bear upon a resolutely heterosexual Africa, then the *hors texte* of this encounter is surely the earlier voice of Frantz Fanon.

It is Frantz Fanon who in *Black Skin, White Masks* provides what for many has become the classic position on the relation between Africa, the West, and homosexuality. Fanon's double move consists not only of associating white racism with homosexuality—as in the statement "the Negrophobic man is a repressed homosexual"[18]—but also simultaneously insisting that no indigenous homosexuality exists in Africa. Fanon suggests that while transvestism may occur among some Martiniquans, these men lead normal sex lives and can "take a punch like any 'he-man.'"[19] In Fanon's account then, homosexuality becomes associated on the one hand with racism and colonial oppression, and on the other with effeminacy. In a context in which the black man's sexuality is read simultaneously as excessive as well as castrated, homosexuality comes into focus here, as Lee Edelman suggests, "only as the conflictual undoing of one man's authority by another; it signifies that is, only as a failed, debased, or inadequate masculinity—a masculinity severed from the ground of its meaning in a phallic 'possession' betokening one's legitimate status as a subject."[20] To be sure, at a historical moment when civilized, normative sexuality was read as one located in the monogamous, heterosexual family, and primitive sexuality in a whole host of what are read as abnormalities and "perversions," it is understandable that Fanon would wish to dissociate Africa from the "primitive"—the sexually "perverse." But, as Diana Fuss notes, it is unfortunate that "Fanon does not think beyond the presuppositions of colonial discourse to examine how colonial domination itself works partially through the social institutionalization of misogyny and homophobia."[21] Could it be that a particular form of heteronormativity was a necessary accomplice to the workings of colonial authority?

If in Fanon's framework nationalist struggle must depend on a simultaneous insistence on the creation of a productive black male subjectivity, a subjectivity that is, which does not allow itself to be symbolically "castrated" through any association with homosexuality, it is not clear that this strategy necessarily speaks to all the experiences of all the subjects within the newly forming nations. Not only does this normative order dictate the sexual construction of masculinity, it also, through the extension in which the demands of race supersede those of gender and sexuality, begins to dictate the sexual lives of women. It is thus that we find in Adrienne Rich's seminal essay "Compulsory Heterosexuality and Lesbian Existence" a letter from a Mozambican woman in exile:

I am condemned to a life of exile because I will not deny that I am a lesbian, that my primary commitments are, and will always be to other women. In the new Mozambique, lesbianism is considered a left-over from colonialism and decadent Western civilization. Lesbians are sent to rehabilitation camps to learn through self-criticism the correct line about themselves. . . . If I am forced to denounce my own love for women, if I therefore denounce myself, I could go back to Mozambique and join forces in the exciting and hard struggle of rebuilding a nation, including the struggle for the emancipation of Mozambiquan women. As it is, I either risk the rehabilitation camps, or remain in exile.[22]

Unlike in the contemporary West then, where one may well postulate a lesbian continuum in the midst of a radically discontinuous male homosocial/sexual existence, in colonial-nationalist and postcolonial Africa one often finds both the male as well as female continuums disrupted. Thus, in such a context, just as the national struggle often takes precedence over the women's movement, so it is that the construction of an insistent heteronormativity begins to threaten any existing alternative sexual practices. It is in this sense that one could argue that at least in some African contexts, it was not *homosexuality* that was inherited from the West but rather a more regulatory *homophobia*.

THE HETERONORMATIVE IDEAL: READING
BESSIE HEAD'S *MARU*

If we want to understand the workings of homophobia and the active curtailment of any nonheterosexual desire it engenders, we may find it productive to turn to Bessie Head's 1971 novel *Maru*. *Maru*, as I suggested earlier, has been read by most critics as a romantic tale in which human love triumphs over the banalities of racial prejudice. While through the character of the Masarwa woman, Margaret, Bessie Head pays a considerable amount of attention to the thematics of race, I want to propose that a more productive reading of the novel suggests that it is concerned not only with racial identity and racism but also, and perhaps more significantly, with (hetero)sexual identity and sexism.[23]

What exactly constitutes "sexual" as opposed to any other kind of desire will have to remain an open question in our reading, since that in many ways is a question that the narrative attempts to negotiate. For, if Head's novel is about the circulation of desire between the four major characters, Maru, Moleka, Dikeledi, and Margaret, it is not always clear in which direction the desires flow. We may discern at least two triangular relationships in the novel: the first being the rivalry of Maru and Moleka for Margaret and the second being the unspoken and indeed unacknowledged rivalry between Dikeledi and Margaret for Moleka. But the nature of these two triangular relationships is different insofar as the relationship between the two men over the woman is fraught with a violent tension which leads to murderous intentions at least in Moleka, whereas the relationship between the two women, while occasionally tense, is never seriously put in jeopardy over their simultaneous desire for the same man.

I propose that the most interesting and dramatic moments in Bessie Head's novel pertain not to the heterosexual desires of the characters but rather to their anxieties about their own homosocial relationships. It need be remarked that it is precisely the homo*social* as opposed to the homo*sexual* configuration of these relationships that mark this text as an apt account of the advent of a particular kind of heterosexual normativity in African contexts. Published in 1971 at a time when Christianity had already done its work in rendering any sexuality other than heterosexual monogamy as sinful and immoral, at a time when the colonially inherited legal discourses in many African states had already labeled as deviant and criminalized any sexuality not conforming to the norms of the heterosexual family, and at a time when the discourse around homosexuality was thematized consistently in African literature as a purely Western phenomenon, Bessie Head's *Maru* marks the moment of the ambivalent triumph of heteronormativity.

If precolonial sexualities in various African contexts could indeed incorporate a whole range of acts which may plausibly be read as "homoerotic" or "homosexual" in retrospect, they were never really labeled as such. In such a context then, the continuum between men's sexual relations and men's social bonds need not have been disrupted. But as Michel Foucault suggests of the European context, the emergence of a discourse around such activities also led to a regulation of these activities and this meant that any such precolonial continuums of male or female desires would, in colonial and postcolonial times, have to be radically disrupted. Bessie Head's *Maru* is a text that explicitly thematizes this rupture. In other words, it is precisely the *impossibility* of imagining a continuum of sexuality both between men and between women[24] that this text seeks to mark. To be sure, I will suggest that Head's narrative surreptitiously points to the ambivalence of that rupture and thus renders the will to heteronormativity unstable. Yet it is important to understand that at the most manifest level heteronormativity is what the novel is about.

The most obvious instantiation of this claim may be found in the growing friendship between Dikeledi and Margaret. Their meetings are filled with a love and affection which profoundly marks both the characters. On one such occasion, when Dikeledi offers to lend Margaret a spare bed that she has at home, Margaret is provoked to think through the nature of their friendship: "Margaret looked up, startled. Their friendship was too unfathomable to her, as though she could not make an effort to analyze her feelings towards Dikeledi and it would drift on and on like this, continually getting into deep water."[25]

Margaret Cadmore then, who, after considerable thought has refused to pass as a "colored" woman and has insisted on naming her own racial identity, finds that her feelings for Dikeledi are those which she cannot name.[26] The imagery suggests that the relationship between the two women is dangerously deep—thus "unfathomable"—and indeed is headed towards "deeper water." If by the end of the novel, the two women are seen to so profoundly love and affect one another that they end up increasingly becoming like each other, then at this still early point they both feel uneasy about their mutual feelings. While Margaret's response is to ponder unsuccessfully over their relationship, Dikeledi we are told immediately "dives" not into the unfathomable waters of their growing love, but rather into a packet of Marmite sandwiches and simultaneously into private thoughts about Moleka—and how else are we to read her ludicrous thoughts about Moleka's kisses ("Moleka's kisses taste like Marmite sandwiches. Moleka's kisses taste like roast beef with spicy gravy. Moleka's kisses. . . ," 87) than as the conventional response of what may well be recognized as a "compulsory heterosexuality?"—How else are we to read them other than as performative utterances which in the face of a dangerously homoerotic tenderness insist: "I want Moleka." "I desire Men"?

While Dikeledi is having these thoughts, Margaret we are told "half-consciously" picks up a pencil and sketches her. This is an important moment because it completes a particular flow of desire that continually structures the same-sex relationships in the novel. Here then we have a scenario in which Dikeledi performs an act which establishes her affection towards Margaret; Margaret senses their growing affection with a little unease; Dikeledi displaces any sexual or erotic component of their relationship onto Moleka; and finally, Margaret half-consciously attempts to reclaim Dikeledi.

A similar structure is in effect in the relationship between the two male protagonists Moleka and Maru. The narrator suggests that "the clue to Moleka and Maru lay in their relationship with women" (34). What follows is a classic Girardian drama: Maru and Moleka become rivals for the love of Margaret in which, as Eve Sedgwick puts it, "the choice of the beloved is determined in the first place, not by the qualities of the beloved, but by the beloved's already being the choice of the person who has been chosen as rival."[27] For while Moleka at least has a brief encounter with Margaret before he decides that he loves her, Maru simply follows suit without any such meaningful exchange with Margaret. As Sedgwick suggests in her own readings of such structures, it is important to recognize that in such an erotic rivalry, "the bond that links the two rivals is as intense and potent as the bond that links either of the rivals to the beloved."[28] Indeed, in the case of Bessie Head's novel, it is clear that the bond between these two friends-turned-rivals far exceeds any bonds they establish with the female characters. For as the narrator notes: "When had (Moleka) and Maru not lived in each other's arms and shared everything? People said: 'Oh Moleka and Maru always fall in love with the same girl.' But they never knew that no experiences interrupted the river and permanent flow of their deep affection" (33). Moleka was devoted to the light in Maru's eyes which he could see from across the room and even when "thousands of people noted the dramatic impact of Moleka, . . . he would always cast his eyes across the room to see if all was well with Maru" (34).

Not only is this homosocial relationship, like that between the women, the cause of some unease, it is also responsible for Moleka's crisis. If Moleka senses at some level that his love for Margaret results in his increasing alienation from Maru, he also discovers that his newfound love along with his loss of Maru leaves him temporarily impotent. He has, we are told, "suddenly forgot[ten] everything about making approaches to a woman" (76). As though to spatially map the flow of desire, Head presents us with a Moleka who, at one point starts off to visit Margaret, is distracted and "unconsciously" we are told, "his feet (take) him in the direction of the house of Maru" (79). Moleka stands outside Maru's house for over two hours watching him through the window and by the end of the evening he is described as a changed man who has had a chance of reflecting upon the nature of his love. "He was Moleka," the narrator suggests, "but with something added" (80).

What is the "something" that is added through this gaze? What is the love that Moleka now grasps? His love for Margaret? His love for Maru? For both? Once again, as in the case between the two women, while Moleka himself can never articulate it, the narrator is ever willing to interpolate. In the next scene, when Moleka finds himself in Dikeledi's bed, he exclaims "Dikeledi!" (83). It is the narrator who explains: "He meant: 'Help me! I have lost everything I ever loved.' He meant Maru" (83).

What is important to note then, is that while Bessie Head gives abundant evidence for a strong, loving relationship between the two male protagonists, that relationship can only be explicitly recognized by them within the limits of a nonerotic, asexual friendship. If what we witness here is a classic example of the workings of heterosexual normativity in which the bodies of women become the objects of exchange within a patriarchal sexual economy, then the characters themselves cannot be allowed to fully partake of this knowledge. Thus it is important that when the relationship between Maru and Moleka undergoes a crisis in the face of a potential heterosexual alliance with a woman, only the omniscient narrator has the privilege of making the links. For were this crisis to be acknowledged directly by the characters *as* a crisis of their own love for each other, it would at the same time mean that they would have to acknowledge the deeper structure of the continuum of same-sex desire.

The question of whether the continuum is or is not experienced by the characters is crucial not only to understand the possibilities of homoerotic desire in the text but also to address the important issue of the misogyny of the text. We are told that none of the relationships that either Maru or Moleka have had in the past with women have been productive or fruitful. On the contrary, they are quite definitely harmful to the women—the "victims" we are told, "exploded like bombs" (35). Furthermore, when Moleka is unable to take out his anger directly on Maru, he plans to sexually molest Maru's sister Dikeledi to provoke his anger. Here, Moleka's displacement of his violent feelings towards Maru onto Dikeledi is entirely in keeping with the larger gendered structures of the novel. In this case, rather than using the body of the woman as the space where a homosocial love can be displaced, it is used as the battlesite for declaring war. I want to suggest that while it is the case that the relationship between male homosexuality and patriarchal interest cannot be calculated independent of the specific context of occurrence, in this particular case, it is not *homosexuality* but rather a *homophobia* that directs such misogyny. For homophobia is precisely the name of the insistent rupture of the homosocial/sexual continuum which makes it necessary for the bodies of women to be exploited as the terrain for resolving the intimate matters between men.[29]

In such a context, then, Margaret's dream, which by all critical accounts is the focal point of the heterosexual narrative, becomes increasingly ambiguous. In her dream Margaret sees herself in the midst of a field full of daisies covered by a cloudy sky:

I looked up again and a little way ahead I saw two people embrace each other. I stared quite hard because they were difficult to see. Their forms were black like the house and the sky, but again, they were surrounded by this yellow light. *I felt so ashamed, thinking I had come upon a secret which ought not to be disclosed, that I turned and tried to run away.* Just then a strong wind arose and began to blow me in the direction of the embracing couple. I was terrified. *They did not want anyone near them and I could feel it.* I dropped to the ground and tried to grab hold of the daisies to save myself from the strong wind. At that moment I opened my eyes. (103, italics mine)

When Dikeledi sees the drawing that Margaret makes based on her dream, we are told that she immediately recognizes at least one of the two in the embrace—it is her brother Maru. She is horrified by what she sees and turns to Margaret: " 'You frighten me,' she said, her eyes wide and startled. 'Why?' Margaret asked. 'Do you always see things like that?' Dikeledi asked" (104). If, as most critics read this dream, it is nothing more than Maru's plan for securing Margaret's love through a dream projection, and if it is nothing more than a vision of what is to come in real life—a union between Maru and Margaret depicted very much in a similar setting, the house, daisies, clouds, and all—then why is Dikeledi horrified upon hearing Margaret's account and seeing its depiction? And more importantly, why the sense of the secret that is best not disclosed? And further, if Margaret is the *intruder,* if she is the unwelcome observer of this embrace, then who exactly is Maru embracing?

If the embrace is indeed, as I am suggesting here, an embrace between the two men, a secret embrace, a taboo embrace, then it becomes important to realize that the dream, which after all is supposedly projected by Maru, becomes the vehicle of his desire to reclaim Moleka. And like all the other same-sex flows in the narrative, this one too occurs without the full knowledge of the actor. Thus if Margaret's effort to reclaim Dikeledi is to sketch her in what remains a semi-conscious secretive gesture, if Moleka's feet "unconsciously" take him to Maru's house, then the homoerotic embrace in this dream too is an *unconscious* projection on Maru's part.

Bessie Head's narrative works on three levels corresponding to three different orders of knowledge: those of the characters, narrator, and the readers. The simultaneous workings of these three orders is precisely what make *Maru* so powerfully a novel about the construction of heteronormativity. For *Maru* is not just some seemingly innocent tale of boy meets girl but rather a complicated account of what it means to become a man through the pursuit of a woman. It is a morality tale of the regulation of desire through socially sanctioned channels and about the importance of regulating any excessive homosocial desire. As such, the three orders of knowledge are important—if the characters' order of knowledge represents the confused and indeed fluid flow of desire, the narrator's knowledge provides a more reflexive and regulatory structure. For it is the narrator's role to ensure that the homosocial relations are indeed recognized by the reader as such, and once recognized, are shown to be actively curtailed. But the project of heteronormativity cannot end by merely suppressing homosocial desire—for it to work it also must seek to regulate the discourse of sexuality itself. And it is here that the third order of knowledge in the novel, which, as a silent knowledge which by definition no narrator can provide, reopens the question of what can be said and what must remain silent in a heteronormative world.

It is this third order of knowledge which explains why while in every other case the narrator has eagerly stepped in to elucidate the nature of the homosocial relationships, at the important moment when Margaret discloses her dream, the narrator is nowhere to be found. The work of interpreting the embrace is left entirely to the reader. For while the rhetoric seems to suggest the homosexual possibility, the specific imagery of the dream links it to the fairy-tale ending of the narrative in which the couples are "properly," that is "heterosexually," paired off with Maru marrying Margaret and Moleka marrying Dikeledi.

To understand the possibility of the encoding of a silent knowledge in the narrative is to understand that the triumph of heteronormativity is at best provisional. For while the novel can only explicitly articulate the "truth" of the heterosexual ending, it leaves the possibility of homosexual difference in place. Thus while in Margaret's dream the homosexual embrace is threatened by the gathering "pitch black clouds," the same clouds ominously gather over the skies in the final scene of the heterosexual coupling.[30] And just as in the dream the embrace is disturbed by Margaret's arrival, so it is that Maru and Margaret continue to be disturbed by the force of Moleka's presence in their lives. To make the link between these two scenes even more explicit, Head writes of the now married Maru: "He wanted a flower garden of yellow daisies, because they were the only flowers which resembled the face of his wife and the *sun of his love*" (1). The daisies that reappear here from the dream remind Maru not only of his wife Margaret but also of Moleka—for it is he who has been described earlier as the "sun around which spun a billion satellites" (58), a "sun" who is played off in the narrative against the moonlike Maru.

It is thus that Bessie Head's novel, ostensibly about race, racism, and the problematics of racial passing becomes a novel about sexuality, sexism, and the problematics of sexual passing. Head's project is to mark the construction of heteronormativity in postcolonial African cultures and to mark the sites of alternative sexual knowledges which in such an order must remain unheard. By showing us the constructed rather than "natural" order of heteronormativity, Bessie Head allows us to reopen and rethink our investigations about the existence of a variety of sexual practices in precolonial, colonial, and indeed postcolonial Africa.

FROM SHAKA TO EVITA

Over the past few years, historical and archival research on African sexualities has pointed to several practices which challenge the invention of Africa as resolutely heterosexual.[31] For instance, in his study *The Construction of Homosexuality*, David Greenberg records the following African practices:

1. The *mugawe*, the religious leader of the Kenyan Meru who wears women's clothing and adopts women's hairstyles is often a homosexual and sometimes marries a man.[32]

2. Among the Angolan Kwayama, some male diviners wear women's clothing and become secondary spouses of men whose other wives are female (60).

3. South African Zulu diviners are usually women but about 10 percent are male transvestites (60).

4. Homosexuality associated with male-to-female gender change without necessary religious connotations has been documented among the Nandi, the Dinka, the Nuer, the Konso, the Amhara, the Ottoro, the Fanti, the Ovimbumbdu, the Thongo, the Tanala, the Bara, the Wolof, the Lango, the Iteso, the Gisu, and the Sebei. For some of these peoples the transvestite role was institutionalized, in others probably not (61).

5. Some Nandi women of Kenya have been recorded to have lesbian affairs for the first time as adults (66).

6. Lesbian affairs were virtually universal among unmarried Akan women of the former Gold Coast (now Ghana). Whenever possible, the women purchased extralarge beds to accommodate group sex sessions involving perhaps half-a-dozen women (66).

7. Homosexual relations are common among Nyakusa boys who leave the main village with their age-mates to form a new village on the outskirts (68–69).

What all these examples[33] suggest is that even if we were to allow for a fair amount of "ethnocentrism" on the part of anthropologists who may have, as we saw Amadiume suggest earlier, "read into" the various African societies their own sexual desires, it still leaves the scales relatively unturned.[34] The question at this point, for most scholars, is not whether or not indigenous alternative sexual practices have existed or continue to exist in Africa, but rather, how one understands their historical emergence, the conditions of (im)possibility for identity formations based on these practices and in particular the relationship of these identities to racial and national identities.

This is not to suggest that the project is an easy one. The question of how one talks about "homosexuality" or "bisexuality" in precolonial Africa remains a complicated one, not only because of the historical interpellation of sexual issues within racial schemas, as we have seen in Fanon, but also because the very categories "homosexual" and "bisexual" have come today to take on a cultural and sociopolitical meaning that they could not possibly have had in precolonial African cultures. It is sobering in this context to note, as David Halperin and Jonathan Katz among others have done, that the category of "homosexual" and its supposed opposite "heterosexual" are relatively recent Western inventions.[35] While the many sexual acts performed ever since the Greeks may, in retrospect, arguably be placed under the rubric of either of these categories, the force of these conceptual categories remains recent and only of dubious use in considering older periods. Furthermore, as John D'Emilio reminds us of the American context, industrialization and capitalism were necessary preconditions for the mobilization of a "gay identity" and it follows that in contexts such as colonial America or precolonial Africa, where industrialization and capitalism had yet to make their full impact, no such identity formation could take place.[36] Yet, as Greenberg's work shows, it is important that neither the inadequacy of the terms, nor our own inability to fully understand sexual *identities* in the premodern West or in precolonial Africa should lead us to the false conclusion that therefore there were no sexual *acts* performed between members of the same sex.

While the idea that homosexuality is a Western perversion only brought to Africa with colonial contact is one which continues to have appeal among a great number of Africans, it is one that is being actively challenged today by sexual minorities around the continent. Simon Nkoli, an important South African gay activist, suggests that for him the most difficult aspect of "coming out" as a black man in South Africa was the rejection that one felt from one's own ethnic community as well as the racism inherent in the white gay community. For Nkoli, the project has been to simultaneously attempt to build crossracial coalitions within South Africa's multiracial gay community as well as to speak out against homophobia in the black African communities.[37]

Nkoli's struggle, like that of many contemporary black African gay activists across Africa, is a struggle over representation. And as is often the case in such struggles, it is a dual process being on the one hand a search for political representation, civil liberties, and the rights of equal protection under the law, and on the other, for the right to re-present the community in a sympathetic frame, to tell different stories[38] than the ones that have been told about it in history, in the hopes of preparing for better times to come.

The fight for gay liberation in Africa is bound to be a difficult one. But there are signs to show that it will not be fruitless. South Africa's march from Shaka to Evita is one indication of the possibilities for change. With its newly formulated constitution, South Africa became the first nation in the world to specifically name gays and lesbians as deserving equal protection and unprejudicial treatment under the law. Thus today, out of Africa come the reforms which make it more livable to be out in Africa, and indeed, one hopes in the rest of the world.

NOTES

Several colleagues at the University at Albany and audiences at the Modern Language Association provided just the right proportion of critique and support to sustain this project. My largest debts on this project are to the students in my Fall 94 introductory literary studies seminar devoted to gender studies—Gary Lombardo, Sandra Bassett, Shannon Houlihan, and Sue Aistrop in particular always kept me moving, as I hope I kept them. Supriya Nair's critical affirmation of my reading of *Maru* was also integral.

1. While at one point in the novel Joe Golder is referred to as being "queer" (236), the term is not used here as it is in contemporary gay politics in the United States. I choose to use the term "homosexual" here because it more accurately conveys the reading of Golder in the newly independent Nigerian context of the novel. As often is the case in such situations, the choice of categories for the intellectual historian are complicated—should one use the word "queer" and insist upon its different signification in the Nigerian context, or should one, instead, shy away from the term, so heavily overdetermined by its contemporary American connotations, and choose a term which currently has relatively less political valence? While the term "queer" is quite appropriately used in discussions of some of the more recent events unfolding in South Africa and elsewhere in sub-Saharan Africa, I find that it is of limited value in claiming it for a 1960s context. Yet, this is a terminological issue in much need of debate.

2. Wole Soyinka, *The Interpreters* (1965; reprint, London: Heinemann, 1970), 199.

3. The quotes are meant to remind us of the always ambiguous relation between any inside-outside relation. In the case of Joe Golder in particular, he is a liminal figure—outsider by virtue of nationality (American) but insider by virtue

of "race." Indeed Joe's search is precisely for a better negotiation of this inside-outside position. The fact that Joe Golder is an academic is also of relevance here because it too sets up a familiar dichotomy—that between academic or "bookish" knowledge and lived or "experiential" knowledge. This dichotomy while speaking to the earlier polarity between the inside-outside also looks towards yet another polarity—homosexual versus heterosexual. While in practice all these dichotomies are indeed in flux, my argument is that foundational discourses, whether Eurocentric or Nativist, whether from the political left or the political right, rigidly uphold the dichotomies thereby rendering dialogue impossible.

4. See Alice Walker and Prathiba Parmar, eds., *Warrior Marks: Female Genital Mutilation and the Sexual Blinding of Women* (New York: Harcourt Brace, 1993) for an elaboration of how this problematic works.

5. Elsewhere, I have argued for the use of this term as a more inclusive category than either "African" or "Africanist." In this earlier scenario, the term "African" is usually meant to authenticate a subjective or experiential knowledge while the term "Africanist" is used, either pejoratively or arrogantly, to describe a "learned" (or "bookish") knowledge. But knowledges are neither so easily divided nor is it the case that even if they were, anything would *necessarily* follow from this division. My alternative term African(ist) puts in productive tension the limits of "experiential" knowledge and those of "bookish" knowledge, hence resuming dialogue without erasing tensions.

6. "Why 'Africa' as opposed to the various different cultures of the continent?" is a question that is often asked in African(ist) circles. As indicated in note 1, the level of abstraction used in any discussion is always a factor among other things, of previous discourses on the subject. Since the usual claim is that homosexuality is "un-African" rather than "un-Ibo" or "un-Hausa" or "un-Gikuyu," I have found it best, in my counterargument to stick to the level of abstraction encountered in this claim. Similarly, since historical time periods, whether measured in relation to colonialism (pre-, colonial, post-) or to any other schema are *not* typically factored into these discussions, I have not attempted in any significant way to address them here. It is precisely in these directions (of ethnic and historical specificity) that future scholarship on African sexualities must find its way. As an early effort, I have chosen to retain a wider angle on these matters.

7. See Chris Dunton, " 'Whetyin be Dat?' The Treatment of Homosexuality in African Literature," *Research in African Literatures* 20:3 (Fall 1989): 422–48, and Rhonda Cobham, "Boundaries of the Nation: Boundaries of the Self: African Nationalist Fictions and Nuruddin Farah's *Maps*," in Andrew Parker, Mary Russo, Doris Summer, and Patricia Yaeger, eds., *Nationalisms and Sexualities* (New York: Routledge, 1992), 42–59.

8. Chris Dunton, " 'Whetyin be Dat?,' " 422.

9. Thus for instance, Femi Ojo-Ade writes about Golder, "He is a strange person, full of contradictions and self-hatred." See Femi Ojo-Ade, "Soyinka's Indictment of the Ivory Tower," *Black American Literature Forum* 22:4 (Winter 88): 748.

10. Derek Wright, *Wole Soyinka Revisited* (Boston: Twayne, 1993), 122 (italics mine).

11. W. E. B. DuBois, *The Souls of Black Folk*, intro. by John Edgar Wideman (1903; reprint, New York: Vintage, 1990), 8.

12. James Baldwin, *Notes of a Native Son* (Boston: Beacon, 1955), 122.

13. One could cite several examples of this vis-à-vis the discussion of homosexuality in African(ist) literary criticism. In addition to the example of Joe Golder, the most obvious instantiation of such limitations is the criticism surrounding Yambo Ouologuem's *Bound to Violence* (1968; reprint, London: Heinemann, 1971). In this novel, just about every sexual relationship except one is "bound to violence"—we are presented with incest, bestiality, voyeurism, and rape. Furthermore, none of these sexual encounters are ever presented as loving or tender ones. The one exception is the relationship between Raymond Kassoumi and the Frenchman Lambert. While this relationship is by no means perfect, Ouologuem treats it as a loving relationship and insists on its tenderness. The novel, in other words, leaves open the possibility of reading this same-sex relationship between a black man and a white man as somehow sidestepping the inherent violence of the other relationships. Problematic though its implications might be, critics have chosen to silence the question by suggesting instead that Ouologuem's portrayal of tenderness and love here is either simply a flaw on his part, or else is not inconsistent given the homosexual nature of the relationship. In other words, this latter claim is based on the argument that the relationship is presented no differently from the others in the novel since the *homosexual nature of the relationship itself* is proof positive of the unnaturalness and violence.

14. Michel Foucault, "Appendix: The Discourse on Language," in *The Archaeology of Knowledge* (New York: Tavistock, 1972), 224. One of the external readers of this essay felt that this discussion of Michel Foucault would be familiar to most readers of *Genders*. While shortening and revising it to some extent, I have nevertheless chosen to retain it here. As a writer, I have wanted to be able to write the essay not only for an audience interested primarily in the study of gender and sexuality and only secondarily in African studies, but *also* (and perhaps more politically importantly) for an audience of Africanists who may not otherwise turn to a journal such as *Genders*. If there is to be a dialogue between both these communities, certain ideas taken for granted by each but not intimately familiar to the other must be rehearsed. I feel that the discussion of the production of discourse on African sexuality is thus crucial in such a context.

15. Ifi Amadiume, *Male Daughters, Female Husbands: Gender and Sex in an African Society* (London: Zed Press, 1987), 7.

16. I suggest that it is not enough, in a critical enterprise, to stop an analysis as soon as one encounters such barriers. While being sensitive to that which causes "offense," we need to ask: How does one historicize this condition of being offended? My argument parallels Joan Scott's skepticism of the category of "experience" as the ultimate grounding for historical claims. One has to attempt to understand how "experience" comes to be experienced as such, and the same is true of "offense." See Joan Scott, "Experience," in Judith Butler and Joan Scott, eds., *Feminists Theorize the Political* (New York: Routledge, 1992), 22–40.

17. It may be useful to note here that while I have not been able to locate any other references to the presence or absence of lesbianism among the precolonial

Nnobi, there are indeed records indicating that other African societies having similar institutional set-ups did not preclude lesbian possibilities. Thus Melville Herskovits, "A Note on 'Woman Marriage' in Dahomey," *Africa* 10:3 (1937): 335–41 suggests that while lesbianism may not always be a factor in such alliances it sometimes may be. On the other hand, it is clear that even institutions based on heterosexual norms leave a certain amount of space for homosexual activities. Thus Evans-Pritchard reports that lesbianism was practiced by women in some polygamous Azande households. Also of note in this context is Evelyn Blackwood's more comprehensive survey of the construction of lesbianism in anthropological discourse (Evelyn Blackwood, "Breaking the Mirror: The Construction of Lesbianism and the Anthropological Discourse on Homosexuality," in David Suggs and Andrew Miracle, eds., *Culture and Human Sexuality: A Reader* (Pacific Grove, CA: Brooks/Cole, 1993), 328–40. Gill Shepherd's article on homosexuality in Mombasa (Gill Shepherd, "Rank, Gender, and Homosexuality: Mombasa As a Key to Understanding Sexual Options," in Pat Caplan, ed., *The Cultural Construction of Sexuality* (New York: Tavistock Publications, 1987), 240–70, Renee Pittin's article on lesbian sexuality in Katsina ("Houses of Women: A Focus on Alternative Life-Styles in Katsina City," in Christine Oppong, ed., *Female and Male in West Africa* [Boston: George Allen, 1983], 291–302), and Judith Gay's article on "Mummies and Babies" (" 'Mummies and Babies' and Friends and Lovers in Lesotho," in David Suggs and Andrew Miracle, eds., *Culture and Human Sexuality: A Reader* (Pacific Grove, CA: Brooks/Cole, 1993), 341–55, all cast lesbian relations in the significantly different light of economics, rank, prestige, and possibilities of upward mobility. Once again, as indicated in note 6, I am aware of the dangers of using any one African society as metonymic for the whole of Africa. My listing of these instances from other African societies is not meant to make any claims about the Nnobi themselves. It is rather to counter the often articulated *generalized* claim that homosexuality is alien to Africa.

18. Frantz Fanon, *Black Skin, White Masks* (New York: Grove Press, 1967), 156.

19. Ibid, 180, note 44.

20. Lee Edelman, *Homographesis: Essays in Gay Literary and Cultural Theory* (New York: Routledge, 1994), 54.

21. Diana Fuss, "Interior Colonies: Frantz Fanon and the Politics of Identification," *diacritics* 24:2–3 (Summer-Fall 1994): 20–42.

22. Adrienne Rich, "Compulsory Heterosexuality and the Lesbian Existence," in Henry Abelove, Michele Aina Barale, and David Halperin, eds., *The Lesbian and Gay Studies Reader* (New York: Routledge, 1993), 240.

23. It is important to remark here that the many ambiguities and tensions in the novel are all the more effective not so much in relation to what the narrative explicitly thematizes but rather in relation to that which is necessarily left unsaid. My reading of *Maru* draws upon Deborah McDowell's reading of Nella Larsen's *Passing* in which, as McDowell suggests, the thematization of *racial* passing belies the more dangerous terrain of *sexual* passing. (See, Deborah McDowell, " 'It's Not Safe. Not Safe at All': Sexuality in Nella Larsen's *Passing*," in Henry Abelove, Michele Aina Barale, and David Halperin, eds., *The Lesbian and Gay Studies*

Reader [New York: Routledge, 1993], 616–25). While Head's novel is written in a sociocultural context quite different from that of the Harlem Renaissance, she may be seen to share with Larsen a similar concern: How does one write about the possibilities of alternative sexualities in black cultures without adding fodder to existing primitivist stereotypes? How does one escape normative sexuality without betraying the "race"?

24. Unlike the Western lesbian continuum, this text, racially coded, divides it too.

25. Bessie Head, *Maru* (London: Heinemann, 1971), 86. All further page references will be cited in the text.

26. Remember here that this is a three-tiered structure—"whites" on top, "coloreds" in the middle, and "blacks" at the bottom. While Margaret is "black," she can pass as colored and is indeed on occasion advised to do so. She remains steadfast in her "black" identification.

27. Eve Kosofsky Sedgwick, *Between Men: English Literature and Male Homosocial Desire* (New York: Columbia University Press, 1985), 21. See also Rene Girard, *Deceit, Desire, and the Novel: Self and Other in Literary Structure*, trans. Yvonne Freccero (Baltimore: Johns Hopkins University Press, 1972).

28. Ibid., 21.

29. In her essay "The Traffic in Women," Gayle Rubin suggests that the sexual division of labor is rooted not in biology but rather in the desire to distinguish clearly between what are dangerously fluid gender identities. Further, by erasing the feminine in men and by erasing the masculine in women, sexual desire is also channeled along heterosexual parameters. Rubin writes, "The sexual division of labor is implicated in both aspects of gender—male and female it creates them, and it creates them heterosexual. The suppression of the homosexual component of human sexuality, and by corollary, the oppression of homosexuals, is therefore a product of the same system whose rules and relations oppress women." See Gayle Rubin, "The Traffic in Women: Notes on the 'Political Economy' of Sex," in Rayna R. Reiter, ed., *Toward an Anthropology of Women* (New York: Monthly Review Press, 1975), 157–210.

30. The novel opens at the end and what follows is an extended flashback. To make matters simple, I treat this opening sequence as though it were placed at the ending of the novel since this is indeed where the narrative ends.

31. Above, I use the phrase "from Shaka to Evita" loosely to mark some of the changes that have taken place in discourses of African sexuality. Shaka, the celebrated Zulu king, was in many accounts read to be a repressed homosexual with expansionist tendencies. Much like the discussions surrounding Nazi Germany, fascism, and homosexuality, the argument made was that Shaka's expansionist tendencies were rooted in his repressed homosexuality. One advocate of such a claim was the anthropologist Max Gluckman (see Daphna Golan, *Inventing Shaka: Using History in the Construction of Zulu Nationalism* [Boulder, CO: Lynne Rieger, 1994] for an account). Thus the rise of the Zulu nation was problematically read in the light of a disordered sexuality. The marker "Evita" is a more contemporary one and refers to the white drag queen who has publicly performed for Nelson Mandela and other black South African Nationalist leaders. Here is a new South

Africa which is willing to officially celebrate rather than repress nonnormative gender performativity. (For an account, see Liz Sly, "South Africa's New Laws Give Gays Foothold on Freedom," *The Times Picayune* [New Orleans], October 9, 1994, A-25).

32. David F. Greenberg, *The Construction of Homosexuality* (Chicago: University of Chicago Press, 1988), 60. All further citations will appear in the text.

33. See also Tade Akin Aina, "Patterns of Bisexuality in Sub-Saharan Africa," in Rob Tielman, Manuel Carballo, Aart Hendricks, eds., *Bisexuality and HIV/AIDS* (Buffalo: Prometheus, 1991), 81–90; Mike Coutinho, "Lesbian and Gay Life in Zimbabwe," in Tielman Hendricks and Van der Veen, eds., *The Third Pink Book: A Global View of Lesbian and Gay Liberation and Oppression* (Buffalo: Prometheus, 1993), 62–65; Edward Evans-Pritchard, "Sexual Inversion among the Azande," *American Anthropologist* 72 (1970): 1428–34; Gordon Isaacs and Brian McKendrick, *Male Homosexuality in South Africa: Identity Formation, Culture, and Crisis* (Oxford: Oxford University Press, 1992); T. Dunbar Moodie (with Viviene Ndatshe and British Sibuyi), "Migrancy and Male Sexuality on the South African Gold Mines," in Martin Bauml Duberman, Martha Vicinus, and George Chauncey, Jr., eds., *Hidden from History: Reclaiming the Gay and Lesbian Past* (New York: New American Books, 1989), 411–25.

34. I am aware that many Africanists resist precisely such theorizing, especially as it is done here, with recourse to anthropological models. Anthropology—perhaps with good reason—has been seen to be an enemy of the people in the colonial context, and for this reason I *begin* with the literary discussions and then *end* with the anthropological/conceptual ones. Rather than structuring the essay so that the literary material glosses the anthropological, I have chosen to use the anthropological material as a gloss on the literary. In other words I am saying, "look, we can see these sexualities at work in these literary texts, and so on, and *by the way* the anthropologists *also* confirm these observations" *rather than,* "the anthropologists say this and here is the literary evidence." If this is a rhetorical strategy, it is no less invested in attempting to critique the hierarchical orders of knowledge exchanges across disciplines than it is in simply winning over an audience.

35. See David Halperin, "Is There a History of Sexuality?" in Henry Abelove, Michele Aina Barale, and David Halperin, eds., *The Lesbian and Gay Studies Reader* (New York: Routledge, 1993), 416–31; see also Jonathan Katz, "The Invention of Heterosexuality," *Socialist Review* 90:1 (1990): 7–34.

36. John D'Emilio, "Capitalism and Gay Identity," in Henry Abelove, Michele Aina Barale, and David Halperin, eds., *The Lesbian and Gay Studies Reader* (New York: Routledge, 1993), 467–76.

37. See Eugene Patron, "Out in Africa" (Interview with Simon Nkoli), *Advocate*, no. 616, November 17, 1992, 44–48.

38. Or, in this case, more appropriately, the ability to historicize the silences. See, in particular, Matthew Krause, ed., *Invisible Ghetto: Lesbian and Gay Writing from South Africa.* (Johannesburg: Congress of South African Writers, 1993), and Mark Gevisser and Edwin Cameron, eds., *Definite Desire: Gay and Lesbian Lives in South Africa* (New York: Routledge, 1994).

Public Face, Private Thoughts: Fetish, Interracialism, and the Homoerotic in Some Photographs by Carl Van Vechten

James Smalls

The art and literature of the Harlem Renaissance are primarily a black and white affair, whereas the art, fiction, and life of Carl Van Vechten (1880–1964)—perhaps black America's most notorious philanthropist— reveal many shades of gray. In 1932, Carl Van Vechten gave up his career as a novelist of light fiction and became a full-time amateur photographer. He was introduced to the then-new Leica camera by his friend, the noted caricaturist Miguel Covarrubias, who among other things, satirized Van Vechten's obsession with African American culture in a drawing entitled "A Prediction" in which Van Vechten was showcased with "negroid" facial features.[1] Not long after, *Vanity Fair* took note of Van Vechten's negrophilic tendencies when it derisively declared that he was "getting a heavy tan." Of all the key players in New York in the years spanning the 1920s through to his death in 1964, Carl Van Vechten was perhaps the most well known and the most influential—easily earning a reputation as a connoisseur and chronicler of Harlem and its black inhabitants through his activities as novelist, music and dance critic, patron of the arts, and photographer. As a powerful catalyst in keeping the "Negro in vogue" for almost five decades, Van Vechten was an essential asset to aspiring African American artists and writers. His acquaintance with influential socialite Mabel Dodge Luhan and a stint with the *New York Times* as music critic, afforded him access to personalities of the day and gave him ready entrée into the worlds of dance, music, and theater.[2] He was well connected in both the arts and publishing worlds and gave many African American creative people their first break by introducing them and their work to important whites in key institutional positions—thereby acting as "a kind of midwife to the Harlem Renaissance."[3]

Over a span of more than thirty years, Van Vechten produced thousands of photographs on a variety of subjects. He specialized in portrait photography—in particular, black portrait photography. These "celebrity" photos were highly conscious portraits of African American artists, writers, and other notables and tackled identity formation as desired by the subject and forged by the photographer. They also helped to reinforce the critical observation that Van Vechten was a collector of rare objets d'art and of rare people."[4] In her discussions on photography, Susan Sontag has noted that "photography has the power to turn people into objects that can be symbolically possessed."[5] Van Vechten took full advantage of the possibilities. As will become evident throughout the discussion, the act of photography itself was fetishistically critical to Van Vechten's psychological and social definition. Not only was his intention to use photography as an artistic expression of cultural and racial documentation, but he also employed the medium as a means of popular mythmaking about himself in relation to African Americans. The calculated exploitation of African Americans and black culture was to be his ticket to fame and fortune.

Van Vechten's photographic output is, relatively speaking, rarely discussed in the literature and few have, to the best of my knowledge, seriously analyzed or critically questioned his negrophilic visualizations in photography. His black celebrity photos were praised by many African Americans, for they assisted in the establishment of blackness as dignified and beautiful within the confines of a bourgeois Western art tradition. They were also credited as instrumental in reversing decades of stereotyped black physiognomy by presenting the African American in the most sophisticated dress, manner, and demeanor. As Van Vechten's celebrity photos demonstrate, the African American head became the approved armature around which racial pride and identity were molded. Even though the body is subordinated in these works to focus on physiognomy, the black body and its potential to be hypersexualized was not overlooked by Van Vechten, who eventually found it, embraced it, exploited it, and worshipped it in a series of little-known photographs that I refer to here as his "fetish and fantasy" works.[6]

These highly erotic and provocative photographs were produced in the 1930s and 1940s and focus on the sexually suggestive interrelationship between black and white men either within the artificial confines of the studio or within narrativized fields of nature and culture referenced as "primitive." These images, never publicly exhibited, reveal a more sinister side to Van Vechten's seemingly benevolent social enterprise. Now freed from their archival invisibility (Van Vechten himself requested that these photos not be made public until several years after his death), these images can now be critically assessed. These rare works engage an ambivalent dialogue on the nature of Van Vechten's personal, sexual, and social identities, desires, and history, while at the same time they reflect wider cultural, historical, and theoretical implications centered around the interstices of homoerotic desire, race, spectatorship, and visual culture in modern America. In a nutshell, these images provoke critical interrogation on the relationships between visual representation, homoerotic desire, and spectatorial looking.

These photographs, in conjunction with Van Vechten's literary and philanthropic influences, force the acknowledgment of a fact—that white patronage carried with it a concomitant racial agenda and was motivated by a bias for modernist primitivism that viewed things African and African American as a means through which the patron could enter into what he or she believed was a more authentic relationship with the world.[7] Thus, these works constitute a difficult dilemma for the contemporary viewer in that they beg the question of whether the racial and sexual fantasies they manifest should necessarily compromise the credibility and integrity of white patronage. Should Van Vechten's "fetish and fantasy" photographs, in light of his positive and affirmative deeds and accomplishments as a philanthropist and promoter of African American art and culture, necessarily disqualify or call into doubt his "public face" of sincerity, credibility, and integrity? Do these visualized "private thoughts" reinforce or undermine racist myths about black sexuality and/or about interracial cooperation? Should the discernments of "private thoughts" through representation overwhelmingly dictate or determine our views and judgment of an individual's "public face" and deeds? Ultimately, can we trust representation as definitive or absolute evidence of psychic and social realities?

Van Vechten's "fetish and fantasy" photos spotlight the emotional and social complications that result from the human necessity to satisfy and yet balance private needs and public standing. They exemplify the unstable regions in the intersections of psychic preoccupations (i.e., fantasies) and social realities. As such, they provoke questions that can not be answered with a singular *yes* or *no* response. Clearly, this human necessity was marked by Van Vechten's own race, social status, and sexual orientation. However, my response to and consumption of these photographs are likewise marked, in fairly complex ways, by my own racial designation and sexual preference. In either instance, race, sexuality, and social interactions converge in a cultural space and are revealed as manifestations of "a human thing" to which these fetish and fantasy photographs speak.

As an art historian by training, I have been taught to separate my personal opinions, moral judgments, and fantasies from the interpretation of visual culture. In looking at these photos, however, I find that I must abandon my earlier art historical indoctrination into the social history of art and indulge in an articulation of subjective thoughts, feelings, and fantasies. I have come to realize of late that my training as an art historian in a socially and politically based methodology has limited my abilities to contend with art production as psychosexual residue. My attempt to grapple here with issues of racial and sexual desire and fantasy in these photographs creates an almost schizophrenic split in approach to the topic. On the one hand, I want to look at Van Vechten's "fetish and fantasy" images as socially and historically significant works created during a specific time and place in which elements of the primitive and the modern were employed to define, confirm, and promote a self-constructed self for Van Vechten in relationship to an African American community which was, at the same time, struggling with its own issues of identity. However and on the other hand, I want to suggest how the "fetish and fantasy" images might operate as products of gay interracial desire and fantasy for myself and for the contemporary viewer. To do the latter, I grate against my art historical grain by making no claims to neutral observation in taking my own subject position into account as a gay black man whose principal but not exclusive object of desire is white men. I thus have a personal stake in this inquiry—an emotional involvement that intervenes in my intellectual interest in and interpretation of these photos.

As already mentioned, interracial representations such as those created by Van Vechten allow for intervention in important contemporary debates centered around the complex interstices of race, homosexuality, and visual culture. This conversation was, for the most part, begun by contemporary cultural theorist Kobena Mercer, whose most recent work on Robert Mapplethorpe's photographs of black male nudes brings into sharper focus the complexities involved in racial and homoerotic relations both inside and outside of representation.[8] Mercer rethought his previous negative reading of Mapplethorpe's work by critically interrogating his own viewership and identification with homoerotic networks of looking. His rethinking of these issues revealed ambivalences and ambiguities in his personal response to such representation. As Mercer had discovered and as Van Vechten's work helps to clarify, interracial gay relations (in representation and in social reality) involve complex multidirectional exchanges of psychological and emotional needs and desires. Race and racial difference become significant and crucial aspects of exchange.

So, by asking the question of whether or not Van Vechten's "fetish and fantasy" photographs should adversely compromise his credibility and integrity as patron to black America, I raise the possibility, as did Mercer with Mapplethorpe's photos of black men, that the issues implicit in these images are more complex, ambivalent, textured, and less easily read as "black and white" racist discourse. Unlike Mercer, whose strategy for reassessing Mapplethorpe's imagery was predicated on anger and ambivalent "structures of feeling" as a black gay male spectator, I approach Van Vechten's "fetish and fantasy" works from the standpoint of surprise, admiration, and emotional delight in their interracial and erotic suggestiveness. I like these photographs. Nevertheless, in this discussion I want to assume that there are implied power relations in gestures of white mastery and black male appropriation and I would care to first read these works as negative exercises in racist dynamics implicating a white male imaginary. I begin with the premise that the "fetish and fantasy" works labor toward the corporeal in such a way that the black body, with all its (re)constructed constituent cultural and ethnographic parts, is fashioned into a legitimizing vision of racial and cultural idolization and marvel—a fantasy construction that benefited Van Vechten and therefore the gay white male imaginary. In addition, I want to examine how these photographs lay bare the destabilizing function of fetishism, primitivism, and spectatorship in the reception and reading of racialized homoerotic visual imagery. In many ways, this essay continues the conversation started by Mercer, and hopefully will add to it.

Even though the ideas generated from Mercer's rethinking of Mapplethorpe's black nudes parallel and draw significant critical connections to Van Vechten's imagery in terms of the dynamics of reading and reception of gay interracial representation, I would like to point out that there are notable differences between Mapplethorpe and Van Vechten, particularly in terms of content, social context, and historical specificity. The social and historical background for Mercer's rethinking of Mapplethorpe's work is the 1980s, the tragedy of AIDS, censorship and political controversies over federal arts policy and funding, and the emergent influence of the fundamentalist Christian Right. In noteworthy contradistinction, the circumstances and context for the production and reception of Van Vechten's imagery during the 1930s and 1940s are noticeably different and center around issues of race relations, white patronage and the tradition of philanthropy, and the fashionability of modernist cultural practices that include primitivism and all of its neo-Freudian associations. Thus, throughout this discussion I keep in mind that Van Vechten's images were fashioned under modernist and not postmodernist conditions even though their confluence of art and life, as well as their kitschlike matter-of-factness, give them a curious postmodern flavor. Therefore, any employment of contemporary theoretical paradigms onto modernist representation is done so with caution.

The question of what these works may have meant to or how they may have served the social aims and personal fantasies of Van Vechten and his contemporaries is, I believe, more immediate and significant than is how they operate on a theoretical or social level for contemporary spectatorship. However, the latter dynamic can not be ignored. Also significant here is the issue that, whereas Mapplethorpe's homosexuality was no secret to his audience, there were efforts made both during Van Vechten's lifetime and after his death to publicly hide his sexual orientation.[9] Both sexual and racial taboos during the 1930s and 1940s exerted considerable pressure on keeping individuals and their desires closeted in ways very different from the more "liberated" environment of the 1980s. This situation does, undoubtedly, affect not only the genesis, look, and execution of imagery but also complicates interpreting their intended and actual function.

The last significant difference between the work of Mapplethorpe and that of Van Vechten that I would like to clarify is that the former was obsessed with racialist imagery in which the black body and its aestheticized parts are scopically focused on in the masculine economy of the gaze thus fixing "race" in an ideological construction of otherness. The process has negative incriminating implications for the white gay imaginary. Van Vechten's imagery, however, is different in that its playful and yet bland focus on interracial relations diffuses the tendency to scopically fix, fetishize, or objectify the body as only marked by race. There is a difference between racial and interracial representation. Interracial visualization has complicating implications for the discourse surrounding spectatorship because it allows for a dissolution and mobility of subject position boundaries that not only impact upon the viewer's interaction with race and sex but become indicative as well of the mobility and confluence of the photographer's psychic and social needs and desires. I will return to this very important dynamic later in the essay. However, suffice it to say for now that it is with the racial/interracial divide that my argument differs most from that of Mercer.

Van Vechten's "fetish and fantasy" photographs served a psychic and social need for the photographer. They attempt to equate interracial erotic intercourse with interracial social cooperation by giving a visual record to fantasies of male interaction that revel in the sexually and racially forbidden. Ironically, in attempting a deliberate dislocation of conventional moral sensibilities through the production of such transgressive visual imagery, Van Vechten reinforces his own perceived racial/cultural enlightenment. These photographs, in social and historical conjunction with the black celebrity photos, as well as with much of the literature Van Vechten himself wrote prior to 1932, exemplify an attempt to satisfy and to resolve a conflicted need to legitimate his negrophilic sympathies publicly and to satisfy his homoerotic desires privately, while laying claim to an "enlightened" engagement in contemporary notions of the primitive and, therefore, in the modern. Thus, these images for Van Vechten are the result of an insistent polarized tension between public appearance and private needs; between an inner reality and an outer theatricality; between serious objective concern for a black subject and a highly subjectified racial and sexual exploitation; and between strains of contention brought on by a concurrent split between negrophilic and negrophobic identities. It is with his erotic interracial images that Van Vechten's public persona as patron and his private sexual and racial fantasies merge and conflict. This conflict ultimately reflects and parallels the ambivalences that plague past and present gay social and sexual interracial relations in America.

THE PRIMITIVE, THE FETISH, AND THE RACIAL

If the "history" in art history can limit the emotional experience of representation—which I believe it often does—then the other extreme, "theory," can be just as confining in its disregard for social/historical/political/ideological context. That is to say, some academic critical theories of spectatorship or of ideology critiques are insular from any sense of practical application or lived experience as they also tend to fix subject positions by race or sexuality. Thus, as with history, theory can also "get in the way" of deciphering the interworkings of desire and fantasy that often have a serious impact on the lived social components of sexual and racial interaction. After all, a myopic focus on the theoretical aspects of fetishism and primitivism was what initially convinced Kobena Mercer that Mapplethorpe's images of black men were racist and ill-intentioned, which by extension, targeted Mapplethorpe the man as a racist in his social/sexual life. This is not to say that theory can not be useful, for it was also through a process of wading through theory that Mercer came to realize that the sexual fetish, the racial fetish, and their psychic effects upon the viewer were not necessarily interchangeable.[10] What Mapplethorpe's black nudes and Van Vechten's fetish and fantasy images confirm and reinforce is the observation that the set boundaries between theory, history, and desire are arbitrary and fluid. The strict application of unique theoretical paradigms such as fetishism or primitivism to Van Vechten's work, for example, highlight unexplainable flaws that support the limitations of theory.

In his critical reexamination of Mapplethorpe's images of black men, Mercer begins by questioning fetishism as a legitimate theoretical paradigm for evaluating racialized representation. He rails against fetishism as an ethnocentric "master discourse"—a discourse that seduces in its conspicuous absence of race. Whitney Davis's informative essay titled "HomoVision: A Reading of Freud's 'Fetishism' " fuels Mercer's complaint in that it underscores the ethnocentricity of Freudian and post-Freudian theory.[11] Freud himself never dealt directly with the racial fetish. Surprisingly, given the advantage of hindsight, Davis, in his deconstructive approach to Freud's "Fetishism," does not consider it either. The closest the author comes to it is in distinguishing the fetish-image from, what he terms, the "fetish-effigy" (i.e., the transient objects attached to or belonging to the fetishized object).[12] In Van Vechten's case, the contrived interrelational actions between the figures, "ethnic" attributes, and the mere sight of skin color differentiation become the "fetish-effigy" serving as "sign" for the intrapsychic or fetish imago.

As a theory, fetishism is very complex and problematic on several fronts, and race as a historical and theoretical construction complicates the matter even further. In his reassessment of Mapplethorpe's black male images, Mercer recontextualized his previous argument of "erotic objectification and aestheticization of racial difference" by positing an alternative reading of fetishism as a negative characteristic. To do so, Mercer first acknowledged that "fetish" or "fetishistic" carry negative connotations that society has conditioned its members to believe and accept. Thus, inherent in the concept of the fetish and fetishism is a moral position which had informed his earlier reading. In this regard, Mercer acknowledges the usefulness of fetishism as a theoretical tool for "conceptualizing issues of subjectivity and spectatorship in representations of race and ethnicity," but he also warns against its pitfalls.[13]

In a similar vein, Davis stresses, in his dissecting of Freud's "Fetishism," the importance of distinguishing fetishism and fetishistic practice from other psychological interests such as obsession, phobia, voyeurism, homosexual longing, mourning, and sadism.[14] These preoccupations predominate in Van Vechten's racial and interracial imagery. Voyeurism, narcissism, and a focus on modernist technique reign in a couple of photos in which a sole black male subject is used to suggest sexual play (illustration 6.1). Here, Van Vechten uses the photographic technique of double exposure and the artistic principle of collage to create an illusion in which a black male subject suggests the sexual position "69." This and other images play upon sexual and racial innuendo and are more in keeping with modernist experimentation in subject matter, lighting, double exposures, composition, and so on. The fragmenting, doubling, and serializing of body parts owes much to jazz imagery and to contemporary Cubist explorations of form. Such treatment of the body also implies a certain amount of violence in fetishistic fashioning and looking. But as Mercer learned and as becomes evident with Van Vechten's interracial nudes, this approach is not inherently negative or dehumanizing. Seen as a legitimate means of sexual/racial transgression, the Van Vechten photo consciously "stages" a sexual act in the guise of modern collage art. It serves to give a visual record to all the taboo things designed to simultaneously satisfy sexual and artistic urges, as well as to gratify Van Vechten's need to "épater le bourgeois."[15]

This image and others like it must have served a particular psychic and social need for Van Vechen who considered such photos more "artistic" than his better known black "celebrity" head shots and, as such, more in keeping with his true self as a modernist. As an experiment in the visual manifestation of "private thought," this image (unusual, yet ideationally consistent with Van Vechten's body of photographic works) was fashioned to clarify, justify, or assuage his "public face" status. As a photographic experiment, this and other images underscore his indulgence in sexual

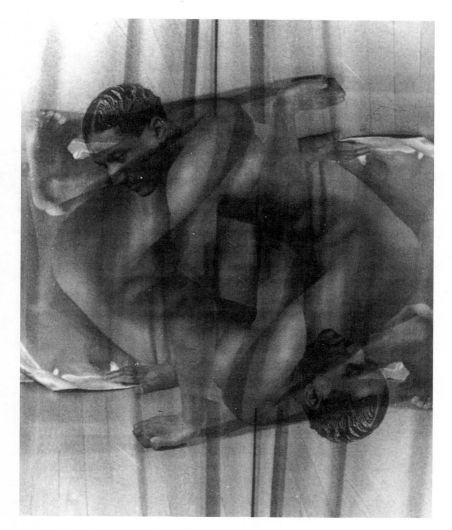

FIG. 6.1 Yale Collection of American Literature, Beinecke Rare Book and Manuscript Library, Yale University.

and racial fantasies through fetishistic contrivance and voyeuristic posturing. Not only does the element of voyeurism come into play as the subject's limbs confusingly and suggestively intertwine as would body parts in an orgy, but the very act of photographic manipulation in the darkroom and reconfiguration of the male body in the studio are themselves revealing of Van Vechten's apparent need to sexually and, in this case, racially manipulate and control. In its seductive and voyeuristic spying onto a racialized spectacle of the male object of desire, this image equates a self-conscious narcissism and hedonism with self-recognition of the master subject. Moreover, it constitutes evidence of the intermachinations of race and sex as decisive and necessary factors in Van Vechten's photography.

As evidenced by illustration 6.1, Van Vechten used photography itself as a fetishistic practice for exposing the primitive attraction of white to black. He made significant use of a black and white medium to play off and construct dualistic meanings through focus on the contrastive aspects of race and culture funneled through a "homovision."[16] The medium itself served to assist in the codification of a schema in which contrived elements of the racial, sexual, and artistic interweave in a matrix of defining relationships between the races. The photographer's endeavor to unify the primitive and the modern and his attempts to project an impression of a mutual and harmonious relationship between black and white men are rendered through formal means of patterning and, in particular, careful choices of background designs, studio props, and poses. All of these were very carefully considered in the (de)(re)construction of interracial and intercultural relations.

Primitivism and fetishism are related events. So too are fetishism, the stereotype, and colonialism. The intricate interworkings of these phenomena cannot be fully unpacked here, but suffice it to say that the stereotype, like the fetish, has negative connotations due to the process of objectification that both entail.[17] Both depend upon a dialogue between "fixity" and "ambivalence" in the ideological construction of otherness. This discourse, in turn, allows for the continuation of colonial fantasy in that black subjects come to stand in as fixed ideas about the nature of sexuality and otherness. Certainly, in much literary and visual discourse, black people have been at the center of colonial fantasy. The construction of that fantasy is merely a complex articulation of the tropes of fetishism by which individuals control and order a mass of complex information so as to successfully project values and beliefs onto people, places, and objects of fear and desire.[18] All three phenomena—primitivism, fetishism, and colonialism—conspire to constitute "a system of multiple beliefs, an imaginary resolution of a real contradiction."[19] Primitivism is a movement predicated upon an obsession with fetishism. It is the racial and sexual fetish that constitutes the theoretical inner-workings and provides the nurturing ideological base for primitivist discourse in modernist practice.

Van Vechten's "fetish and fantasy" photos engage in modern primitivist practice by employing two kinds of fetish in a modernist context—the racial or epidermal and the sexual. As the cultural theorist Homi Bhabha has noted, the former aspect of the fetish differs from the latter in that the former can never be hidden as a secret and is significant in the signifying chain of both "negrophobia" and "negrophilia."[20] The "charm" of Van Vechten's "fetish and fantasy" photos is that they successfully confuse philic and phobic attitudes about race for both the spectator and for the master subject in their interracial erotic indulgence. In allowing for a play back and forth of negrophilic/phobic fetishistic tendencies, Van Vechten makes sex (more accurately, homoerotic desire) a prevalent open secret.[21] Because fetishistic representation makes present for the subject what is absent in the real, Van Vechten's photos can be characterized as visualizations of a masculine fantasy of mastery and control over the "objects" represented and depicted.[22] This is an inherent trait in the problematic aspect of fetishism because it resides in colonizing discourses and as such automatically sets up a negative colonizer/colonized relationship of power.[23]

The stereotype operates much in the same fashion as does the fetish— as a scene or site of fantasy and defense or as a desire for an originality which is threatened by the difference of race, color, and culture.[24] What complicates the matter is that Van Vechten produced imagery that is both racial and interracial. Both black and white men are subjected to the same negative relationships of power, both are susceptible as "virgin territory to be penetrated and possessed by an all-powerful desire to probe and explore an alien body."[25] Thus, fetishism and the fantasy of mastery are intensified and complicated by a combined interracial and homoerotic investment. So, in discussing Van Vechten's photography in the context of fetishism and fetishistic practice, I distinguish between his "racialized" nudes in which a sole black subject is contextualized in an artificial studio environment or in a natural setting read as "primitive," and his "interracial" images in which black and white men are similarly narrativized as they interrelate on primitive and erotic levels. With both kinds of images there is a question of a "fantasmatic emphasis on mastery" and black male appropriation by the white male subject inherent in the conception and presentation of these nudes. In either instance, it is spectatorship and the dynamics of gay male fantasy that become critical to a deciphering of meaning.

The relationship between fetishism and spectatorship is not only crucial to an understanding of Van Vechten's imagery, but is also central to the human psychic and social thinking about images, objects, and individual relationships to one another. Illustration 6.2 well illustrates the interracial and spectatorial point. In the confines of the studio environment, two male figures—one white and the other black—are placed against a curtain backdrop with arms raised above their heads and bodies poised in a mirroring contrapposto stance. The foregrounded white figure has his back and buttocks exposed to the viewer while the backgrounded black man is frontally positioned to reveal both his face and penis. Both figures are "feminized" in that their bodily positions recall poses typically associated with women in Western art. Both figures are objectified as passive objects of desire. In the relationship between black and white body, however, the white man takes on a more passive role in his vulnerability to anal penetration. A difference in skin color has replaced the "norm" of sexual difference. The black male figure becomes the phallic counterpart to the anally receptive white man. An erotic fantasy based on desired relations of sexual power and fetishistic practice between the races is set. However, this image, like so many others in the interracial series, is not bound by a single fantasy reading of white over black power relations. This is particularly true when potential shifting subject positioning and spectatorship are considered. I shall address this phenomenon later.

In a way, illustration 6.2 is subversive of usual racial stereotype in that it shows a white man in a position of vulnerability and potential aggressive fetishistic looking. Contrarily, in several of Van Vechten's racialized nudes, white mastery over the racial other is assumed and pronounced. For example, in a couple of his racialized photographs in which a sole black figure implies a white presence in the gaze, the black man becomes, as a product of white construction, an ethnographic representative of "Africa." In these images, the black figure is scantily swathed in African fabric as a "sign" of his Africanness. In one photo, the black subject frontally faces the camera in confrontation with the viewer. His upper torso is heavily draped in African cloth while from the waist down he is shown naked with penis exposed. The black man's African "essence" is reduced to his penis and to a scrap of fabric on which are noticeable African designs. The black man is "ethnicized," sexualized, and objectified

FIG. 6.2 Yale Collection of American Literature, Beinecke Rare Book and Manuscript Library, Yale University.

as a specimen of study by the author. He becomes a sign of a whole range of racial and sexual expectations related to a fixed concept of the primitive. In yet another "racialized" photo akin to illustration 6.2, the black figure is situated in an artificial studio setting with his lower half covered with kente cloth. He is shown bending over as if to pick up or place something on the ground. The back part of his wrapping is conspicuously open, allowing for his buttocks to peer through. His left hand is placed atop his backside so as to draw the viewer's attention to his exposure. The implications here are not only racial/ethnic but sexual as well. The exposed buttocks are perhaps intended to stimulate a fantasy of anal penetration. Thus, contrary to his phallic position in illustration 6.2, the black man in other racialized photos can alternately be ascribed to a passive or anally vulnerable position. This kind of implied subversion of the stereotype in representation may have been viewed by Van Vechten as a form of enlightenment and mutuality of desire between the races—both of which were confused with the notion of interracial cooperation in social life.

Van Vechten's compositional placement of black against white in the visual arena facilitates the imaginary projection, acknowledgment, and identification with fantasies about racial and cultural "difference" and the attempted disavowal of that difference. However, the differences are fetishized, objectified, and in some cases presented as serious ethnographic documents of mutual racial and cultural embrace and cooperation. What makes Van Vechten's representation peculiar and particular is that skin is not the principle "signifier" of fantasy in his interracial images. He perceives all expressions of interracial exchange—be they psychic or social—as fetish. Skin remains, however, a significant element in Van Vechten's work, for the fetish is always experienced in contrastive terms to the white male body even when the white body is conspicuously absent from the internal visual frame. Van Vechten's own subject position and interests as white author of the visual text makes this so. In his case, the fantasy of mastery is intensified and complicated by, what I perceive as, a distinct and deliberate authorial projection into his images.[26]

This projection, in alliance with the racial fetish, the stereotype, and homoerotic desire, assists in the formation and affirmation of a social self predicated on a play between mastery and pleasure as well as on anxiety and defense. By positioning himself as author and voyeur both inside and outside of the visual text, Van Vechten completes a cycle of cathartic union with or repulsive fear of the black man. Thus, the specular effect of these photographs takes on added meaning. On the one hand, Van Vechten projects himself as gallantly embracing black people and, on the other hand, he privileges himself as disinterested spectator to witness and record blacks embracing their racialized and sexualized selves as well. Furthermore, Van Vechten cleverly plays with the idea of black and white on multiple levels. Again, on an artistic/photographic level, he uses black and white photography to pattern black and white bodies in black and white poses or situations of polarized tension—opposites do indeed attract. The attraction/repulsion aspect of these images is underscored by the black/ white patterning of the studio backdrop environments and erotic tension between the figures.[27] The result is more scientific than artistic as the black and white imagery holds together and creates fantasy energy likened to the push-pull effect of the proton and electron in the atom.

All of Van Vechten's "fetish and fantasy" photos share in common the sense of studio control and artificiality combined with the spontaneous vision of the snapshot as ethnographic document. The documentary aspect of his working method makes significant connection to the primitive concept of the mask as "a portrait completely on the surface, evident, unequivocal . . . the stereotype . . . being first of all a social, historical product, [containing] more truth than any image claiming to be 'true'; it bears a quantity of meanings that will gradually be revealed."[28] Particularly for Van Vechten, the mask was significant in that it exposed far more than it concealed. Theatrical contrivance and the mask come together and play significant roles in his photograph of a black man displaying an African mask to the viewer. Here, the spectacle of the body is racially, culturally, and sexually coded. The black model dutifully, perhaps even resentfully, displays to the viewer the object of his racial origins while the mask in a pendant photo (illustration 6.3) representing the same model holding the same mask over his genitals, transforms the black subject into a sign and symbol of exotic culture and sexual powers. The black figure's frontal nudity, the mask, and what is behind the mask work in concert as items of attraction and spectator curiosity. The black man simultaneously displays and "wears" the mask. The spectacle of the auction block is evoked with the objectifying display of the exposed black body and its cultural correlates (i.e., the primitive) scripted onto it. The mask conceals and yet reveals the mysteries of the black man to the spectator. He not only flaunts his essence to the supposed privied observer, but is himself transformed into an ethnographic item of note for the discriminating eye of the "expert." The theatrical backdrop reinforces the stereotype as a floral pattern is used to evoke the feel of the "primitive" in nature.

The spectacular exploitation of the black body as sexual object and item of ethnographic curiosity grew out of the historical practice of minstrelsy.[29] In displaying his own mask/penis to the white photographer/ spectator, the black man literally becomes a spectacle upon a minstrel stage—a black performer in blackface. Not surprisingly, Van Vechten

FIG. 6.3 Yale Collection of American Literature, Beinecke Rare Book and Manuscript Library, Yale University.

was, in his social life, an avid fan of minstrelsy—defined here as a form of racial entertainment extolling the complications of revealing and hiding true identity behind a mask or facade of blackness (hence Covarrubias's caricature of Van Vechten in blackface). The photographer's love of minstrelsy is recounted in an anecdote in which he persuaded the wealthy socialite Mable Dodge to allow two African American performers to entertain at one of her parties. Dodge recorded that "while an appalling Negress danced before us in white stockings and black buttoned boots, the man strummed a banjo and sang an embarrassing song. They both leered and rolled their suggestive eyes and made me feel first hot and then cold, for I had never been so near this kind of thing before; but Carl rocked with laughter and little shrieks escaped him as he clapped his pretty hands."[30]

Van Vechten's male nude photos are especially likened to the concept of blackface minstrelsy in their ultimate purpose of displaying and fetishizing the black male body in the frozen spectacle of a combined ethnographic and erotic contemplation. In each photo, nudity is a significant requirement marking the black body as icon of study and fantasy. The designation of the black body as performative and spectacular was essential to early twentieth-century modernist practice. Since the mask and minstrelsy often operate within contrived theatrical spaces, it was logical that Van Vechten would find both attractive given his penchant for artificiality, the theater, and his passion for collecting people and objects. Houston Baker, Jr., reminds us that the mask is not only a "thing" but is also a "space of habitation" that encapsulates "a family of concepts or a momentary and changing array of images . . . that group people."[31] The mask is also used in social, cultural, and sexual ritual. It is a form that exemplifies the white man's "repressed spirits of sexuality, ludic play, id satisfaction, castration anxiety, and a mirror stage of development."[32] Further, and on a Freudian level, the mask is, as a disembodied face, also likened to decapitation and castration. The mask, with all of its metaphoric associations with primitivism, fetishism, psychosexual display and concealment, was a meaningful and useful item and idea to master for both the black and white modern artist. As Baker describes it, the mask as a concept and as a physical thing operates as a means to exemplify "the mastery of form" and "the deformation of mastery."[33] The attempt by Van Vechten to master the mask as face, body, and modern idea is in fact implicit in the dichotomy between his black celebrity photos and his fetish and fantasy images. Analysis of these two bodies of photographic work also reveals the inherent problematics of mastery that "deformation of mastery" implies. Furthermore, Van Vechten's close association with the world of the theater made him especially drawn to the potential complications surrounding the mask and masquerade as aesthetic and social instruments for multiple meanings of deception and revelation. To master the mask and to take advantage of all that it implied was to be modern.

Playing upon the idea of the mask as a sign and process of cathartic union with the other, Van Vechten's fantasy of racial and cultural mastery is coupled with an aspect of voyeuristic spectacle in a rather unusual photograph showing a nude black man beholding an African statuette (illustration 6.4). The angular positioning of the model's back, arms, buttocks, and legs intentionally mimics and recalls the very angular forms of the object held by the subject. Here, Van Vechten plays on the idea of the photographer's "objective" ethnographic documentary eye contemplating the black man who holds and contemplates his own primitiveness (i.e., a likeness of his own body). The impression is one of serious ethnographic study and cataloguing of the primitive body.[34] It is also a clear visual statement of physical and cultural possession on the part of the intended spectator. Both black man and statuette are conceived as works of art—acquired, owned, and fashioned to the beholder's desires. In another photograph with the same model set in a dance pose, the figure's nudity and angular form work to evoke a sensual primitiveness in the dance while turning the subject into an object of racial and cultural distinction. The subject has become the very African statuette that he held in the prior photo.

In both instances, the voyeuristic scrutiny of the photographer's gaze is justified in a study of the study of angular form and movement. By viewing the black subject in this manner, Van Vechten could successfully objectify and fetishize the black body and transfer it onto the legitimizing cultural aspect of African art and the ethnology of black dance. No doubt, these images satisfied Van Vechten's multiple intentions—they appeased his penchant for collecting and documenting peoples and culture and allowed for the exercising of his fantasy as voyeur of primitive and narcissistic practices. Furthermore, as contrived visual displays of homoerotic, interracial, and intercultural activities constructed within highly artificial and controlled spaces, they satisfied his need to collect and document black people in relation to his own specific conception of the black man's ancestral link to Africa.

In his initial reading of Mapplethorpe's representation of black men, Mercer suggested that the photographer's work constituted aggression in the act of looking and in the process dehumanized black men. The question of dehumanization in fetishistic practice surfaces not only in

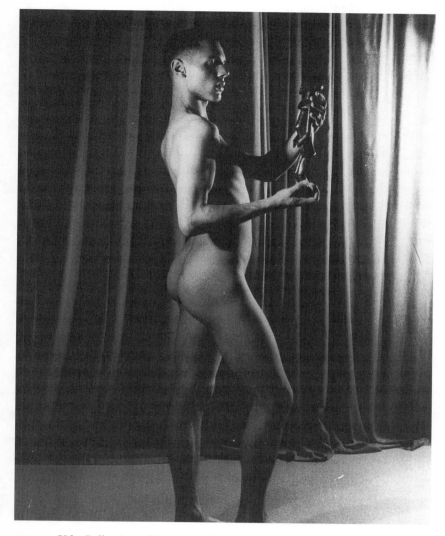

FIG. 6.4 Yale Collection of American Literature, Beinecke Rare Book and Manuscript Library, Yale University.

representation but in theory as well. Again, according to Whitney Davis, fetishization is not necessarily dehumanizing if we consider a theoretical point of fact—that in order to dehumanize one has to have a "total" recognition of the other from which acts of "dehumanization" represent a deflection of deviance—a notion which derives from the quandary and questioning centering around the possession or lack of the penis in oedipal schematics.[35] Real subjectivity, Davis contends, is only a continuum of states of "dehumanizing" the other. A real subject perceives the other according to his or her own unconscious beliefs and desires, that is to say, according to his or her own subject position. Thus, the object of desire is "inherently" partial and fragmented vis-à-vis the subject.

The imaginative role and subject position of the spectator must also be considered, for the fetishistic practice of looking can and does play a significant role in determining and shaping our fantasies and desires. Fetishistic looking and fetishistic practice are, however, not necessarily related occurrences. Fetishistic looking is part and parcel of the psychical dynamics of desire and, as such, shades into but cannot be equated with fetishism as acting out sexual practice. The differentiation parallels the whole dynamic explained earlier between theoretical structures in relationship to social practices—the two phenomena contribute to one another but are not the same thing. What theory and representation (a visible explication of theory and/or practice) make clear is that desire and the act of looking are complex and ambivalent psychic mechanisms inherently constitutive of fetishism itself. In this regard, Davis speaks of "humane fetishisms" that do not necessarily involve the dehumanization of the fetishizing subject or fetishized object. For Van Vechten, photography itself then functioned as a "humane" fetishistic practice—as the playing-out of the intrapsychic or intersubjective formation of desire in a controlled racial, erotic, and social fantasy.

As a combination of Mercer and Davis makes clear, fetishism as a theoretical scheme is not very helpful in the analysis of racialized and homosexualized imagery because Freud's account on fetishism ignores completely the element of race in fetishistic practice and, as well, is "embedded in the patriarchal system of sexual division . . ."[36]—thus failing to satisfactorily integrate homosexuality or a consideration of homoerotic desire. Both Davis and Mercer rightly conclude that fetishism is limited in terms of deciphering the "circuitry through which individual desire must circulate."[37] Along a similar vein and as Davis notes, fetishism affirms a heterosexual subject position and operates to "dehomosexualize fetishistic looking."[38] The dehomosexualizing process is evident with illustration 6.2 in its feminizing of the subjects and the setting in fantasmatic opposition of penis and anus. Van Vechten's interracialism tries to ascribe a "normalizing" heterosexual male/female, active/passive paradigm to homoerotic expression. Race and racial difference are defined in gendered terms. That is to say, phallic/black/masculine is set against anal/white/feminine. Further, this interracial joining of black and white parallels the phenomenon of androgyny itself in that both attempt to perceive the marrying of opposites into a unified entity or encounter of harmony. Thus, illustration 6.2 would give visual support to Davis's conclusion regarding the role of homosexuality in fetishism as "the reality of fetishism and fetishism . . . [as] . . . the imaginary of homosexuality."[39] The sight/site of interracial union in Van Vechten's photo confirms that "there can be no real or imaginary looking . . . which does not sustain some degree of homosexuality and fetishism."[40] Thus, Van Vechten's artistic evocation of interracial harmony is based on a gay subjectivity that is inherently fetishistic and racialized—a condition which is, as Mercer concluded in his reassessment of Mapplethorpe, not automatically racist nor necessarily a bad thing.[41]

The flaw of fetishism as a master discourse is exposed through the blaring contradiction between critiques of fetishism as a means for reinscribing racist and heterosexist norms, and attempts to recuperate a version of fetishism that is "humane" and inescapable. The almost vertiginous oscillation between these two poles is at work in Van Vechten's imagery and is a core feature of Freud's ambiguous theorization of fetishism. Within the context of colonial discourse, Homi Bhabha has addressed the flux and flaw of fetishism as foundation for the construction of both negrophobic and negrophilic structures. Mercer has underscored Bhabha's observations in his discussions of skin color as fetish in Mapplethorpe's imagery. Both contemporary theorists expose fetishism as the "splitting of conscious and unconscious belief that is relevant to the ambiguous axis upon which negrophobia and negrophilia intertwine."[42] Thus, the intrinsic and troubling flux and reflux of fetishism encoded in Van Vechten's photography simply exposes the complicated and unfixed nature of a theoretical paradigm as it invades representation that speaks to the interstices of human desire and racial difference.

LURE OF THE PRIMITIVE AND LOSS OF SELF

In early twentieth-century modernist practice, white engagement with the primitive was viewed as a sign of social and artistic sophistication—a purifying regression through simplification and the satisfaction of primal urges. Africa was, to employ a term used by Michel Leiris, "Edenic"—a conceptualized site of "ritual intoxication" for whites.[43] Indulgence in the primitive was considered as one way to put aside or momentarily suspend one's racial and cultural identity and become "one" with the other. As shall be elaborated more fully below, blacks also partook in the intoxication of the primitive as defined by whites but for altogether different reasons. Taking pleasure in the losing of self in the other served to disrupt historical, spatial, and social oppositions between white and black, self and other, Euroamerica and Africa. As an admirer and patron of African American art and letters, Van Vechten shared in his contemporaries' beliefs that persons of African descent retained many of the elemental, spiritual qualities that white people had lost. The idea of unrestrained and aggressive sexuality—a significant feature of cultural primitivism—is employed by Van Vechten as one aspect of a nostalgic regression heightened by the insularity of the studio. His "fetish and fantasy" imagery underscores the critical and social ambiguity that arises out of an attempt to embrace primitivism as an instrument for disidentification with white, patriarchal, bourgeois society. In their capacity as images of avowal—of racial/cultural deification and idolization—Van Vechten's "fetish and fantasy" photographs disallow any real power the black man might have by engaging in stereotypic visual discourse of the primitive. Historically, primitivism as a concept has been automatically scripted onto the black body in a way that the correlate fantasies of racial and sexual otherness are always present.

According to Hal Foster's elaboration on the underlying dynamics of primitivism, two things occur in its modernist form—on the one hand, there is an explicit desire to break down the cultural oppositions of European and "primitive," culture and nature, as well as the psychic oppositions held to underlie them: active and passive, masculine and feminine, heterosexual and homosexual. On the other hand, there is an insistence on maintaining these oppositions. These conflicts of desire occur because the primitivist seeks to be both "opened up to difference" (i.e., racial, sexual, social, cultural) and to be "fixed in opposition" to the other so as to have mastery over it.[44] In Van Vechten's case, this is most clearly seen in several of his interracial nudes in which the themes of male homosexuality, cannibalism, and acts of physical violence—all of which are homologous events in fetishist and primitivist discourse—are linked.

Most significant for my discussion, however, is the social and psychic function of primitivism for Van Vechten himself. Within a modern primitivist visual discourse, Van Vechten's "homovision" has given an intensity of purpose to an explicit signification of racial differentiation. Due to the secretive nature of the fabrication and circulation of these photos, I submit that they have more to do with Van Vechten's racial and social crisis as a private individual and public patron than they do anything else. They also illustrate his dire need to demarcate racial and sexual subject and object and to seek jurisdiction over both. The highly sexualized and racialized aspects of his "fetish and fantasy" photos become simulacra of charms and dangers against the loss of self inscribed in both homoerotic and interracial experience.[45] For example, in a telling photograph from this "loss of self" series, Van Vechten depicts the white man as actively netted by the "primitive" (illustration 6.5). The white victim, willingly snared as prey, will soon be either abused, sacrificed, or devoured by the black man. I believe that the white man is a willing accomplice in his capture because of an apparent lack of resistance on his part. Again, I cannot help but read the netted white figure as an authorial projection— that is, as Van Vechten willingly throwing himself into the pig-sty of primitivist activity and taking delight in slopping about in its mud. In order for Van Vechten to enjoy his status as victim of and lord over the very object he desires, the black man, he "gets primitive" and partakes in the base pleasures and biological impulses that the black man, as representative of an alluring and mysterious need to somehow become more complete, has to offer.

Of course, this primitivized sadomasochistic ritual of sacrifice is based on a manifestation of "colonial fantasy" in which a rigid set of racial and sexual roles and identities are used to construct scenarios of desire in such a way that clearly routes these references to the testimonials of the historical legacies of slavery, bondage, lynching, and to the real consequences of white exploration and exploitation of peoples of African descent. This primitivist discourse in Van Vechten's representation, although extreme in its kitsch/camp feel, has close affinities with serious orientalist/exoticist discourse.[46] For instance, a photograph of a black man serving a white man grapes (illustration 6.6) conveys stereotyped servitude in conjunction with racial distinction, sexual subservience, and implied social hierarchy as does any exotic harem image or story from the nineteenth century. Thus, at first glance it would appear that the ideas behind Van Vechten's "fetish and fantasy" images are not new but are merely contemporary rehash of old stereotyped racial, sexual, and social fantasy

FIG. 6.5 Yale Collection of American Literature, Beinecke Rare Book and Manuscript Library, Yale University.

codes used to solidify existing hierarchical structures between the races. Van Vechten takes these old facts and places them under the scrutiny of modernist critique. If read this way, then these images created by Van Vechten as a measure of authorial projection, clearly have negative impli-

FIG. 6.6 Yale Collection of American Literature, Beinecke Rare Book and Manuscript Library, Yale University.

cations for the gay white male imaginary. However, the interracial character of the works and the potential mobility of spectatorship change all this.

Van Vechten's obsessive fixation on the white man's relationship and proximity to the black male body and the latter's "primitive" rhythms force a decidedly autobiographical note of intersubjective desire and wish-fulfillment onto his photos. Sometime in the 1940s, Van Vechten shot a series of photographs in which black and white men encounter one another in a natural, junglelike setting (illustration 6.7). As visual manifes-

FIG. 6.7 Yale Collection of American Literature, Beinecke Rare Book and Manuscript Library, Yale University.

tations of modern colonial discourse, these photos attempt to simultaneously recognize and disavow differences between the races by producing
for the white man a deceiving space of encounter, knowledge, and embracing of the primitive through voyeuristic surveillance and incitement
of sadomasochistic interplay. In all instances, the white man's encounter
with Africa is a desired one—one in which he is a visitor or lost stranger
to the black man's "natural" habitat in nature. The white man willingly
becomes the docile and passive object of foreplay who deserves and wants
to be netted, tied up, sodomized, and cannibalized. This state of affairs is
most explicitly revealed in yet another series of photographs created
around the same time as those mentioned above in which themes of
sacrifice and ritualized enactments of violence and sexual violation between black and white men are most noteworthy. In these, it is the
mystique of the black man's "Africanness" set in contrastive conjunction
with a "willing" and receptive white man, that operate to signify transgressive sadomasochistic fantasies and desires for both the white and black
male subject. The implications of sodomy, cannibalism, and sadomasochism become Van Vechten's projections of a particular modern subjectivity
onto a constructed interracial primitivism.[47]

Van Vechten's fantasy of becoming one with the other continues with
two incredible photographs showing a white man draped over an African
drum while in the masochistic "jouissance" of a self-sacrifice to "Africa."
In one of the two images, the white man is represented nude, bound at
the hands and feet, and draped over an African drum (illustration 6.8). He
is about to be stabbed, disembowled, sacrificed by the black man who
crouches before him clutching a knife. The floral backdrop attempts to
impart a sense of primitivized place. The counterpart photo evokes the
white man's complete loss of self and willing sacrifice to "Africa" as an
ideal. In it, the white man is alone, nude and uncomfortably splayed over
the drum. The plain backdrop and glittery floor material emphasize the
artificial and theatrical setting for an offering taking place on an African
drum-as-altar. Because he is alone and fed up only to the viewer's gaze
(who was initially and intentionally Van Vechten himself), the offering of
self becomes a private affair (if the idea of authorial projection is accepted)
for Van Vechten who desires to be sacrificed on the shrine of Africa,
thereby identifying himself as both a captive and martyr.

Van Vechten's loss of self is achieved by pairing contradictory elements
of impotence and aggression, passive spectatorship and acts of cruelty. For
the photographer, these images constituted attempted flirtations with

FIG. 6.8 Yale Collection of American Literature, Beinecke Rare Book and Manuscript Library, Yale University.

boundary dissolution and transcendence—boundaries that most likely tested and affirmed his need to maintain separation, difference, and control over African Americans while convincing himself through artistic reinforcement of completely surrendering himself over to them. These contrived fetishistic acts of racial and sexual fantasy not only serve as psychic or fantasmatic reinforcement of Van Vechten's very public social role as a patron and philanthropist of African American art and culture but also function to resolve conflicts of racial difference and homoerotic desire through sadomasochistic wish-fulfillment in his perceived passive surrender and self-sacrifice to black men. In a Freudian sense then, Van Vechten's sacrifice becomes "a symbolic version of cannibalism and a sacred, transcendental version of suicide—a version in which the voluntary destruction or offering of self achieves social significance."[48]

In a curious series of "fetish and fantasy" interracial photographs in which a loss of self thematically predominates, Van Vechten evokes a quasi-ritualistic atmosphere of white worship of and supplication to the black body/penis. In one of these (illustration 6.9), a white man is shown on his knees with his back to the viewer. He raises both hands as though in supplication before a standing black man who looks down upon the white figure while holding a goblet in each hand. The artificiality of the studio environment draws the viewer's attention to the activity taking place between the two figures. The position of the white man and the compositional placement of his head at the black man's crotch suggests fellatio. The setting, props, lighting, and positioning of the figures all give a pious feel to a profane encounter. Again, Van Vechten is working in opposites to heighten sexual and social fantasy. Interestingly, this photo clearly relates to illustration 6.2 in its encoding of a passive/active dynamic in racial division.[49] Clearly, the mechanisms of sadomasochism and sexual/racial fetishistic practice—both being significant dynamics contained within the tradition that paved the way for modernist primitivism—are the operative agents in these and other images created by the photographer.

If the potential for authorial projection is kept in mind, the oscillation of the white master subject between sadist and masochist parallels a desired alternation between active and passive positions vis-à-vis the black body/penis. This is a dynamic of power that is, in this instance, ascribed to the white master subject. However, due to the interracial character of these images, the subject-position mobility of the author is also allowed to the viewer. Again, this is a point I will discuss in the following section. For now, I want to reiterate that images like these were extremely significant for defining and maintaining Van Vechten's psychic link to a social life. By focusing in on the homoerotic in racial difference and by placing that fantasy within a highly artificial atmosphere of harmonious solemnity, images such as illustration 6.9 heighten a sense of white capitulation and racial cooperation that is then transferred by Van Vechten to the social domain. In pushing the theme of utopic interracial harmony in ritualized gestures and contrived settings, Van Vechten's photos succeed at playing upon a conflictual fusion of racial power, fear, and desire by the white master subject.

Whereas his earlier novels had manifested a serious moral commentary on the inversion of accepted values, these photographs are more private, playful, and "therapeutic" reveries on the photographer's own trans-

FIG. 6.9 Yale Collection of American Literature, Beinecke Rare Book and Manuscript Library, Yale University.

gressive violations of a perceived barrier between himself and the African American community. In a way, these photographs constitute a kind of "visual slumming" as one form of violation. In his social life, Van Vechten loved to go "slumming" into Harlem and, in fact, bragged that he had started that trend.[50] His "fetish and fantasy" photographs indulge in a desire to taste the forbidden fruit of the black man, whose "goods," both sexual and cultural, are as tempting and satisfying as the prohibited fruit in Eden (illustration 6.6). These photos bring to light the significance of racial perception in creating works of art and encourage the viewer to see primarily but not exclusively through the white man's gaze and subject-position. The spectator is coerced into adopting fantasies of sadomasochism and interracial intercourse by accepting manipulated cultural readings catalyzed by racial difference. Van Vechten's gaze upon the racial body inscribes a "look" which implies hierarchical ordering of a superior/inferior identity. Colonial and primitivist visual tropes of an alternating slave/master relationship are used to create a description of white capitulation and "sacrifice" as a means of achieving a semblance of racial and cultural awareness. And yet, these photos allow for the fantasmatic possibility of multiple subject positionalities and interpositionalities that complicate even further the interconnections between fantasy, desire, and race.

SPECTATORSHIP

On one level, Van Vechten's "fetish and fantasy" nudes could be read as modes of representation fashioned to "facilitate the [white] imaginary projection of certain racial and sexual fantasies about the black male body."[51] Yet on another level, they are classic expressions of ambivalence in that they exemplify the fracturing or multiplicity of homoerotic desire and interracialism into complicated psychic, social, and spectatorial emotional effects. The psychic/social divide of fetishism is particularly significant to Van Vechten's work and yet that division is often blurred because his imagery bears a markedly intersubjective function as fantasmatic reinforcement for construction and maintenance of his social self. His works, due to their intended private nature, further underscore the psychological, therapeutic, and cathartic function of art that is so often espoused by many romantics.

The intrapsychic components of fetishism, sadomasochism, and homoeroticism are all tied into the construction and interworkings of desire and feature as necessary components for Van Vechten's concept of modernity. However, what Mercer's critical work on Mapplethorpe makes clear is that fetishistic practice in representation must not only consider identification by the master subject but must also take into account the subjective positioning of the spectator—be he actual or intended. Viewer subjectivity and spectatorship are critical considerations for any reading of Van Vechten's interracial nudes. What Van Vechten's images succeed at doing is provide for the construction of multiple positionings by the viewer as voyeur, masochist, sadist, or fetishist. They offer the spectator, regardless of race, multiple erotic fantasy choices from which to choose.[52] That is to say, I can, if I so desire, identify with the white man's subject and object position and he with mine. By eliding and replacing the black man with my imaginary self in illustration 6.9, for example, I can identify as sadist; by doing the same in imagery where the black man is subservient (illustration 6.6), I identify as masochist. By not transpositioning myself at all, I become voyeur or I can place myself into the scenario as a third person in a "ménage à trois"—all of these "democratic" possibilities can be erotically and fantasmatically stimulating for both subject and object of desire.[53]

These sorts of complications provide a window onto the ambivalences and intricacies of desire and fantasy that can not always be definitively pinpointed and explicated by theory. Van Vechten's "fetish and fantasy" images are visual exercises in how fantasies can be generated by the mobility of subject positionalities. For Van Vechten, sadomasochism and racial difference work in conjunction to satisfy any subject position. As a black gay spectator, my identification with the black figure is possible and probable but is not always fixed and assured. Inherent in this dynamic of desire are subcurrents of sadomasochism, the fantasy mechanisms of which I am certain Van Vechten understood. S/M structures are automatically inscribed in the binary oppositions in the visual suggestion of slavery/mastery, active/passive, phallic/anal, black/white, and so forth. These are polarities that also speak to an inherent instability because they attempt to construct an artificial framework that consolidates and naturalizes structures of power.

Spectatorial mobility in the fantasmatic allows me to easily elide or erase the black figure and replace him with myself in either a position of control or submission. Thus, Van Vechten's black figure can function as a rival or accomplice in encountering the object of my desire—I make the choice. And herein lies the attraction to the "fetish and fantasy" images for this viewer. The desired object and desiring subject are not fixed but are mobile depending upon my wants/needs as spectator. Unlike Mapplethorpe's imagery, or even that of Van Vechten's contemporary George Platt Lynes, where the element of "where to look" is limited and dictated by the author, Van Vechten's "fetish and fantasy" photos do not command a "categorical" identity or subject position for the spectator. Such a fluid fantasmatic legitimizes and seriously complicates the relationship of power between white and black men. Thus, I am and I am not "used, laid bare, and overdetermined from without" by white eyes in the realm of fantasy.[54] Neither and yet both spectator and object become powerless and powerful at some point. For myself, this dynamic does not destabilize me or promote any ambivalent "structure of feeling" as Mapplethorpe's black nudes had done for Mercer. On the contrary, I find my control of the fantasy to be an important element in further stimulating erotic desire.[55] Any tension between black and white or active and passive positioning not only parallels an S/M dynamic but can, in my view, operate as a necessary aspect of the fantasy for the gay black or gay white desiring subject.

Thus, Van Vechten's "fetish and fantasy" photos emphasize ambivalent interracial relations of looking and desiring that often destabilize any subject/object dichotomy in terms of seeing and being seen. Voyeurism, objectification, fetishization, S/M dynamics—all necessarily come into play if the fantasy is to be maintained. These scenes and their related issues invite the spectator into what Mercer refers to as "those messy spaces in-between . . . binary oppositions . . . that ordinarily dominate representations of difference."[56] The shifting subject positionings and numerous permutations of racial and homoerotic fantasies elicited from Van Vechten's visual imagery exemplify the complexities of desire in which questions of race, homosexuality, social identity, and power enter into the psychic and lived relations between black and white men. These kinds of responses cannot be explained solely by theoretical paradigms because the problem with theory is that it tends to be removed from our lived experiences which are based, in significant part, on fantasies and desires—interests that reside in those "messy spaces." As visual manifestations of gay and racial fantasy and desire, Van Vechten's photos help illuminate and bridge those gaps.

PARALLEL DESIRES

The dialogue between the primitive and the modern in early twentieth-century American culture forced many African American artists and writers to also succumb to fetishistic expectations in their work. Since primitivism and primitive behavior were defined by the dominant culture as a state existing before Christian morality, homosexuality would then be justified in such a context.[57] Despite the individuality and semi-independence that history has ascribed to the African American artist, it was Van Vechten who not only commanded awe and respect from a modest portion of them and others from the African American community in Harlem, but it was he who also singlehandedly dictated or coerced the homoeroticizing and sensualizing of the black male body for them.[58] Whereas gay white artists such as Van Vechten found emotional solace and urgent social significance in engaging in mixing erotics with "Africanisms" to inform an avant-garde agenda, for the African American intelligentsia of the early modern period, homosexuality and Africanness were discontinuous problematics. Homosexuality, either black or white, was a taboo topic only dealt with indirectly.[59] The problem of the gay black relationship to Africa germinated in the work of Alain Locke—African American leader and philosopher of black cultural production from the 1920s to the 1950s. Locke argued for the need for African Americans to study their origins in Africa and to apply what they learned to artistic production. According to David Bergman, "Locke's interest in Africa . . . [was] . . . at least partly motivated by a desire to create a cultural context for black homosexuality."[60] In his writings on African and African American art, Locke himself couched his sexual politics in ambiguous and enigmatic terms.[61] Since gay black men of the early modern era sought legitimation of desire in an African past just as did whites, they easily adopted similar primitive features or ideas in representation. Perhaps this is why it was easy for Van Vechten to dictate a primitivized homosexuality to African American artists.

Unlike the use of the black body by whites to promote a self-conscious avant-gardism, the goal of the black artist in the employment of similar primitivist and fetishist tropes was to relocate from the social and artistic margins to a site of mainstream acceptance by the white status quo. That is to say, African American artists were aware of the psychological need of whites for Harlem and for the primitivized black man. To supply what was in demand was not necessarily viewed as a negative thing. As Nathan

Huggins has suggested, the indulgence by whites in Harlem as a heart of darkness and in black men as its drumbeats, "provided some black men a positive image of themselves, and, most important, it brought downtown money uptown."[62] Thus, acknowledgment by the dominant culture of the black man's "forces" and the mechanisms of capitalist economics allowed for or forced, in many cases, the African American artist to evoke the primitive in his art. But once again, this should not necessarily be deemed as negative complicity on the part of African Americans as is typically perceived today. Thus, the employment of racial and sexual fetishism in the works of black artists such as Richmond Barthé, Richard Bruce Nugent, and Charles Cullen, raises important cultural and political issues surrounding the relationship between black self-representation and white patronage.

Ironically, in latching onto primitivism and the racial fetish, both blacks and whites used the black body as linkage to a primitive modernism but did so with different objectives. Interestingly, very few African American artists included the black nude body in their work. When they did, they objectified it and fashioned it as an item of consumption to suit contemporary aesthetic or artistic trends such as Art Deco or Cubism. For example, the African American artist and writer Richard Bruce Nugent, who was also a close acquaintance of Van Vechten, created highly sensualized, stylized, and decorative graphics of black nudes for *Fire!!*, a radical magazine published in 1926 by young African American writers and artists. Nugent concentrated on male figures whose rendering was sexually and sensually provocative. His erotic drawings paralleled his scandalous short story of miscegenation, androgyny, and homoeroticism, called "Smoke, Lillies, and Jade." Nugent was an outrageously flamboyant personality whose reputation as a notorious "out" homosexual even surprised Van Vechten himself.[63]

Of all the African American artists who incorporated the racialized and eroticized male nude into their art, the sculptor Richmond Barthé (1901–89) is perhaps the most notable. The major theme of his work was the nude or nearly nude black male figure in the act of the dance. Barthé attempted to sanctify homoerotic desire and Africanity in his most visibly famous statue, *Feral Benga* (1935, The Newark Museum), by combining a European feature often associated with homoerotic desire (i.e., Michelangelesque forms), and angular physical movements identified with an impulsive African primitivism. Despite the differences in media, Barthé's works are similar to Van Vechten's in their juxtapositioning of racial focus and the sensual worship of the black male physique in motion.[64] Van Vechten and Barthé were not only friends, but the latter is rumored to have shared in Van Vechten's homoerotic interest in and attraction to black men.[65]

Barthé's work is unique and relevant to the issues at hand in the fact that as visual products of a black man, his pieces complicate the approach to racial pride through application of the racial fetish, spiritual/religious sentiment, homoerotic sensibility, and bodily sensuality—features that were, for the most part, sanctioned by Van Vechten.[66] Barthé's mode of black bodily representation parallel's Van Vechten's in that his sculptures combine Western standards of bodily beauty as well as African ones, thereby drawing appeal from primitivists and fetishists as well as European classicists. Furthermore, Barthé followed Locke's lead in setting up polarities in his sculptures between ancient and contemporary, classic and modern, European and African, pagan and Christian. With Locke's work serving as ideological example for African American artists to follow, Greece and Africa became synonymous in their classical embodiments— both were defined as "rigid, controlled, disciplined, abstract, heavily conventionalized."[67] In attempting to visualize this amalgamation in his sculptures of black male nudes in the act of primitive dance, Barthé's works play out in visual form the interworkings between homoerotic desire, spiritualism, and European/African classicism. In this respect, they closely parallel the ideas behind Van Vechten's "fetish and fantasy" photographs.

Barthé's novel blending of the spiritual with the physically sensual is analogous to an attempted balancing of the primitive and the modern during the early modern period. His admixture of spirituality and sensuality, in fact, dovetailed with the historical moment in that the most significant motivation for primitivism in modernism was the wish to "be physical" as coextensive with "being spiritual."[68] Because Barthé's works are similar to Van Vechten's in their juxtapositioning of racial/ethnic focus and homoeroticism (i.e., sensual worship of the black male body), they exemplify that ambiguous moment when aspects of the primitive and the modern coexist. Treating the black body in this way is especially problematic for the African American artist, for when the black physique becomes both a product and property of the white elite (Barthé's sculptures were highly praised, accepted, and purchased by whites), it is transformed into an objectified cultural product whose very "blackness" (an essentialist concept brought about by Locke's New Negro movement and a racialist approach to art) becomes suspect.

Thus, I believe that Barthé's and Van Vechten's employment of a combined homoeroticism and racialism in representation operated not to bolster any sense of racial pride or racial denigration on the parts of the artists but to point to a modernism in which elements of the primitive and the homodesirous had to coexist in tension as evidence of modern interracial relations on a psychic and social level. Both artists' appropriations of race and culture imply a certain amount of dependency on and support of a traditional, patriarchal model of (Euro)culture for describing the black male body. Both exhibit a dependency which appropriates an abstract, universalizing concept of "Africa" and locates it within a matrix of a Europeanized and sexualized black masculinity. The work of both artists underscore the links between a racialist approach to art and modernist primitivism—a combination that resulted in moments of social and sexual ambiguity and ambivalence for both the black and white male artist and spectator. In other words, both Barthé's male nude sculptures and Van Vechten's interracial photography exemplify the ambiguous moment when aspects of the primitive and the modern exhibit awkwardness in their attempts to integrate and coincide.

Based on Van Vechten's privately circulated male nude photos, his significant involvement in the worlds of theater and dance, as well as a series of recently unearthed pornographic scrapbooks produced by him in the 1950s, it goes without saying that he was undoubtedly gay and was particularly attracted to black men in a private way far surpassing the confines of his public displays of cultural benevolence.[69] His homosexuality was a given both in and out of the black community. I am less concerned with harping upon the identification of Van Vechten as gay or in viewing his "fetish and fantasy" photographs as "queer" expression in a sexually repressed period and more interested in interrogating how the photographer's homoerotic sensibilities overlap and parallel with the racial fetish and the act of photography as both psychological and social reinforcement for a self-constructed self.

Van Vechten's role as patron to the African American community in Harlem during the first half of the twentieth century helps to explain the parallel desires that some African American male artists may have had for the eroticized and primitivized black male body. His involvement in the New York gay subculture also helped shape how black men were perceived and received in both art and life by gay white men.[70] As experimental works in patterning and contrasting arrangements in black and white, and as visualized intersubjective reinforcements for a public posture, Van Vechten's interracial male nude images were fashioned "for his eyes only" and for those of his most intimate circle of gay friends and other cultural types who not only had strong interests in primitivist modernism and its connection to the avant garde, but whose penchant for the homoerotic and the racial also made for a "naughty" underground environment of interracial bedfellows. Exactly who slept with whom makes for good gossip but is not important here. Suffice it to say that Van Vechten's "fetish and fantasy" images as well as interracial images created by his friend and contemporary George Platt Lynes, constitute cultural evidence of a phenomenon in early twentieth-century gay modernist circles in which racial distinction became a significant factor in a homoerotic attraction which may or may not have been mutual for all involved.

Based on my own emotional response to both Van Vechten's and George Platt Lynes's imagery, and not on any "hard" documentary evidence, I suspect that the predominantly white urban gay subculture of the 1930s and 1940s consciously utilized race, racial difference, and the homoerotic as group-defining instruments of power and identification with a cultural avant-garde elite. I have also suggested that many African American men who identified with this white cultural avant-gardism were complicit in this self-defining interracialism. Unfortunately, there is no existing documentation that tells us precisely how whites or blacks of Van Vechten's intimate circle responded to his interracial imagery. We do have, however, written evidence of the erotic pleasures taken in interracial representation by George Platt Lynes, whose male nudes express parallel Van Vechtenian ideas on interracial sexuality.[71] Lynes and Van Vechten were very close friends and fellow New Yorkers who had met each other in Paris in the 1920s as members of the circle of Gertrude Stein. The careers of both photographers parallel in that Lynes's ambition before photography was to become a writer. Also, both started their careers as photographers with portraits of celebrities in the literary, art, and theater worlds.

However, as was not the case with Van Vechten, Lynes's homosexuality was public knowledge, especially among the American expatriates in Paris. As a photographer, Lynes was more famous and celebrated than was Van Vechten whose notoriety rested primarily on his role as patron and philanthropist. Due to the implicit and explicit social and legal pressures of the period, neither Lynes nor Van Vechten could openly display their intensely homoerotic and interracial photographs. Their public exposure would have proven too shocking for an audience in which homosexuality was taboo and interracial coupling, particularly between the sexes, was suspect. This in turn restricted their circulation to a close circuit of confidants. Nonetheless, both photographers no doubt saw their male nudes as private exercises in modernist practice and as a means of psychically and socially reaffirming their roles as white men in command of aesthetic, racial, and sexual matters. Lynes's fixation on and control over black men and their crotches was indicated in a letter written by Lynes to Bernard Perlin:

"Tomorrow I've a date with D., that 'wonderful gentle good-looking (super body!) Negro' I [have] inherited." In a subsequent letter Lynes continues: "The brown boy I inherited . . . is heaven—affectionate and good, beautiful in the lean long muscular way, chocolate and ashes-of-roses, and (you guess where and how) fantastic, wonderful."[72]

Lynes's use of the word "inherited" underscores an enthusiastic desire to collect and possess racial bodies, while his allusion to the black man's phallic endowment points to the stereotype of the hypersexual as an essential component in the description of racial difference for the white master subject. Even though attitudes such as this negatively indicts the gay white male imaginary in the exploitation of race and sex, it also speaks to the realities of intersubjective fantasies that were not only enjoyed by the white master subject but also, in many instances, by the eroticized object of desire—the black man. In other words, Lynes's description might be deemed racist and stereotyped, but it is also erotic. Racism and eroticism often work in concert to reinforce one another in fantasy and desire. The fixation on racial stereotypes can not only add considerable pleasure to the object of desire for the subject, but its very status as a taboo and its social regard today as politically incorrect can work inadvertently to stimulate attraction for the spectator regardless of race. As Van Vechten's "fetish and fantasy" works have helped to explain, sadomasochistic currents and subject position mobilities can and do intensify the ambivalence of desire inherent in such encounters. To indulge and clarify, I will use another more explicit letter written by Lynes to Bernard Perlin which further implicates the white photographer in "negative" yet erotically stimulating pleasures indulged in a voyeuristic approach to the interracial couple:

"I asked B. if he'd be willing to pose with D. A little to my surprise he said yes, so I asked D. to come along. He did. I photographed . . . them together in all sorts of close-contact suggestive sentimental sensuous poses . . . D. would have been willing, but I thought B. wouldn't. . . . But then . . . everything did happen . . . and the sight of that big black boy screwing that super-naked little white bundle of brawn was one of the finest I've ever seen."[73]

It is the sight or vision of gay sadomasochistic power relations underscored by racial opposition ("big black boy"/"white bundle of brawn") that structures the photographer's enthusiastic and intensely erotic description. Lynes revels in his own spectatorship. More specifically, he makes reference here to a series of art photos in which white and black and all black men engage in sexual foreplay leading up to and including the sex act.[74] Although Van Vechten never made such explicit statements regarding race and sexual attitudes in his correspondences, the chances are good, based upon his "fetish and fantasy" images and prominent status in the gay subculture of New York, that he wholeheartedly shared in Lynes's libidinous interracial fantasies.[75]

The interracial male nudes of Van Vechten and George Platt Lynes are significant in that they are evidence, among other things, of these men's erotic use of race and racial difference in a burgeoning gay subculture in New York spanning the period from the 1930s to the end of the 1950s—a subculture in which race and racial difference were evidently of primary importance. As Lynes's and Van Vechten's photos and their exchange between individuals suggest, race and racial distinction were not only significant factors in the power operations within the gay subculture of the 1930s to the 1950s but also route our attention to the complex avenues of sexual and racial desire of both blacks and whites in erotic fantasy and in social arenas. It is clear that for Van Vechten, his gay proclivities overlapped with his desperate social attempts to project himself as the "Messiah" of African American culture. He needed concocted images of a harmonious interracialism as a personal vehicle of reinforcement in order to convince himself that he indeed possessed a level of prestige and power of which he may not have been thoroughly convinced that he actually had. In his social life, Van Vechten desired desperately to be part of black cultural strides but more often than not encountered walls of resistance and mistrust by many African Americans.[76] Despite his desires to "infiltrate" the black community and move beyond the confines of spectatorial periphery, Van Vechten remained an outsider. So, his interracial male nudes operate as modes of fantasy or desire to infiltrate and be accepted by the black man. Also, what these photographs make clear to me is that there must be a distinction made between a historical racism that negatively impacts upon the real social lives of individuals and a psychic racialism, that is, focus on racial difference and stereotypes in the realm of desire that form the basis of erotic fantasy in representation.

CONCLUSION

By now, it should be obvious why the public has not been allowed to see these "fetish and fantasy" photos, for they expose the private thoughts and desires of a man who publicly promoted himself as an affirming advocate for African Americans, their creativity, and culture. Without a doubt, racial and gay subtexts and pretexts percolate below the surface of Van Vechten's photographs. In the end, his photos draw critical attention to the artifice of the forced racial, sexual, and cultural roles and identities ascribed to blacks by whites. They therefore point to a "constructedness" of race and racial difference within a homoeroticized field, thereby reminding us that pleasures can ultimately be political even when left publicly unacknowledged.[77] They can be said to make ambivalent the "political unconscious" of white masculinity as they expose a need to have jurisdiction, claim, and control over black cultural and white subcultural arenas while at the same time hypocritically posturing a semblance of objectivity and enlightened sympathy.

The white pre-Stonewall gay subculture in which individuals like Van Vechten officiated perhaps needed the tropes of black primitivism and the intricate dynamics of fetishism in order to distinguish and empower itself within its own societal stigmatic status as a repressed minority. It was through interracial and homoerotic imagery that gay white males attempted to distinguish themselves by exercising control over the representation of the bodies of others. It was an engagement that could seriously indict Van Vechten and force suspicion and condemnation of his homoerotic and negrophilic motivations and intentions. However, as I have tried to suggest in this essay, Van Vechten's photos are not as simple and clear-cut as might first appear in their delineations of power relations between blacks and whites. His interracial nude photos underscore the observation that racial and sexual desire are intersubjective constructions that are mobile and fluid. With them, the master subject (i.e., the spectator) can constantly transgress identities, positions, and roles. They in fact constitute aspects of interracial gay desires that are as complex, ambivalent, and multiple as was Van Vechten's personality.

Considering the possibilities and potential subject-position mobilities that Van Vechten's works elicit, it may be too hasty and simplistic to dismiss him as a racist and to believe that blacks were merely his helpless victims—fodder for the mill of white imagination. These "fetish and fantasy" images force the viewer to acknowledge that the flow of desire and power can be multidirectional. African Americans also can and do exhibit, proclaim, and exercise fantasies of racial domination, phallic endowment, and exploitation. To what extent were African Americans themselves responsible for or participants in their own representation in Van Vechten's visual output is an important question to be considered. In some instances, as Van Vechten's "fetish and fantasy" photos give evidence, the black man himself can be complicit in his own fetishization. This is a controversial statement, but I believe that it lies at the very heart of fantasy in gay interracial relations. By allowing myself to be fetishized and by reveling in that process from my own subject position as a gay black male spectator, I can also maintain the illusion of cooperation and wrest a certain amount of power and control over the white man. This is not a form a self-hatred or internalized racism but can represent one way in which the black man can use a fantasy that may or may not be his own for empowerment. Such ambivalences of fantasy catalyzed by Van Vechten's interracial representation give a more complex poignancy to the notion of being "in bed with the enemy."

The complexity of the relationships between interracialism, homoeroticism, and fantasy as I have posed them here, calls into question the very validity of representation as definitive evidence of social and/or psychic truth. As cultural constructs created from elements of fantasy and social reality in varying proportion, Van Vechten's "fetish and fantasy" photos speak to the very problem of trusting representation as evidence of an author's moral, political, or ideological convictions. Fantasy is just that, and is not reality even though both are usually based on each other. In the case of Van Vechten, based on his relationship to the straight and gay African American communities and his engagement in modernist primitivism, one must question what pleasures and cultural/political agendas are being played out on all sides. I suppose that the problem is not so much about being able to fetishize, primitivize, racialize, or eroticize—we all do that—but rather who is doing it and why. It is this interrogation that alerts me to the organic and unfixed quality of Van Vechten's representation, especially in its conjunction with homoerotic desire and race.

My intention in this essay has not been to present Van Vechten as yet another disturbing figure of early modernism. What I have tried to do with his "fetish and fantasy" photographs is to show how they operated then and now as visualized psychic and social expression that make us frustratingly aware of the ambivalences and complexities involved when racial difference and homoerotic desire collide. Van Vechten's "fetish and fantasy" images give food for thought as to how we might incorporate these ambivalences and complexities into determining the intensity and quality of our real gay and interracial social lives.

Van Vechten's fractured complexity as an individual, in addition to his multiple identities as writer, collector, photographer, and philanthropist, make his life, work, and intentions fascinating and rewarding avenues of future investigation and analysis. As an important figure in early twentieth-century modernist thought and practice, Van Vechten lives up to our expectations in that "the woof of his thought is a charming destroyal of all accepted standards, the web of his thinking is a delicate but constructive anarchy."[78] "Web of thinking" and "constructive anarchy" are indeed appropriate descriptions for Van Vechten's brand of modernity, for what his images do if anything are to keep us continually confused and conflicted.

NOTES

This essay is a revised version of a paper presented at the groundbreaking "Black Nations/Queer Nations?: Lesbian and Gay Sexualities in the African Diaspora" conference held in New York City in March 1995. I would like to thank Martin Duberman, Jonathan Weinberg, and Margaret Vendryes for their leads, comments, and insightful revelations about Van Vechten.

1. On Covarrubias and his contributions to the Harlem Renaissance, see David Levering Lewis, *When Harlem Was in Vogue* (New York: Oxford University Press, 1981); Nathan Irvin Huggins, *Harlem Renaissance* (London: Oxford University Press, 1971); Adriana Williams, *Covarrubias* (Austin: University of Texas Press, 1994); Covarrubias's drawing is part of a sequence of a collection called "Negro Drawings" published in 1927. It was Van Vechten who played a significant role in launching Covarrubias's career as a caricaturist.

2. Keith F. Davis, *The Passionate Observer* (Kansas City, MO: Hallmark Cards, 1993), 13.

3. Huggins, 93.

4. Ibid., 94.

5. Susan Sontag, *On Photography* (New York: Doubleday/Anchor, 1989), 14.

6. True to the history of forced invisibility and nonconsequentiality of black and gay lives in America, the biography of Van Vechten's most used black model, Juante [Allan] Meadows, goes unrecorded whereas the career and life of Van Vechten's most favored white model, Hugh Laing, is most thoroughly documented. Out of an enormous number of correspondences, Juante Meadows was mentioned in only one of Van Vechten's letters: see Bruce Kellner, ed., *Letters of Carl Van Vechten* (New Haven: Yale University Press, 1987), 180. These images are all located in the uncatalogued Van Vechten collection at the Beinecke Rare Book and Manuscript Library at Yale University.

7. For a more apologetic approach to white patronage, see Jeffrey C. Stewart, "Black Modernism and White Patronage," *The International Review of African American Art*, 11, no. 3 (1994): 43–46. Also see Huggins and Lewis for more condemnatory views of white patronage as negative influence on African American art, artists, and culture.

8. Mercer's essays on the subject have appeared in various sources. In 1994, he incorporated them into a single chapter entitled "Reading Racial Fetishism: The Photographs of Robert Mapplethorpe," in his book *Welcome to the Jungle: New Positions in Black Cultural Studies* (New York: Routledge, 1994), 171–219. This is the source I will use throughout this essay. Mercer mentions Van Vechten in his writings, referencing him only as "white photographer of black literati in the Harlem Renaissance." Apparently he was unaware of the photographer's interracial nudes.

9. There is strong evidence to indicate that his marriage to the actress Fania Marinoff was an arrangement of convenience; see Kellner.

10. Mercer, 190.

11. See Whitney Davis, "HomoVision: A Reading of Freud's 'Fetishism,'" *Genders* 15 (Winter 1992): 86–118.

12. Ibid., 110. Very few scholars have tackled the racial fetish as a theoretical and social problem/phenomenon, let alone within the confines of representation. This is, however, beginning to change, particularly with the works of contemporary cultural critics such as Stuart Hall, Homi K. Bhabha, and Kobena Mercer.

13. Mercer, 190.

14. W. Davis, 88.

15. In his writing as well as photography, Van Vechten used the black head and body to promote an antibourgeois stance inherent in the rebelliousness of early twentieth-century modernism—a position "indulgent of free love, feminism, homosexuality, the mixture of 'high' and 'low' culture, and support of abstraction and Cubism"; see Stewart, 43–46.

16. "Homovision" is a term I am borrowing from Whitney Davis and refers to a consideration of the formation and role of homosexuality and homoerotic desire in fetishism and fetishistic practice. See Whitney Davis, "HomoVision: A Reading of Freud's 'Fetishism,'" *Genders* 15 (Winter 1992): 86–118.

17. For a highly nuanced discussion of the intermachinations of these phenomena, see Hal Foster, *Recodings: Art, Spectacle, Cultural Politics* (Seattle: Bay

Press, 1985); and Homi K. Bhabha, "The Other Question: Stereotype, Discrimination and the Discourse of Colonialism," *The Location of Culture* (London: Routledge, 1994), 66–84.

18. On how the stereotype works on and in representation, see Richard Dyer, *The Matter of Images* (London: Routledge, 1993).

19. Foster, 198.

20. On skin fetishism as an articulation of the "ethnic signifier," see Stuart Hall, "Pluralism, Race, and Class in Caribbean Society," *Race and Class in Post-Colonial Societies* (Paris: UNESCO, 1977), 150–82; also see Victor Burgin, "Photography, Fantasy, Fiction," *Screen*, 26 (Spring 1980), reprint in Victor Burgin, ed., *Thinking Photography* (London: Macmillan, 1982), 177–216; Bhabha.

21. "Open secret" is a term used by Eve Sedgwick in her assessment of the clandestine and unarticulated knowledge of the homosexual and the homoerotic within homosocial structures; see Eve Kosofsky Sedgwick, *Between Men: English Literature and Male Homosocial Desire* (New York: Columbia University Press, 1985).

22. Bhabha, 80. This characterization is problematic in many respects. It assumes in its gender specificity that fetishism and fetishistic practice are the exclusive domain of men. It does not allow for the possibility of women as having fantasies of mastery and control.

23. The theoretical and psychoanalytic sources on fetishism are numerous. To start, see William Pietz, "The Problem of the Fetish," *Res*, 9 (1985): 5–17; 13 (1987): 23–45; and 16 (1988): 105–23. See Freud's "Project for a Scientific Psychology" (1895), *Standard Edition of the Complete Psychological Works of Sigmund Freud*, ed. James Strachey et al. (London: Hogarth Press, 1953–74), 24 vols.; 1: 295–387; especially pt. 1, secs. 1–18; Sigmund Freud, "Fetishism" (1927), *Standard Edition*, 21: 147–57; Christian Metz, *Psychoanalysis and Cinema* (London, 1982), ch. 5; Christian Metz, "Photography and Fetish," *October*, 34 (Fall 1985): 81–90; Steve Neale, "The Same Old Story: Stereotypes and Differences," *Screen Education* (1979/80): 32–33, 33–37; Jean Baudrillard, "Fetishism and Ideology," *For a Critique of the Political Economy of the Sign* (1981); Emily Apter and William Pietz, eds., *Fetishism as Cultural Discourse* (Ithaca: Cornell University Press, 1993).

24. Bhabha, 80.

25. Mercer, 177.

26. For a theoretical perspective on the author as projection, see Michel Foucault, "What Is an Author?," *Language, Counter-Memory, Practice*, trans. Donald F. Bouchard and Sherry Simon (Oxford: Blackwell, 1977).

27. The idea for using patterned backdrops as environments was borrowed from fine art paintings and became an important signature element in Van Vechten's photographic style; see Kellner, 187; also see Keith F. Davis, 35, note 52.

28. Quoted from Italo Calvino, *Difficult Loves*, trans. William Weaver (San Diego: Harcourt Brace Jovanovich, 1984), 228–29. Cited in Jefferson Hunter, *Image and Word: The Interaction of Twentieth-Century Photographs and Texts* (Cambridge, MA: Harvard University Press, 1987), 115.

29. On the history of minstrelsy see Robert C. Toll, *Blacking Up: The Minstrel Show in Nineteenth Century America* (New York: Oxford University Press, 1974);

on the theoretical links between race, the mask, and sexuality, see Eric Lott, *Love and Theft: Blackface Minstrelsy and the American Working Class* (New York: Oxford University Press, 1993).

30. Mable Dodge Luhan, *Intimate Memories, III* (New York: Harcourt Brace and World, 1936), 79–80.

31. Houston Baker, Jr., *Modernism and the Harlem Renaissance* (Chicago: University of Chicago Press, 1987), 17.

32. Ibid., 17.

33. Ibid., 15.

34. Sexual exploitation is implicit in ethnographic photography. For example, in early photos for *National Geographic*, images of Africans (in particular women) focused upon their state of nakedness in nature. For a history of the early use of photography in ethnographic and anthropological practice, see Elizabeth Edwards, ed., *Anthropology and Photography, 1860–1920* (New Haven: Yale University Press, 1992).

35. W. Davis, 108–9.

36. Mercer, 188, 191; W. Davis, 87.

37. W. Davis, 87.

38. Ibid., 103–6.

39. Ibid., 106.

40. Ibid., 107.

41. Mercer, 190.

42. Mercer, 184.

43. Marianna Torgovnick, *Gone Primitive: Savage Intellects, Modern Lives* (Chicago: University of Chicago Press, 1990), 111.

44. Hal Foster, "Primitive Scenes," *Critical Inquiry*, 20, no. 1 (Autumn 1993): 83–85.

45. Torgovnick, 151.

46. For more nuanced discussions of colonialism and related orientalist/exoticist practices, See Edward Said, *Orientalism* (New York: Vintage, 1979); Homi K. Bhabha, "The Other Question: The Stereotype and Colonial Discourse," *Screen*, 24 (6) (November-December, 1983): 18–36; James Clifford, "On Orientalism," *The Predicament of Culture* (Cambridge, MA: Harvard University Press, 1988); also see Torgovnick, 252–53, note 17.

47. On these preoccupations in primitivist practice, see Foster, "Primitive Scenes"; also see Homi K. Bhabha, "Interrogating Identity," *The Location of Culture* (London: Routledge, 1994), 40–65.

48. Torgovnick, 189.

49. Although difficult to verify, it is very likely that these two photographs, as well as some others, were all shot in the same session.

50. Quoted in Huggins, 100.

51. Mercer, 173.

52. Even though gender difference is a significant factor in the dynamics of spectatorship and representation, it is important to remark that these images were not intended for female spectatorship. Because of this, I only consider here the gay male subject position. The complexities and scope of the issues arising out of

straight female or lesbian spectatorship of gay male interracial imagery is not only mind-boggling, but unmanageable in scope for this essay.

53. This kind of complicated dynamic occurs with straight pornography in which the heterosexual male can transpose himself into lesbian scenes.

54. This was the source of Mercer's initial angry response to Mapplethorpe's black male nudes; see Mercer, 193.

55. In this regard, my own subject position response was reinforced by other African American gay men at the Black Nations/Queer Nations? conference who, upon seeing several of these "fetish and fantasy" photographs, expressed subjective sentiments of an aroused excitement and erotic stimulation that these images stirred in them.

56. Mercer, 209.

57. Within the discourse of primitivism, homosexuality is often linked with castration and cannibalism; see Torgovnick.

58. See Stewart, 45, also see Eric Garber, "A Spectacle of Color," in Martin Duberman et al., eds., *Hidden from History: Reclaiming the Gay and Lesbian Past* (New York: Meridian, 1989), 318–31; George Chauncey, *Gay New York* (New York: Basic, 1994), 227–67.

59. David Bergman, *Gaiety Transfigured: Gay Self-Representation in American Literature* (Madison: University of Wisconsin Press, 1991), 176.

60. Ibid., 176–77.

61. Interestingly, the function of Locke's sexual politics in the formation and fostering of a racialist art for African Americans has never been even remotely considered in the literature. See Jeffrey Stewart, ed., *The Critical Temper of Alain Locke* (New York: Garland, 1983).

62. Huggins, 90.

63. In one of his letters, Van Vechten wrote: "Also as I went out William Pickens caught my arm to ask me who the 'young man in evening clothes' was. It was Bruce Nugent, of course, with his usual open chest and uncovered ankles. I suppose soon he will be going without trousers"; see Kellner, "Letter to Langston Hughes," (11 May 1927), 95–96. Of course, Van Vechten photographed Nugent, who became one of his "collected" acquaintances. Nugent's ("out")rageous personality supposedly limited his audience and career; see David Levering Lewis, "Harlem My Home," in Mary Schmidt Campbell et al., *Harlem Renaissance: Art of Black America* (New York: Abrams, 1987), 71.

64. As far as I know, only Eric Garber has observed and acknowledged that "Richmond Barthé's gay sensibility was evident throughout his work." See Garber, 330; also see Eric Garber, "'Tain't Nobody's Bizness: Homosexuality in Harlem in the 1920s," The Advocate, 13 (May 1982): 39–43, 53; also, it should come as no surprise that Barthé and Nugent were close friends and shared an interest in combining racial identity with homosexual identity.

65. Apparently, Barthé found Van Vechten to be an indispensable ally when he was in need of black male models. This is substantiated by an Easter card dated March 21, 1940, in which Barthé thanked Van Vechten for sending him nude photographs of Allan Juante Meadows—the black model used in most of Van Vechten's "fetish and fantasy" photos. See Van Vechten Collection-Correspon-

dence from Richmond Barthé, Beinecke Library, Yale University. The card says: "Many, many thanks for the photographs of Allen Jnanlejegarhadutha [sic] Meadows. The photographs are grand but I'm sorry he couldn't relax more." Barthé refers here to the tension and stiffness detected in Meadows's demeanor. Barthé later created a statue of Meadows as a nude piper (whereabouts unknown). I would like to thank Margaret Vendryes for bringing this reference to my attention and with sharing with me her dissertation research on Barthé.

66. Barthé was very religious and declared that his work was "all wrapped up with my search for God. I am looking for God inside of people . . . ," Gary A. Reynods and Beryl J. Wright, eds., *Against the Odds: African-American Artists and the Harmon Foundation* (Newark, NJ: The Newark Museum, exhibition catalogue, 1989), 154. Also see Winslow Ames, "Richmond Barthé," *Parnassus*, 12 (March 1940): 10–17; Margaret Breunig, "Sculptures by Barthé," *Art Digest*, 19 (1 April 1945): 56; Howard Devree, "Exhibition Review: Richmond Barthé," *Magazine of Art*, 32 (1934): 232; William H. A. Moore, "Richmond Barthé—Sculptor," *Opportunity* (November 1928): 334; "The Passing Shows: Richmond Barthé," *Art News*, 44 (1 April 1945): 28; "Sculpture of Unusual High Quality by Richmond Barthé," *Art News*, 37 (18 March 1939): 9; "The Story of Barthé," *Art Digest*, 13 (3 January 1939): 20.

67. Bergman, 177.

68. Torgovnick, 228.

69. The pervasive presence and social significance of a visible homosexual enclave in New York during the early part of the twentieth century has been acknowledged by Garber in "A Spectacle in Color" as well as by Chauncey in *Gay New York*. In several of Van Vechten's letters, love affairs with other men are casually mentioned. On the pornographic scrapbooks, see Jonathan Weinberg, " 'Boy Crazy,' Carl Van Vechten's Queer Collection," *The Yale Journal of Criticism*, 7, no. 2 (1994): 25–49. Also of note is the fact that during the 1930s and 1940s it was especially within the entertainment enclaves of the theater and the dance where a vibrant black and white pre-Stonewall gay subculture emerged and thrived.

70. We know that in his role as lord over the "glitterati" of New York, Van Vechten was involved in the life of the black gay community in Harlem. He attended and officiated over many of the drag balls held there such as those at the Rockland Palace Casino and the Savoy; see Bruce Kellner, *Carl Van Vechten and the Irreverent Decades* (Norman: University of Oklahoma Press, 1968), 201.

71. See James Crump, "Photography As Agency: George Platt Lynes and the Avant-Garde," in George Platt Lynes, *Photographs from the Kinsey Institute* (New York: Bulfinch Press, 1993), 137–47.

72. Letter from George Platt Lynes to Bernard Perlin (24 October 1952); quoted in Crump, 152.

73. Letter from George Platt Lynes to Bernard Perlin (6 January 1953); quoted in Crump, 154.

74. To my knowledge, these photos have never been published and remain in the archives of the Kinsey Institute for Sexual Research.

75. Unfortunately, Van Vechten does not mention Lynes's photographs in any

of his copious correspondences. Nor does Lynes ever mention seeing works by Van Vechten. This does not mean, however, that the exchange never happened. The secretive, underground nature of homoerotic and interracial linkages must have fueled these kinds of exchanges. Also, the private and closeted nature of Van Vechten's visual imagery showing a coupling of homoerotic and interracial desire, is consistent with his attempts to fashion and control his public and private persona.

76. Formidable resistance came from W. E. B. DuBois who was the most important and influential leader among the black middle class. DuBois, deeply disturbed and troubled by Van Vechten's salacious novel *Nigger Heaven* (1926), decried any artistic focus on black sexuality. He criticized Van Vechten's approach to black sexuality, labeling the novel a "caricature of half-truths . . . astonishing and wearisome hodgepodge of laboriously stated facts, quotations and expressions illuminated here and there with something . . . near . . . cheap melodrama"; quoted in the *Crisis* (December 1926). Nathan Huggins points out that Harold Cruse, in his *The Crisis of the Negro Intellectual* (New York: Morrow, 1967), 35, believes that blacks and Harlem paid a high price for Van Vechten's patronage. Langston Hughes, James W. Johnson, and Van Vechten's biographers think he gave more than he got; see Huggins, *Harlem Renaissance*, 314, note 8.

77. Mercer, 141.

78. Quoted in preface to Edward Lueders, Carl Van Vechten, (New York: Twayne, 1965), n.p.

PART THREE

Dissident Sexualities:
Historical Perspectives

SEVEN

Love + Marriage = Death

Sander L. Gilman

THE PROBLEM: THE EIGHTEENTH CENTURY

At least in a lesser-known variation of Jonathan Swift's oft-quoted poem, Strephon loves Chloe to no little degree because:

> Her graceful mien, her shape and face,
> Confessed her of no mortal race:
> And then, so nice, and so genteel;
> Such cleanliness from head to heel:
> No humours gross, or frowzy steams,
> No noisome whiffs, or sweaty streams,
> Before, behind, above, below,
> Could from her taintless body flow.[1]

Pure Chloe, "a goddess dyed in grain/Was unsusceptible of stain" (457), until, of course the wedding night, when Chloe having drunk "twelve cups of tea" needed "to leak" (459). Strephon hears his pure beloved "as from a mossy cliff distil" and "cried out, 'Ye gods, what sound is this?/ Can Chloe, heavenly Chloe piss?' " (459).

Strephon seems to understand the actual physicality of his object of desire when the smell of Chloe's urine "struck his nose: He found her, while the scent increased/As mortal as *himself* at least" (459). For Strephon, all's well that end's well, for his realization of Chloe's physicality enables the marriage to be consummated.[2] And yet the happy end in which Strephon seems to have overcome his idealization of Chloe's body disguises a repressed moment.

What is missing with Strephon's realization that Chloe is a physical human being is the possibility of disease. Chloe, as the object of desire, may be "human" to the degree that she micturates, but the border of that "humanity" lies at the impossible notion that she has a sexually transmitted disease. Once this repressed fear is articulated the reader can understand what has been left unstated in Jonathan Swift's often-cited discussion of Strephon and Chloe. For Swift, the idea of Chloe's infection is impossible to both the writer and his creation, the lover. Yet Swift wrote another satiric poem about another union that, like the poem of Strephon and Chloe, stresses the physical but without that pair's happy end. Indeed, it is a poem in which the idea of infection is necessary to this vision of the marriage bed. It is not a pseudo-Arcadian marriage but a May-December marriage of a fifty-two year old minister and "a handsome yound imperious girl" (243). The minister desires the younger woman as a sign of the power of his old age; she desires her marriage to provide her with social status. The result is quite different from the marriage of Strephon and Chloe. Here, the new wife cuckolds the minister over and over again after the wedding night, using the same artifice of beauty employed by Chloe ("She at the glass consults her looks" [243]) yet to a much different end. "But now, though scarce a twelve month married,/His lady has twelve times miscarried,/The cause, alas, is quickly guessed,/The town has whispered round the jest" (245). His sweet wife has gonorrhea and infects him, shortening his life. He has been constantly cuckolded, and her lovers' having given her "a plenteous draught/Then fled, and left his horn behind" (245). The cuckold's horn is associated with the sexual transmission of disease in the marriage bed.

Thus the minister "Gets not an heir, but gets a fever;/A victim to the last essays/Of vigour in declining days. He dies" (246). And the young widow immediately turns to the rake with whom she has been cavorting and whom she marries "for his face":

> And only coat of tarnished lace;
> To turn her naked out of doors,
> And spend her jointure on his whore:
> But for a parting present leave her
> A rooted pox to last forever. (247)

Her attraction for the physical being of her lover kills her as certainly as the minister's attraction for her beauty has killed him. Strephon will not die of love; the minister certainly has. Chloe's physicality is represented by her micturation, the widow's immorality by a case of syphilis. Death enters the frame only in the latter case.

The underlying difference between these two readings of the frailty of the flesh and its relationship to the madness of love has to do with the absolute location of danger in the form of sexually transmitted disease. Swift has split the idealized, "good" love object from the dangerous, "bad" love object. Each is idealized for different reasons and yet this division assures that the "good" love object can never be infectious. The passion that true love generates is the guarantee that this is the case. The "bad" object will always be the source of illness. The calculation that leads to such a choice of sexual object may blind the lover to this, as in the case of the minister, but it is not true passion. In this arbitrary dichotomy, passion protects. In a recent book, Otto Kernberg notes:

Sexual passion reactivates and contains the entire sequence of emotional states that assure the individual of hiw own, his parents', the entire world of objects' "goodness" and the hope of the fulfillment of love despite frustration, hostility, and ambivalence. Sexual passion assumes the capacity for continued empathy with—but not merger into—a primitive state of symbiotic fusion (Freud's "oceanic feeling"), the excited reunion of closeness with mother at a stage of self-object differentiation, and the gratification of oedipal longings in the context of overcoming feelings of inferiority, fear, and guilt regarding sexual functioning. Sexual passion is the facilitating core of a sense of oneness with a loved person as part of adolescent romanticism and, later, mature commitments to the beloved partner in the face of the realistic limitations of human life, the unavoidability of illness, decay, deterioration, and death.[3]

Kernberg's comment on the nature of sexual passion as that which provides access to the complexity of the object of desire's reality implies the splitting of the "good" object of desire from the "bad" and dangerous one. Yet Kernberg, too, splits the anxiety about venereal disease from his analysis of sexual passion. Why is such a split necessary? Strephon's passion constructs Chloe as the idealized object of desire, and his realization of her physicality enables him to evolve into an awareness of her humanity (and her mortality). But his very creation of her as the "good" object blinds him from the possibility of becoming aware of the object of desire's potential for disease and for betrayal. The death that Kernberg evokes is a "natural" death, that of an old age together with the beloved, not the horrors of sexually transmitted disease passed from the beloved. The "bad" object brings death into the immediate present in the act of betraying the marriage bed. Both are rooted in the "love madness" that shapes the idealized object of desire. This is also true of the minister, who married a beautiful, young girl as a sign of his station. He is blind to her potential for destruction because he wishes to believe his own image of his object of desire. Swift is careful to show that this "love madness" has corrupt, material origins (in contrast to that of Strephon) and that this makes it impossible for him to recognize the betrayal that he experiences. Strephon's "love madness" leads to an acknowledgment of Chloe's physicality and yet such a move from unquestioned idealization to the "good" love object blinds him to her potential for disease and betrayal.

Swift splits the idealization of the love object ("love madness") into a "positive" world in which nonmaterial desire, with its blindness, gives way to insight and reproductive sexuality and a "negative" world in which desire for status, with its stress on the material, leads to blindness and death. Swift, in most things more satirical than his contemporaries (and ourselves) is unable, even in an ironic tone, to imagine Chloe as even potentially the source of illness and death. The pure beloved can be a human being even with all of those physical needs that we deem unspeakable because they seem to violate the imagined purity of the beloved. The (male) lover, Swift shows in the tale of Strephon and Chloe, cannot simultaneously hold two antagonistic thoughts about one's beloved—the first, a total idealization of the object of desire and, the second, the notion that the idealized individual possesses all of the mundane realities of human physicality including the potential for disease. There are limits in Western culture to the internal image of imagined purity. As human beings our culture shapes us to understand urine and excrement as disgusting, but with this understanding of the disgusting nature of excretion we also come to understand excrement as separate from us. We enter into human society through the labeling of inherent aspects of our own body as repellent and different from us.

Quite different is our anxiety about disease and its location. If excrement is always separate from us, disease always seeks to enter us; it lurks within us; it penetrates us from outside, like the "bad" lover. She (and in Swift's world the object of desire is always gendered "feminine") represents the anxiety about castration translated into a form of syphilophobia. In locating the source of disgust beyond ourselves, we seem to free the object of desire from not only the physical aspects of the body but from being the source of any illness. How can the one I love hurt me, especially through the very act of love? And being outside of our imagined selves, the "good" and the "bad" objects are clearly separated in our fantasy. Only a "bad" object will want to and is able to hurt me.

The division of "good" and "bad" objects of desire may be necessary psychologically, because it is impossible in reality. There is no way of separating the potential for infection and the potential or actual violation of the marriage bed from the idealized object of desire. We cannot, as Swift does, locate danger only in the materiality of the "bad" woman as the source of illness. Only in sexual passion, the domination of the lover by his or her fantasy of the object of desire as "love madness," is it possible to construct an object of desire that refuses to link the physicality of the lover as approachable, real, and tangible, with the possibility for disease, infection, and death. "Love madness" or sexual passion may thus be a necessary quality of our construction of the object of desire. For the idealized object of desire must essentially be without stain. When we imagine the object we love, we suspend all images of disgust. And yet it is the repression of our own potential for infection and death that colors the object of desire.

Sex, with implied risk for the male and its focus on the corrosive nature of the female genitalia, is as marked in early modern culture by disgust as much as is excretion—if not more. In his account of Strephon's sexual passion, Swift sees this learning process about the idealized other as the true good, for the "Beauty [that] must beget Desire" (460) must give way to the sense of the object of desire as human. It is this inner fascination that can cause sexual excitement but which can also block its consumma- tion.[4] Judith P. Butler notes that " 'sex' is an ideal construct which is forcibly materialized through time."[5] Such constructions are a "process of materialization that stabilizes over time to produce the effect of bound- ary fixity and surface we call matter" (9). Such boundaries are those between fear or disgust and pleasure but also those potentially between excretion and disease.

Early in Freud's work, he restates the tension between the physicality of the object of desire and its idealized manifestation. And Freud's re- statement of the moment is much less ironic than Swift's:

it is only in the rarest instances that the psychical valuation that is set on the sexual object, as being the goal of the sexual instinct, stops short of its genitals. The appreciation extends to the whole body of the sexual object and tends to involve every sensation derived from it. The same overvaluation spreads into the psychological sphere: the subject becomes, as it were, intellectually infatuated (that is, his powers of judgment are weakened) by the mental achievements and perfection of the sexual object and he submits to the latter's judgments with credulity. Thus the credulity of love becomes an important, if not the most fundamental, source of authority. (*Standard Edition [SE]* 7:150)

"The credulity of love" or "love madness" weakens rationality and suspends judgment. The love object is perfect and such perfection excludes any notion of disease. Indeed, the idealized "genitals" that are the focus of such a passion are imagined genitalia that only give pleasure and cannot be diseased. It is the "overvaluation" of the body of the object of desire that clouds the lover's judgment and "perfects" the object of desire without those aspects that lead to disgust. Perfection here is a culturally constructed category which excludes everything that could evoke disgust.

Such an "overvaluation" places the body of the object desired as beyond the limits of the censuring mechanisms of society that make us read our bodily functions as corrupting and corrupt. It is the basis for the construction of the role of both the masochist, whose pathological state confuses the "real" object of desire with the object of desire who punishes because of desire, and the idealized object of desire, who is beyond physicality. It is difficult enough for Western society to keep simultaneously in mind the double function of the genitalia, as reproductive and excretory organs, except in St. Augustine's Pauline view of the body as inherently corrupt or, pathologically, as an aspect of the act of sexual fetishization. It seems almost impossible to add to this the idea that the genitalia can also be the source of disease and yet this comes to play a major factor in the representation of the female genitalia as the source of danger for the male in the fantasy of the eighteenth century.

In the eighteenth century, Johann Wolfgang von Goethe had his fictional protagonist Wilhelm Meister "bound by invisible bonds" to his Marianne after he observed her urinating. William Wordsworth's response to this scene in the novel was to be "struck with such disgust that he flung the book out of his hand, would never look at it again, and declared that surely no English lady would ever read such work" and/or so expose herself?[6] Even imagining a fictional character seeing his beloved urinating evokes Wordsworth's disgust. What is unstated is the danger that is evoked here by the genitalia—for the disgust associated with observing the beloved's micturation reveals the dangerous genitalia of the woman. For the male they are symbolically dangerous because of the evocation of castration anxiety in the male observer, but this generalized anxiety in the eighteenth century takes the concrete form of the anxiety about sexually transmitted disease and its impact on the male. Thus these texts, written by males, stress or repress the potential for infection as a sign of the anxiety generated by the physicality of the woman's body.

In Swift's world, the minister's infection is the result of hiw own desire to possess that which transgresses against the norms of his culture. Here, the disgust represented in Swift's poem is aimed not only at the infected and infecting woman but at the violation of the marriage bed by the materiality of both parties, a violation certainly evoked by the literary trope (reaching back to Chaucer) of disgust toward the May-December relationship. He becomes the masochist who has created his own masochistic scenario. He has created an object of desire, who, however, punishes him through her sexuality, the same quality that he found most attractive in her youthfulness.

Such disgust is seen, of course, only from Swift's male perspective. Roy Porter and Lesley Hall point out that married women tolerated, or at least were forced to tolerate, their husbands' violation of the marriage bed. They quote from a report by James Boswell that one of his female friends would have rather had her husband take "a transient fancy for a girl, or being led by on's companions after drinking to an improper place" than have had her husband keep "a particular woman."[7] Here, the anxiety about the loss of status as the object of desire seems to have outweighed the anxiety about sexually transmitted disease. Given the ease with which men could remove themselves from the obligations of the family, the danger of the mistress to the wife's status seemed greater than the risk to her person. Thus women, too, could repress the anxiety about sexually transmitted diseases that permeated their society.

The woman as sexual object in the first poem by Swift we discussed, the tale of Chloe and Strephon, may be imagined pissing but not infected. And yet certainly the potential for such a state of illness exists in all human beings. "Natural" functions such as excretion that we label as disgusting are contrasted with the "unnatural" transmission of sexually transmitted diseases in the marriage bed in the boundary we draw between the "good" and "bad" objects of desire. This boundary has no equivalent reality in the world. Those aspects, such as excretion, that society labels as shameful and disgusting, are, as Freud notes, forces that stand in opposition and resistance to the libido (*SE* 7:159). And yet even more disgusting, as Freud illustrates in the case of Dora, for example, is Western society's response to sexually transmitted diseases which are also intimately tied to the libido.

The anxiety about sexually transmitted disease is linked to the fear of the shattering of the "good" object of desire. The disgust arises from the image that the marriage bed has been violated and this heightens the sense of outrage at the destruction of the "good" beloved. The difference between Strephon and Swift's minister is that Strephon benefits in his learning about the "natural." He and Chloe will consummate their marriage and reproduce. His "good" object remain "good." Neither adultery nor cuckoldry is possible in their world. The minister is destroyed by never acknowledging his unnatural act—the materiality that was responsible for his May-December marriage. He is never aware that this act is the cause of his pain and his death. Shame and pain are the two moments that separate the two actions—excrement is, at least according to Dean Swift, natural, but disease, specifically, sexually transmitted disease within marriage, is unnatural, like the marriage in which it occurs. It is evil because it destroys the male and *his* potential progeny. The question of male anxiety about identity and bodily integrity is central to this trope.[8]

The scholarly literature on the violation of the marriage bed, on adultery, at least from Edward Westermarck's creation of the study of marriage as the model for sociological study to the present, has focused on the problems of inheritance.[9] Reproduction and property were linked and the violation of the marriage bed was reduced to the problem of lineage. Adultery was thus merely a problem of defining who would or at least who should inherit property and name. With few exceptions, the discussions of the literary representations of adultery have followed this economic model.[10] I argue that there is a second, perhaps more immediate, problem addressed in the anxiety about the violation of the marriage bed, and that is the anxiety about disease and death. Adultery and virginity become two linked concepts. For the perfection of the virgin also "guarantees" the absence of sexually transmitted illness as well as the ability of the male to pass his name and property down to his "real" heir.[11]

Sex, as Roy Porter and Lesley Hall remind us in their study of sexual knowledge in England, is closely bound to the idea of marriage in European culture: "From the seventeenth century, marriage recurs as a central element in discussions of sexuality. Emphasis on marriage may represent a concession to moral norms: 'for married only' can cover a multitude of explicit detail ... [they are] presented as being for the benefit of the married, in fact a sound support for monogamy in a dangerous age."[12] Sexuality, or at least the discourse about sexuality, can be fixed within the discussions of marriage. Porter and Hall carefully illustrate how knowledge (and myths) about the physicality of sexuality, and knowledge (and myths) about infection come to be mutually understood and yet constantly separated within the British discourse of uxoriousness. Such a discourse about monogamy masks the anxiety about the violation of the boundary set about sex, in which it is permitted and healthy within marriage and dangerous and potentially infection outside of marriage. This myth needs to be reinforced by society to preserve within marriage the one "safe" space for sexuality.

Thus we have framed our problem—the special question of love, fantasy, trust, and belief in "marriage" as the prophylaxis against disease. Here, marriage comes to be understood as defined by ideas of fidelity and trust as well as love. But it is also the creation of the illusion of the perfection of the object of desire, an illusion which can reach the stage of madness when it does not mature in the light of the realities of human desire, physiology, and temperament. How very problematic this is can be judged by Dean Swift's second poem in which the death of the old man is caused *by* his marriage—admittedly in the views of the eighteenth century, an imbalanced marriage, a marriage that was "diseased." Yet both of these are readings of a masochistic scenario in which the lover creates an idealized object of desire: Strephon, his faultless Chloe; the minister, his youthful bride. Each is "betrayed": Strephon learns that his bride is physical as she urinates; the minister ignores his being cuckolded and becomes infected. These are mirror-images of the madness of love and the ability to construct an idealized object of desire in one's fantasy. Swift's first poem represses the possibility of disease; the second obsesses about it. The mutual exclusion of these two models of desire illustrate that the representation of pure desire and the healthy body must be separated from the fear of corporeal corruption of the body through sexually transmitted disease. This is coupled with a powerful moral lesson (for, Swift, too, was a minister). Swift's texts show the tension that can exist when the body of the beloved is pure but when the male can never truly know that this is the case.

'AS YOU LIKE IT': SEVENTEENTH-CENTURY VARIATIONS ON THE THEME

It is not only in the ironic world of Swift but within a strong Western tradition of comedy that madness, sex, marriage, safety, and illness are linked. It is in the world of comedy, in Shakespeare's *As You Like It*, that the worlds of life and love and death and betrayal come to be associated with the idealization of the object of desire and the problem of disgust.[13]

For Shakespeare links love, desire, physical illness, madness, and melancholy in complicated ways to provide a mirror for the folly of believing
that marriage cures all!

As You Like It is a comedy. It is a comedy that has recently been of
interest because of its complicated pattern of sexual disguise: boy actors
playing young women dressing as young men. It is a comedy, like all of
Shakespeare's comedies, about the problems of generations: how the
errors of the older generation are made good by the younger generation.
The play is, I will show, even more complicated. For it is at the same time
a play about love and a play about disease—specifically the disease syphilis, which both comes from and results in melancholy and which is
associated with the love madness that is at the center of this comedy.

The plot of the comedy is rather simple. Rosalind, the daughter of the
deposed Duke Senior, and her cousin Celia flee into the forest of Arden
disguised as Ganymede and his sister Aliena. There they meet Orlando
who has also fled from the "envious court" of Duke Frederick, where he,
like Rosalind, was mistrusted because his father, Sir Rowland de Boys,
was an opponent of the new duke. Rosalind and Celia take with them the
court fool Touchstone and find in the forest the men of Duke Senior's
court, among them the sad Jaques, the arch-melancholic.[14] After various
confusions all is made right: the "real" court of Duke Senior is restored,
Rosalind is betrothed to Orlando, Celia to Oliver, his brother, Touchstone
to the country maid Audrey. Only the sad Jaques remains isolated in the
forest at the close of the play.

As You Like It harbors, however, the ghost of illness much like Hamlet's
father's ghost haunts *Hamlet*. And it is an illness tied to love—both to the
idea of love as the means of creating an idealized object of desire as well
as love as that dangerous stage in which, as we have quoted Freud, the
"powers of judgment are weakened" (*SE* 7:150). Madness is caused by the
fixation on the object of desire and is also the act created by love. Madness
seems to be an illness suffered by the males in the comedy. It may seem
in its first form to be pleasant, but it is a madness nevertheless. On
entering the Forest of Arden, Touchstone and Rosalind (who is disguised
as the tall, handsome youth Ganymede) overhear the rustic lover Silvius
speak to Corin of his overwhelming love for Phebe in which his love took
the form of "many actions most ridiculous/Hast thou been drawn to by
thy fantasy?" (2, 4). Hearing this, the fool Touchstone comments on the
power of love madness to distort the realities of daily life and to make
them seem that which they are not:

I remember, when I was in love I broke my sword upon a stone and bid him take
that for coming a-night to Jane Smile; and I remember the kissing of her batlet
and the cow's dugs that her pretty chopt hands had milked; and I remember the
wooing of a peascod instead of her, from whom I took two cods and, giving her
them again, said with weeping tears "Wear these for my sake." We that are true
lovers run into strange capers; but as all is mortal in nature, so is all nature in love
mortal in folly. (2, 4)

Here is the "fantasy" about which Silvius speaks in its most comic reality.
For the object of desire that is created has nothing to do with the physical
reality of the beloved. The milk maid is confused with the objects she
touches and with all nature that becomes identified with the beloved. She
is the "good" object of desire who cannot be anything but perfect.

   This reduction of the lover to the fool has its ultimate, masochistic
expression, not in the comic world of the rustic and the fool, but in the
discourse of the court and the city. Rosalind, with her ways of the court,
identifies with the Arcadian peasant's madness: "Jove, Jove! this shepard's
passion/Is much upon my fashion." Madness and love are intertwined;
true love is the madness that creates the object of desire and yet Rosalind's
understanding of love madness and the confusion of the self with the
object of desire is cast in a quite different tone.

   In the third act (3, 2), Rosalind (still dressed as the young man Ganymede) confronts her own imagined lover, Orlando, with the charge
that he could not love Rosalind since he shows no true madness in his
physiognomy:

A lean cheek, which you have not, a blue eye and sunken, which you have not, an
unquestionable spirit, which you have not, a beard neglected, which you have not;
but I pardon you for that, for simply your having in beard is a younger brother's
revenue: then your hose should be ungartered, your bonnet unbanded, your sleeve
unbuttoned, your shoe untied and every thing about you demonstrating a careless
desolation; but you are no such man; you are rather point-device in your accoutre-
ments as loving yourself than seeming the lover of any other.

The lover can only be seen as a lover in representing madness (with the
deshabille of madness, the disorder of the body). Rosalind, in male disguise, describes the act of the creation of the object of desire as the act of
madness: "Love is merely a madness, and, I tell you, deserves as well a
dark house and a whip as madmen do: and the reason why they are not so
punished and cured is, that the lunacy is so ordinary that the whippers are
in love too. Yet I profess curing it by counsel." Here, the masochistic
scenario is stated quite directly. For male lovers should be beaten (as the

insane are imagined to be treated) to cure the symptom of their madness. Their madness is their fantasy about the nature of their female beloved. This is represented in their physicality, the disarray, and the treatment must be a whip or isolation in "a nook merely monastic." They must be made to act "love mad" as an antidote to their love madness. This will "wash your liver as clean as a sound sheep's heart, that there shall not be one spot of love in't" (3, 2).

The male lover's complaint is love madness, which arises in the liver, according to Robert Burton's discussion in *The Anatomy of Melancholy*, and is represented by a numbing of the senses as in all madness. It seems to be clearly gendered. Only men can suffer from it; only they can cure it in other men. The cure, like the illness, has as its primary symptom the inability to see the object of desire as anything but idealized. The loss of an accurate measure of the reality of the object of desire becomes the symptom that leads to other forms of madness. It is the "reality" of the female beloved that must be restored if the male is to be cured of his illness. Rosalind (as Ganymede) in her rationality mocks such male lovers and argues that they should be treated like all other mad *men* with confinement and punishment. And yet she, too, feels desire for Orlando, a desire that constructs him as her love object. Her desire may indeed represent itself as a type of love madness, in terms of the gender confusion caused by her disguise as a young man.

Madness is, however, not represented in the play only by these lovers. Love madness in the male is a positive image of insanity. It is the madness also associated with the pairing of couples in the comedy. It seems to be benign because it relates to pleasure. Yet one of the most famous mad *men* in the Shakespearean comedies, "Monsieur Melancholy" (3, 2), the sad Jaques, is the red thread that connects all aspects of the drama. We hear of the melancholy Jaques well before we meet him, when he is described as weeping for the deer, "the poor dappled fools," his companions have slaughtered. One such deer has only been wounded and seems too to weep. Jaques identifies himself with the wounded deer:

> "Poor deer," quoth he, "thou makest a testament
> As worldlings do, giving thy sum of more
> To that which had too much": then, being there alone,
> Left and abandon'd of his velvet friends,
> "Tis right": quoth he; "thus misery doth part
> The flux of company:" (2, 1)

The image of the weeping stag has its analogies in the emblem literature of the day.[15] It is the representation of damaged masculinity and also the image of the wounded cuckold, the male who has been damaged by the violation of his marriage bed. The horned stag is a figure that we have already met in Swift's poem on marriage. The cuckold is the fool who has trusted the madness of misapprehension and who truly believes in the perfection and cleanliness of the object of desire. Jaques is the male wounded by his beloved and yet the image is more complicated, as the stag over which he weeps has been wounded by his fellow male courtiers in the Forest of Arden.

The cuckold's wounding, however, is not merely the wounding of the soul but also of the body. The theme of the horn is echoed often enough in the play as to make it a leitmotif linking the forest, sexuality, and cuckoldry.[16] Thus, Touchstone comments:

A man may, if he were of a fearful heart, stagger in this attempt; for here we have no temple but the wood, no assembly but horn-beasts. But what though? Courage! As horns are odious, they are necessary. It is said, "many a man knows no end of his good": right; many a man has good horns, and knows no end of them. Well, that is the dowry of his wife; 'tis none of his own getting. Horns? Even so. Poor men alone? No, no; the noblest deer hath them as huge as the rascal. Is the single man therefore blessed? No: as a walled town is more worthier than a village, so is the forehead of a married man more honourable than the bare brow of a bachelor; and by how much defence is better than no skill, by so much is a horn more precious than to want. (3, 3)

Touchstone's ode on horns echoes in the exchange between Rosalind and Orlando in which Rosalind, still seen by Orlando as his friend Ganymede, recounts the dangers of the marriage bed in terms of the snail's "horns, which such as you are fain to be beholding to your wives for" (4, 1). Men get their "horns" from their wives' betrayals and these horns are a sign of their madness in believing the inviolability of the marriage bed. The final repetition of the theme of the horn returns to the relationship of sad Jaques to the wounded stag. As the hunters sing after the kill:

> Take thou no scorn to wear the horn;
> It was a crest ere thou wast born:
> Thy father's father wore it,
> And thy father bore it:
> The horn, the horn, the lusty horn
> Is not a thing to laugh to scorn. (4, 2)

But what is there that is dangerous about the violation of the marriage bed and its results? It is the prospect of death by syphilis, the physical result of the violation of the marriage bed. For the "velvet" on the stag's horns—that sign of spring and sexuality—is also read by Shakespeare in *Measure for Measure* as a sign of syphilitic infection, called the French pox, as well as pain and early death.[17]

Jaques has been wounded, like the horned stag, but wounded by love. He is aware that his illness may be directly caused by a woman, yet her illness has been caused by a man. For the cuckold's status is created by another male's presence in the marriage bed. His illness is syphilis and it haunts his solitary life. Jaques is a sufferer, like Hamlet, of both physical and psychological ills.[18] But his world is one that may well lend itself to a rereading. Jaques's melancholy is thus his means of reinscription through his illness. He "will through and through/Cleanse the foul body of the infected world,/If they will patiently receive my medicine" (2, 7). Cure is to be found in the madness of melancholy that sees through the madness of life. Melancholy now serves as the medicine to cure the foul body world of its infection; it is both the symptom of disease and its cure. The infection, as we have seen, seems to be the result of Jaques's "love madness," his reliance on the false belief of his lover's purity, but in the world of the Forest of Arden, Jaques's "illness" is understood as resulting from his libertine life:

DUKE SENIOR: Most mischievous foul sin, in chiding sin: For thou thyself hast been a libertine, As sensual as the brutish sting itself; And all the embossed sores and headed evils, That thou with licence of free foot hast caught, Wouldst thou disgorge into the general world. (2, 7)

Jaques has been "cuckolding" others and has been punished for it by contracting an illness. He is the libertine who has infected the marriage bed of others and has himself been infected by his actions. Sexual passion must, according to the image in the comedy, construct the pure object of desire. Jaques becomes the exemplary syphilitic in this world of love in *As You Like It*.

That Jaques is syphilitic is accepted in the critical literature on Shakespeare as early as the nineteenth century.[19] But what his syphilis means has never been explored. It is a sign of his role as the infected and the source of infection within the sexual economy of the comedy. It is also the source of his worldview, his melancholy, and his illness is in turn shaped by his manner of seeing the world. Jaques's syphilis can account for his morose version of the seven ages of man, for as David Beverage argues, "The Duke's point is well taken, for Jaques's famous "Seven Ages of Man" speech, so often read out of context, occurs in a scene that also witnesses the rescue of Orlando and Adam. As though in answer to Jaques's acid depiction of covetous old age, we see old Adam's self-sacrifice and trust in Providence. Instead of "mere oblivion," we see charitable compassion prompting the Duke to aid Orlando and Orlando to aid Adam."[20] In his soliloquy "All the world's a stage," Jaques speaks of "the lover,/Sighing like furnace, with a woeful ballad/Made to his mistress' eyebrow." This stage of love madness in the male may lead to the fullness of middle age but the syphilitic male is condemned to die in "second childishness and mere oblivion,/Sans teeth, sans eyes, sans taste, sans everything" (2, 7).

Read as the account of the progression of a syphilitic male's infection from youth through the age of infection into the dotage of tertiary Luis, or even a quicker progression into the rotting of age, Jaques's soliloquy signals the most pessimistic course of life and decay. It is a decay that is outlined in the curses of Timon of Athens who damns the inhabitants of Athens with the symptoms of syphilis (4, 1). Yet it is also an awareness of himself as infected and the source of infection, of danger. Shakespeare's syphilitics, unlike Swift's minister, become self-conscious markers of the presence of illness in the world, especially in the world of comedy.

The relationship between syphilis and melancholy is an old trope in the medical literature of the seventeenth century. Melancholy comes from syphilis, as Robert Burton notes in *The Anatomy of Melancholy*[21] or predisposes one to syphilis, as Girolamo Fracastoro, who coins the name syphilis, notes: "for those whose veins are swollen with black bile and throb with thick blood there is in their case a greater struggle and the plague clings more tenaciously.[22] In his work on contagion, Fracastoro comments that the symptoms of syphilis are melancholy, lack of appetite, thinness, and sleeplessness.[23] Yet there is more to the relationship between the two illnesses than causation. Both have their roots in the domination of Saturn in the heavens and both provide an image of character. The syphilitic, like sad Jaques, rails against his fate: " 'So someone sighing over the springtime of his life and his beautiful youth, and gazing with wild eyes down at his disfigured member, his hideous limbs and swollen face, often in his misery railed against God's cruelty, often against the stars.' "[24] Here Jaques's very monologues become a sign of the illness. And it is an illness of the marriage bed, of love madness that has disguised the dangers that lurk within love relationships. Thus in Agnolo Bronzino's *Venus, Love, and Jealousy* (1546), the sign of the viola-tion of Venus's marriage bed and her cuckolded husband Hephaistos, is the representation of the black-skinned syphilitic, in pain, his hair falling out; in its parallel piece, *Venus, Cupid, Folly, and Time* (c. 1545), it is the melancholic, in the traditional position, hand on head, into which the syphilitic is transformed.[25]

Jaques's melancholic comments identify the source of his infection as one of the "women in the city." This charge is a commonplace by the time we get to Addison and Steele's *Tatler*, published on December 7, 1710, with its "Admonition to the young Men of this Town" concerning the dangers of sexually transmitted disease for young men (and the poten-tial loss of their noses).[26] Jaques's melancholy is the result of syphilis and his libertinage and is inflicted on him because of the infections coming from a woman. But it is his love madness that caused him to be unable to distinguish between a proper object of desire (as exemplified by the lovers in *As You Like It*) and the "woman of the city." His wounding is the result of his presence in another's marriage bed. It is a sign of his false reliance on the superficial values of the "city," the place of seduction and disease.

Syphilis in the world of Shakespeare's drama is not without at least an attempted cure. The common cure for syphilis (as well as gonorrhea) during the sixteenth century was mercury. It was, as Porter and Hall note, "a 'cure' [that] many perceived as worse than the disease, unpleasant, long-drawn-out, and causing noticeable physical stigmata."[27] And Shake-speare's understanding of the implications of such treatment is clear. In *Henry V*, Pistol comments about his wife who is being treated in the hospital for syphilis: "to the spital go, And from the powdering tub of infamy/Fetch forth the lazar kite of Cressid's kind" (2, 1). The effect of mercury poisoning, using sweating baths, is similar to syphilis itself—the loss of hair, the marking of the skin, and the development of a stinking breath, that marks one as one under treatment. These are public signs. Thus, in the eighteenth century, in *Joe Miller's Jestbook*, there are a series of jokes about sore gums, constant salivation, loose teeth, and the strong metallic smell to the breath.[28]

Jaques's treatment, however, is to be different. He is the self-aware syphilitic, quite different from Swift's minister. He is aware of his dan-ger—to the "women in the city." After all of the lovers are united and the court is about to be restored, Jaques separates himself out from the world made right. He exiles himself. All of the male characters, with the exception of Jaques, have the potential for love and marriage. Yet the madness that is love, a madness that sees beyond disguise in clothing and beyond gender roles, cannot imagine the betrayal of the marriage bed.[29] And this potential violation is represented in the comedy by Jaques, who can never marry for he is marked by another madness, melancholy, that stems from his libertinage, from his indulgence in polluting sexuality. The answer to Jaques's madness and infection is the answer of the leper, whom the syphilitic still mirrors in the seventeenth century. He must be banished once order is restored. He gives all of the characters their appropriate measure of love, but he remains alone in the Forest of Arden, "at [the Duke's] abandon'd cave" (5, 4). Thus Jaques undertakes his cure of love madness, as Rosalind claims she was able to do and change the "mad humour of love to a living humour of madness; which was, to forwear the full stream of the world, and to live in a nook merely monastic" (3, 2). Here Jaques also mirrors Timon of Athens's image of withdrawing from human companionship, which he is denied as a syphilitic, and is condemned "to the woods; where he shall find/The unkindest beast more kinder than mankind" (4, 1).

But what of the three pairs of lovers united at the end with Jaques's blessing? Only Touchstone and his rustic lover are "cursed" with a short stay within the happy madness that is love. But, of course, it was also Touchstone alone who recognized the possibility of corruption within his marriage bed. He states the case for his "love" most directly in the same terms that Shakespeare used for Jaques's melancholy, the image of the horned stag:

TOUCHSTONE: Truly, and to cast away honesty upon a foul slut were to put good meat into an unclean dish.

AUDREY: I am not a slut, though I thank the gods I am foul.

TOUCHSTONE: Well, praised be the gods for thy foulness! sluttishness may come hereafter. But be it as it may be, I will marry thee. . . . Amen. A man may, if he were of a fearful heart, stagger in this attempt; for here we have no temple but the wood, no assembly but horn-beasts. But what though? Courage! As horns are odious, they are necessary. It is said, "many a man know no end of his goods:" right; many a man has good horns, and knows no end of them. Well, that is the dowry of his wife; 'tis none of his own getting. Horns? Even so. Poor men alone? No, no; the noblest deer hath them as huge as the rascal. Is the single man therefore blessed? No: as a walled town is more worthier than a village, so is the forehead of a married man more honourable than the bare brow of a bachelor; and by how much defence is better than no skill, by so much is a horn more precious than to want. (3, 3)

Audrey may be foul and disgusting but she is not a slut—at least not now. The fool Touchstone and the melancholic Jaques know that the result of the violation of the bed of love is disease and death. Here in the comedy lies the potential for betrayal, but it seems to be distanced from the other loving pairs. Shakespeare's subtlety here is quite different from Swift's anxiety. He recognizes the potential for death and sex to be closely linked. Certainly, like Swift, he sees danger in reducing passion to materiality and commerce. As Dromio of Syracuse says of a prostitute in *The Comedy of Errors*, "she is the devil's dam; and here she comes in the habit of a light wench: and thereof comes that the wenches say 'God damn me;' that's as much to say 'God make me a light wench.' It is written, they appear to men like angels of light: light is an effect of fire, and fire will burn; ergo, light wenches will burn. Come not near her" (4, 3). Death lies in the action of the unfaithful female lover. It is from her that the illness of melancholy and syphilis spreads. Yet it is also possible in the world of *As You Like It* for lovers to be infected. The prostitute is the woman of the town, but never that far from the other objects of desire in the comedy.

All the "pure" lovers are united and the royal court is restored at the conclusion of the comedy. The world turned topsy-turvy is righted again. Only Jaques remains in the Forest of Arden, now the place of exile from healthy mankind. His remaining in the forest is the end of the action but not the end of the play. Shakespeare has added a quite unusual ending: the boy actor who had played Rosalind, who was also crossdressed as a boy, appears at the conclusion of the comedy on the stage and holds her/ his epilogue as a man, warning all the young women of the town against infection by the men. "If I were a woman I would kiss as many of you as had beards that pleased me, complexions that liked me and breaths that I defied not," says the boy who has played Rosalind. Be aware of those men bearing the marks of the treatments for syphilis—bad breath, spotty skin, and thinning of hair and beard. Here, the echo of Timon of Athens's curse resounds again: "down with the nose, Down with it flat; take the bridge quite away Of him that, his particular to foresee, Smells from the general weal: make curl'd-pate ruffians bald; And let the unscarr'd brag- garts of the war Derive some pain from you" (4, 3). The smell of the syphilitic, the syphilitic's mottled skin, the loss of hair, the scarred visage, all are public signs of the disease and its mercury cure that make the syphilitic the bearer of the mark of opprobrium.

This double-edged warning states the counter lesson. For if Jaques knows that he has been infected (and will infect) through his libertinage in the city, his self-exile in the forest is also in the message that the actor/ Rosalind brings. Beware, young women, he says, of licentious men who will infect you and make you into "women of the city." The idealized state of marriage, the resolution of the sexual tensions of the comedy, sex without fear of death, is not a possibility for Jaques (or even, the epilogue whispers, for the lovers). For there are those men, Shakespeare argues in his epilogue, who still live in the cities (unlike Jaques) and can infect you. Beware of those men when you, young woman, invite them into the marriage bed. Unlike young men, you do not suffer from love madness, you can make real choices based on the signs and symptoms of your lovers. Shakespeare thus is able to accomplish what Swift could not. He shows how very slippery the idealization of the lover can be and how "love madness" can easily become the stuff of physical illness and betrayal.

CONCLUSION AND A NEW BEGINNING

The universal preoccupation with the purity of the love relationship, with the anxiety that love and marriage (or at least a permanent relationship based on the madness of love) could lead to death through infection, is a powerful trope of the present age. The new-yet-old suggestion for the control of STDs and of AIDS has again been broached—the marriage bed, celibacy, and—love. In the 1880s, the French physician Alfred Fournier had proposed marriage as the ultimate prophylaxis for syphilis.[30] Recently, the proposal has reappeared as a desire to locate safety, the safety of the idealized object of desire, in the world of marriage.[31] This medical version of the moral obligation to "Just say no" is the simple restatement of the desire for the *guaranteed* purity of the marriage bed that Shakespeare had already shown as impossible, at least in the world of the comedy. Here "love" as the cure for AIDS has become a means to assure public health.

Love has come to be a key word in the most recent public health advertising about AIDS. The Austrian AIDS organization has presented a studied series of "art" posters representing heterosexual and homosexual partners, as aestheticized Others under the motto "Protect Out of Love" (S 25319–24).[32] In the world of the public health advertising poster, "Love" is defined as caring and protecting and the "natural" extension of sexuality. For the hidden message is that the use of condoms is a sign of caring, thus removing sexuality from representation as brutal, coarse, ugly, and destructive. The pure love of the comedy is the antithesis of the sex embodied in Jaques's illness. Today, risk is represented in the broadest possible way. Thus the image of the healthy, beautiful family is central to AIDS education. The German AIDS-*Hilfe* presents a gender-balanced family (father, mother, one male and one female child) with the motto: "Because I Love You" (25182).

A parallel image is to be found on a poster aimed at Native Americans. With a male and female in silhouette with the motto "Love carefully—Preserve your heritage—Know your partner!" (25248). The elegance of the image, especially the complex calligraphy of the word *Love* points to the preservation of the "race." The "love" implied is, of course, related to sex, but it is extended to the image of preserving the group. "Love" is caring and no violation of the marriage bed is permitted, as this will impact negatively on the isolated world of the lovers. The result of such a violation of the marriage bed is death. A photograph of a shrouded body on a gurney, its feet exposed and presented to the audience in the manner of Andrea Mantegna's Christ, his feet exposed to our view, is labeled, "Don't Let Love Sweep You off Your Feet" (28181). Love comes to be a very dangerous basis for protection from disease.

In the age of AIDS, all love relationships become as suspect as in the world of *As You Like It.* Let us turn to the most recent work of the hottest (or at least the most discussed) contemporary British writers, Martin Amis. Amis's comic novels span the beginning of the age of AIDS. In his first novel, *The Rachel Papers* (1973), the teenage protagonist, Charles Highway, discovers that sex can lead to disease, gonorrhea specifically, but it seems only from someone who was foreign and "wasn't very good looking" (89). Having had sex with her on a lavatory floor, he develops an intense case of the clap. Foreignness, ugliness, and bodily functions are closely linked in Amis's protagonist's image of the "bad" love object that combines both illness and difference.

Charles Highway spots his "true love" Rachel at a party and assumes that she is Jewish because of her dark hair and eyes. When this is resolved, when she says that she is not Jewish, his love for her transcends the physical, including the question of disease. Rachel is (ironically) seen as physically perfect. "Neither of us defecated, spat, had bogeys or arses. (I wondered how she was going to explain away her first period, overdue already.) We were beautiful and brilliant and would have doubly beautiful and brilliant children. Our bodies functioned only in orgasm" (180). This mock idealization of the beloved exists until he finds "a stray pair of panties under the armchair. As I lit the fire I picked them up to kiss and sniff at. After I had been kissing and sniffing at them for a while I turned them inside out. I saw: (i) three commas of pencil-thick pubic hair, and (ii) a stripe of suede-brown shit, as big as my finger. 'Fair's fair, for Christ's sake,' I said aloud. 'They do it too' " (181).[33] Here the Swiftian awareness is an awareness of the physicality of the "good" beloved, and yet one still quite separate from the foreign girlfriend who infected him. Yet does the beloved insist that they use condoms only because she is not on the pill? Well, what of the "huge notice on the mantelpiece" of Rachel's room?: "FOR THE LOVE OF GOD DON'T LET HIM TOUCH YOU/HE HAS AN UNUSUALLY REVOLTING DISEASE" (97).

Amis's *The Rachel Papers*, with all of its subsequent scandal, is a novel of sexual self-discovery which centers on the revelation that all human beings, as sexual beings, are also dangerous to themselves and to others. Yet it also manages to create a boundary between the "good" (uninfected) and "bad" (infected) objects of desire. The characters of the novel create objects of desire and sex objects that are separate and yet are quite aware of the artificiality of these constructions. But this is, again, only within the world of the comic, where satire is the central mode of representation. "Love" makes the object of desire pure, but this purity is always suspended and held up to questioning.

In the age of AIDS, even STDs are no longer a joke, not even in satirical novels. In 1995, well into the age of AIDS, Martin Amis published his most recent novel of marriage and betrayal, *The Information*.[34] One of the central figures in the novel, Richard Tull, has decided to revenge himself on his friend, the popularly successful novelist Gwyn Barry. To do so he implements a series of minor and rather mordent attacks, one of which concerns a "fan" of Barry who has become enamored with him through his television appearances.

Barry is renowned in England or at least on English television for his "Uxoriousness," his happy and loving marriage to Lady Demeter (35, 42). Theirs was "a match made in heaven" (65). This also seems the case in Tull's often repeated statements of sexual desire for his wife Gina. Marriage is the state of perfect desire, or at least it seems, in the novel. One must remember, however, that in Britain there was still the ghost of the 1937 divorce law reform in the popular consciousness. Marriage could be annulled if one party could be shown to have married while "suffering from communicable venereal disease."[35] In Amis's novel the protagonists' marriages appear to represent the idealization of a state of marriage yet are constantly shown to be the source of danger. The anxiety about infection lurks always in the background.

Tull proposes to have the seventeen-year-old Belladonna seduce his rival Barry, in order to besmirch his friend's reputation. And Belladonna, tricked out in punk dress and black eye-liner, is indeed "deadly" (67). Hers is not the illness of literary biography which Tull is condemned to spend his time reviewing, such as that of William Devenant, who "got a terrible clap of a black handsome wench that lay in Axe-yard . . . which cost him his nose" (95). For such risks to the poets in the age of AIDS are minor. In the age of penicillin, syphilis holds few fears.

Tull fantasizes that he had acted upon Belladonna's sexual invitation and allowed her to perform fellatio upon him: "There was one favorite in particular: the kind of sexual intercourse that involved not an exchange of bodily fluids so much as a full transfer" (135). This is the image of safe sex (at least for the male). Safe sex is a major subtheme of this 1990s novel. Sex, disease, and the violation of the marriage bed have now become the theme that links eros and thanatos, love and death. For, as it turns out, in the course of the novel, Belladonna is revealed as being HIV+: "She ain't mega-well. She's *positive*, man" (339), says the boy-friend who had initially approached Tull to sell him the information about Belladonna's fantasies about his enemy. Thus the marginal attempt at muddying his name by associating him in a sexual adventure with a minor turns out to be a question of life and death. The adventures in the realm of seduction were indeed flirting with the potential for infection:

"You remember that weird little sister I brought round to see you—Bella-donna?" He waited with his head down. "What happened?"

"That would be telling now, wouldn't it."

"Naturally." He waited. "You didn't fuck *her*, did you?"

"Are you out of your mind? Or do you just think I am. A little spook like that. . . . I need that. Not to mention the risk of disease. . . . No. I just let her give me a blow job." (357–58)

Barry then turns, in what appears to be a moment of concern, to his friend and asks: "*You* didn't fuck her, did you?" (358). This moment of concern is the final twist to the plot. It is not Tull's "trap" that is the center of the novel, but rather his friend's behind-the-scene manipulation of Tull's life. For as becomes evident as the novel unravels, it is indeed Barry who has been directing the action all along. He has been in control of Tull's life in every detail. He is anxious when his "friend" informs him about Belladonna not because of his potential infection from her but because he has been having weekly sex sessions with Tull's idealized wife, Gina. These meetings, paid for and delivered, have enabled Tull to write his final, awful novel. And the final scene of Amis's novel is the staged discovery by Tull of this fact when he walks in on his wife performing fellatio on Barry. It is the same position that enables the infection to spread only one way—according to the myth created in the text—from the man to the woman. It is precisely what Tull imagines doing with Belladonna. There is no safe haven for the anxiety about sex and disease in the age of AIDS. The safety of the marriage bed in the age of AIDS is only conceivable in terms of black humor.

The violation of the marriage bed is the source of humor from the seventeenth to the twentieth century. Cuckolds are funny, at least to male readers, who, idealizing their own narcissistic pleasure, can never imagine being anything but seducer. The humor of sex is tied to the idealization of the object of desire created by the male—the beautiful woman, pure beyond belief, who could never be anything but faithful. The antithesis, the woman who infects, lies on the other side of that arbitrary boundary. She is the destroyer of men. Yet it is the male, too, who infects, who corrupts. This is not the stuff of humor—it is the anxiety of the male who imagines himself being infected in order to infect. The social conventions of marriage are thus the fantasy construction in which safety lies. It is a safety that shields the male from the world of illness, the world of disease. Purity in the marriage bed is the idealization of the object of desire as beyond infection, beyond disease, beyond the aging process, beyond death! Here we can remind ourselves of Otto Kernberg's description of the ages of sexual passion that end in the acceptance of decay and death as part of the natural process of aging together. The narcissistic projection of the idealized self into the world and its concretization as the object of desire excludes all of these possibilities.

Three variations on a theme—Shakespeare, Swift, and Amis—point to the anxiety about disease that lies within comic representations of the marriage bed. Not only anxiety about the future lineage defines this danger: the cuckold dies from his cuckoldry, betrayed by the love object he has constructed in his love madness. The male's anxiety about not only his heirs but his own body, at risk for infection from the women of the city, is placed within the comic world. It is that aspect of this world that denies the power of satiric distancing, where the anxieties of the body transcend the framing power of the genre. Jaques remains isolated by his libertinage in the forest; Swift's minister dies of his cuckoldry; Amis's failed writer sees his ideal object of desire vanish as he observes his friend have oral sex with her. In all cases, the object of desire—the male's fantasy of the woman as idealized figure—comes to be revealed as the castrating adulteress who carries with her the potential for the male's destruction. And yet in all of these images the dichotomy of the infecting woman and the infected male is undercut to show us how all participants are involved in the dance of sex and death, blinded by the self-delusion of the purity of the marriage bed. Love + marriage = death.

NOTES

1. *The Complete Poems of Jonathan Swift*, ed. Pat Rogers (New Haven: Yale University Press, 1983), 455. On Swift's better-known text see: Ashraf H. A. Rushdy, "A New Emetics of Interpretation: Swift, His Critics, and the Alimentary Canal," *Mosaic: A Journal for the Interdisciplinary Study of Literature* 24 (1991): 1–32; William Freedman, "Dynamic Identity and the Hazards of Satire in Swift," *Studies in English Literature, 1500–1900* 29 (1989): 473–88; Thomas B. Gilmore, Jr., "Freud, Swift, and Narcissism: A Psychological Reading of 'Strephon and Chloe,' " in John Irwin Fischer, Donald C. Mell, Jr., and David M. Vieth, eds., *Contemporary Studies of Swift's Poetry* (Newark: University of Delaware Press, 1981), 159–68; Peter J. Schakel, "Swift's Remedy for Love: The 'Scatological,' " in John Irwin Fischer, Donald C. Mell, Jr., and David M. Vieth, eds., *Contemporary Studies of Swift's Poetry*, ibid., 136–48; Thomas B. Gilmore, Jr., "Freud and Swift: A Psychological Reading of Strephon and Chloe," *Papers on Language and Literature: A Journal for Scholars and Critics of Language and Literature* 14 (1978): 147–51; C. J. Rawson and Maximillian E. Novak, "The Nightmares of Strephon: Nymphs of the City in the Poems of Swift, Baudelaire, Eliot," in Maximillian E. Novak, ed., *English Literature in the Age of Disguise* (Berkeley: University of California Press, 1977), 57–99. See also Martin Pops, "The Metamorphosis of Shit," *Salmagundi* 56 (1982): 26–61.

2. I am employing the word "marriage" in this essay as shorthand for any explicitly monogamous love relationship whether straight or gay.

3. Otto Kernberg, *Love Relations: Normality and Pathology* (New Haven: Yale University Press, 1995), 45.

4. On this question in the eighteenth century, see Simon Richter, "Medizinischer und aesthetischer Diskurs: Herder and Haller über Reiz," *Lessing Yearbook* 25 (1993): 83–95.

5. Judith P. Butler, *Bodies That Matter: On the Discursive Limits of "Sex"* (New York: Routledge, 1993), 1.

6. On the discussion of the fetishization of urination in literature, see my *Difference and Pathology: Stereotypes of Sexuality, Race, and Madness* (Ithaca, NY: Cornell University Press, 1985), 115–16.

7. Roy Porter and Lesley Hall, *The Facts of Life: The Creation of Sexual Knowledge in Britain, 1650–1950* (New Haven: Yale University Press, 1995), 24.

8. For a crosscultural view, see T'ien Ju-K'ang, *Male Anxiety and Female Chastity: A Comparative Study of Chinese Ethical Values in Ming-Ch'ing Times* (Leiden: E. J. Brill, 1988).

9. Edward Westermarck, *The History of Human Marriage*, 3 vols. (London: Macmillan, 1921). He sees adultery as a mysterious association between husband and adulterer in some societies (1:233, 300–16), but he argues that (1:518–26) the basis for chastity is inheritance. See also John R. Gillis, *For Better, for Worse: British Marriages 1600 to the Present* (Oxford: Oxford University Press, 1985), 79–81.

10. There is an extensive literature on the literary representation of adultery. The following were of interest for this essay: Michael Neill, "Unproper Beds: Race, Adultery, and the Hideous in *Othello*," in Anthony Gerard Barthelemy, ed., *Critical Essays on Shakespeare's* Othello (New York: G. K. Hall, 1994), 187–215; Allison Sinclair, *The Deceived Husband: A Kleinian Approach to the Literature of Infidelity* (Oxford: Clarendon, 1993); Dieter Beyerle, "Ehebruch und krankes Kind: Zu einer Motivkombination in französischen Romanen des 19. Jarhhunderts," *Romanistisches Jahrbuch* 41 (199): 114–38; Naomi Segal, *The Adulteress's Child: Authorship and Desire in the Nineteenth-Century Novel* (Cambridge, MA: Polity Press, 1992); Peter von Matt, *Liebesverrat: Die Treulosen in der Literatur* (Munchen: C. Hanser, 1989); Tony Tanner, *Adultery in the Novel: Contract and Transgression* (Baltimore: Johns Hopkins University Press, 1979); Judith Armstrong, *The Novel of Adultery* (New York: Barnes and Noble Books, 1976).

11. Lawrence Osborne, *The Poisoned Embrace: A Brief History of Sexual Pessimism* (London: Bloomsbury, 1993), especially his chapter on the virgin on 18–40. He does not mention disease at all in this context.

12. Porter and Hall, 277.

13. The following literature is of importance in framing this discussion of Shakespeare's understanding of melancholy and syphilis: Greg W. Bentley, *Shakespeare and the New Disease: The Dramatic Function of Syphilis in Troilus and Cressida, Measure for Measure, and Timon of Athens* (New York: P. Lang, 1989); Greg W. Bentley, "Melancholy, Madness, and Syphilis in Hamlet," *Hamlet Studies: An International Journal of Research on the Tragedie of Hamlet, Prince of Denmarke* 6 (1894): 75–80; Gustav Arthur Bieber, *Der Melancholikertypus Shakespeares und sein Ursprung* (Heidelberg: C. Winter, 1913); Sir John Charles Bucknill, *The Mad Folk of Shakespeare: Psychological Essays*, 2nd ed., rev. (London: Macmillan, 1867); Sir John Charles Bucknill, *The Medical Knowledge of Shakespeare* (London: Longman, 1860); Irving I. Edgar, *Shakespeare, Medicine, and Psychiatry: An Historical Study in Criticism and Interpretation* ([London]: Vision, 1971); Johannes Fabricius, *Syphilis in Shakespeare's England* (London: Jessica Kingsley, 1994); Lemuel Matthews Griffiths, "Shakspere and the Practice of Medicine," *Annals of Medical History* 3 (1921): 34–43; David Hoeniger, *Medicine and Shakespeare in the English Renaissance* (Newark: University of Delaware Press, 1992); Nicolas Jacobs, "Saffron and Syphilis: *All's Well That Ends Well*, IV.v.1–3," *Notes and Queries* 22 (1975): 171–72; Aubrey C. Kail, *The Medical Mind of Shakespeare* (Balgowlah, N.S.W.: Williams and Wilkis, 1986); A. O. Kellogg, *Shakespeare's Delineations of Insanity, Imbecility,*

and Suicide (New York: Hurd and Houghton, 1866); Raymond Klibansky, Erwin Panofsky and Fritz Saxl, *Saturn and Melancholy: Studies in the History of Natural Philosophy, Religion, and Art* ([London]: Nelson, [1964]); Hans Laehr, *Die Darstellung krankhafter Geistezustande in Shakespeares Dramen* (Stuttgart: Paul Neff Verlag, 1898); Wolf Lepenies, *Melancholy and Society*, trans. Jeremy Gaines and Doris Jones (Cambridge, MA: Harvard University Press, 1992); Bridget Gellert Lyons, *Voices of Melancholy: Studies in Literary Treatments of Melancholy in Renaissance England* (London: Routledge and K. Paul, [1971]); Francis R. Packard, "References to Syphilis in the Plays of Shakespeare," *Annals of Medical History* 6 (1924): 194–200; Herman Schelenz, *Shakespeare und sein wissen auf den Gebieten der Arznei- und Volkskunde* (Vaduz, Liechtenstein: Topos Verlag, 1977); Robert Ritchie Simpson, *Shakespeare and Medicine* (Edinburgh: E. and S. Livingstone, 1959); H. Somerville, *Madness in Shakespearian Tragedy*, with a preface by Wyndham Lewis (Folcroft, PA: Folcroft Press, 1929; 1969 printing); Macleod Yearsley, *Doctors in Elizabethan Drama* (London: J. Bale, Sons, and Danielsson, ltd., 1933).

14. On the figure of Jaques see: Alan Rickman, "Jaques in As You Like It," in Russell Jackson and Robert Smallwood, eds., *Players of Shakespeare, II: Further Essays in Shakespearean Performance by Players with the Royal Shakespeare Company* (New York: Cambridge University Press, 1988), 73–80; J. C. Bulman, "*As You Like It* and the Perils of Pastoral," in J. C. Bulman and H. R. Coursen, eds., *Shakespeare on Television: An Anthology of Essays and Reviews* (Hanover, NH: University Press of New England, 1988), 174–79; Devon L. Hodges, *Renaissance Fictions of Anatomy* (Amherst: University of Massachusetts Press, 1985); Robert B. Bennett, "The Reform of a Malcontent: Jaques and the Meaning of *As You Like It*," *Shakespeare Studies* 9 (1976): 183–204; Robert Ray, "Addenda to Shakespeare's Bawdy: *As You like It*, IV.i.201–18," *American Notes and Queries* 13 (1974): 51–53; M. D. Faber, "On Jaques: Psychoanalytic Remarks," *University Review*, Kansas City, Missouri 36 (1969–70): 89–96, 179–82.

15. Michael Bath, "Weeping Stags and Melancholy Lovers: The Iconography of *As You Like It*, II, i," *Emblematica* 1 (1986): 13–52, and E. Michael Thron, "Jaques: Emblems and Morals," *Shakespeare Quarterly* 30 (1979): 84–89; Winfried Schleiner, "Jaques and the Melancholy Stag," *English Language Notes* 17 (1980): 175–79; Claus Uhlig, "'The Sobbing Deer': *As You Like It*, II.i.21–66, and the Historical Context," *Renaissance Drama* n.s. 3 (1970): 79–109.

16. Compare Alan Macfarlane, *Marriage and Love in England: Modes of Reproduction 1300–1840* (Oxford: Basil Blackwell, 1986): 239–44, on adultery and inheritance in Western culture; and 240, horns on male.

17.

LUCIO: I grant; as there may between the lists and the velvet. Thou art the list.

FIRST GENTLEMAN: And thou the velvet: thou art good velvet; thou'rt a three-piled piece, I warrant thee: I had as lief be a list of an English kersey as be piled, as thou are piled, for a French velvet. Do I speak feelingly now?

LUCIO: I think thou dost; and, indeed, with most painful feeling of thy speech: I will, out of thine own confession, learn to begin thy health; but, whilst I live, forget to drink after thee.

FIRST GENTLEMAN: I think I have done myself wrong, have I not?

SECOND GENTLEMAN: Yes, that thou hast, whether thou art tainted or free.

LUCIO: Behold, behold, where Madam Mitigation comes! I have purchased as many diseases under her roof as come to—

SECOND GENTLEMAN: To what, I pray?

LUCIO: Judge.

SECOND GENTLEMAN: To three thousand dolours a year.

FIRST GENTLEMAN: Ay, and more.

LUCIO: A French crown more.

FIRST GENTLEMAN: Thou art always figuring diseases in me; but thou art full of error; I am sound.

LUCIO: Nay, not as one would say, healthy; but so sound as things that are hollow: thy bones are hollow; impiety has made a feast of thee. (1, 2)

18. Greg Bentley, "Melancholy, Madness, and Syphilis in Hamlet, *Hamlet Studies: An International Journal of Research on the Tragedie of Hamlet, Prince of Denmarke* 6 (1984): 75–80.

19. Sir John Charles Bucknill, *The Medical Nature of Shakespeare* (London: Longman, 1860): 108, refers to Jaques's syphilis as "that disease which engrossed so much attention at that time by its novelty and prevalence." More recently, see Johannes Fabricius, *Syphilis in Shakespeare's England* (London: Jessica Kingsley, 1994), 224–28 on Jaques as syphilitic.

20. David Bevington, "Introduction," William Shakespeare, *As You Like It* (Toronto: Bantam, 1980), xx.

21. Robert Burton, *The Anatomy of Melancholy*, ed. Holbrook Jackson (New York: Vintage, 1977), 1:2, 376 citing Botaldus.

22. *Fracastoro's Syphilis*, ed. and trans. Geoffrey Eatough (Liverpool: Francis Carins, 1984), 65.

23. Hieronymus Fracastoro, *Drei Bucher von den Kontagien* (1546), trans. Viktor Fossel (Leipzig: Johann Ambrosius Barth, 1910), 69.

24. *Fracastoro's Syphilis*, 57.

25. See my *Sexuality: An Illustrated History* (New York: John Wiley, 1989), 148–49.

26. Donald F. Bond, ed., The *Tatler* (Oxford, 1987), III, 317–22.

27. Porter and Hall, 135.

28. Gilman, 205.

29. On the nature of gender relationships, see: Lesley Anne Soule, "Subverting Rosalind: Cocky Ros in the Forest of Arden," *New Theatre Quarterly* 7 (1991): 126–36; Jan Kott, "The Gender of Rosalind," *New Theatre Quarterly* 7 (1991): 113–25; Hsiao-hung Chang, "Transvestite Sub/Versions: Power, Performance, and Seduction in Shakespeare's Comedies" (Diss, University of Michigan, 1991); Jean E. Howard, "Crossdressing, The Theatre, and Gender Struggle in Early Modern England," *Shakespeare Quarterly* 39 (1988): 418–40.

30. Alfred Fournier, *Syphilis and Marriage*, trans. Alfred Lingard (London: D. Bogue, 1881); *Syphilis et mariage*, 2nd ed. (Paris: G. Masson, 1890).

31. Gerard Tilles, R. Grossman, and Daniel Wallach, "Marriage: A Nineteenth-Century French Method for the Prevention of Syphilis: Reflections on the Control of AIDS," *International Journal of Dermatology* 32 (1993): 767–70.

32. All references are to call numbers in the Print and Photograph Division of the National Library of Medicine, Bethesda, Maryland.

33. Martin Amis, *The Rachel Papers* (New York: Vintage International, 1992).

34. All quotes are to Martin Amis, *The Information: A Novel* (New York: Harmony Books, 1995). See also Julian Loose, "*The Information* by Martin Amis," *The London Review of Books* 17 (May 11, 1995): 9; David Nicholson, "*The Information*. By Martin Amis," *Book World* 25 (May 7, 1995), 3.

35. Porter and Hall, 241.

"With This Ring I Thee Own":
Masochism and Social Reform in *Ulysses*

Laura Frost

I am awfully angry with you. I do wish I could punish you for that. I called you naughty boy because I do not like that other world. Please tell me what is the real meaning of that word? Are you not happy in your home you poor little naughty boy? I do wish I could do something for you. Please tell me what you think of poor me. . . . I have never felt myself so much drawn to a man as you. I feel so bad about. Please write me a long letter and tell me more. Remember if you do not I will punish you. So now you know what I will do to you, you naughty boy, if you do not wrote.[1]

Leopold Bloom receives this faltering epistle from Martha Clifford, aspiring dominatrix, with trembling excitement. More than the potato in his pocket, Martha's letter burns in Bloom's mind as he wanders the streets of Dublin on June 16, 1904. In spite of fancying himself a literary man, Bloom is enraptured by these awkward, repetitive, and far from threatening lines.

Throughout *Ulysses*, Joyce represents Leopold Bloom's masochistic games with humor: his titillating mock-trial in Nighttown, his excitement at Bella/Bello Cohen's "heel discipline" (433), and his correspondence with Martha. Indeed, it is Joyce's humor, a feature Gilles Deleuze suggests is constitutive of masochistic pleasure,[2] that points out the paradoxes of Bloom's desires. For Bloom is not only the most famous modern masochist:[3] he is also "the world's greatest social reformer" (392), formulating schemes for everything from "the development of Irish tourist traffic in and around Dublin" (590) to the installation of public restrooms for women and the distribution of state funds to women to compensate them for the pain of childbirth. Bloom's constant quest for erotic subjugation—

his fantasies of and efforts to realize exaggerated forms of domination and submission in sexual scenarios—is maintained alongside his apparently oppositional inner monologues and impromptu barroom lectures on his sweeping aspiration "to amend many social conditions, the product of inequality and avarice and international animosity" (571).

These curious contradictions within Bloom's psyche have not been addressed in much depth by prevailing psychoanalytic approaches. Instead, Bloom's sexuality has been typically treated as an expiation of guilt, or as an Oedipal rebellion against the Father, or the so-called phallic mother: generalized entities that tend to overshadow the subject's more subtle, ambiguous, and historically specific experiences in the world.[4] Just as the connection between Bloom's fantasies of erotic domination and his interest in specific types of sociopolitical reform is not immediately apparent if we adhere to a developmental or strictly intrapsychic interpretation of masochism, it is similarly obscured by Joyce's suggestion—and a standard interpretation of modernist texts—that the artist is "like the God of the creation," sitting "behind or beyond or above his handiwork, invisible, refined out of existence, indifferent, paring his fingernails."[5] Moreover, Joyce's ambiguous representations of sexologists Havelock Ellis, Krafft-Ebing, and Magnus Hirschfeld,[6] and the baffling, chaotic metamorphoses of gender and sexuality of characters in *Ulysses* have led many critics to the understandable conclusion that sexuality, for Joyce, is largely a function of intertextuality, language games, or epistemological provocation with a multiplicity of "meanings" meant to frustrate systematic ideological readings. The specific cultural references that are the very fabric of Bloom's masochistic fantasies have gone largely unnoticed. Implicated in Bloom's relationship with Martha Clifford, for example, is a constellation of sociopolitical issues and historical preoccupations otherwise veiled by Joyce's claims to political neutrality.

My account of masochism in *Ulysses* will trace a series of specific textual and cultural references embedded in Bloom's erotic fantasies and elaborate on his appropriation of a historically situated dialogue about gender politics. I agree with Richard Brown that we need "a renewed sense of the importance of subject-matter in Joyce's fiction"; although Brown does not address masochism *per se* in depth, he proposes that Joyce's writing "seems importantly connected to attitudes about marriage, to the scientific interest in sexuality, to non-reproductive priorities in sex and to women, that we characterize as modern" (9). Demonstrating how

Bloom's masochistic fantasies are created from his conscious concerns with distributions of social and political power, Joyce shows erotic fantasy to be saturated with references that exceed, contradict, or do not necessarily register on psychoanalysis's scale of interpretive priorities. Furthermore, Joyce illustrates the paradoxes and reversals in fantasies of erotic domination: that is, how masochistic fantasy articulates sociopolitical concerns *and* introduces contradictory attitudes about those issues. Masochism and masochistic identifications in *Ulysses* take up, and in some ways parody, topical discussions of power and resistance: specifically, early twentieth-century debates about women's rights.

This investigation turns on an understanding of how the unconscious is influenced by those elements that psychoanalysis calls "the here and now"—the subject's everyday experiences and encounters—and political ideology. From the debate around Freud's "seduction theory" to recent feminist work on sexual response,[7] questions of how our politics influence our fantasy life, and how to approach (or admit) those fantasies that contradict our political position, have remained unresolved—mainly because they raise disturbing questions about the limits of political commitment in the realm of the unconscious. Recent work on masochism (and the larger category of erotic domination or S/M) has attempted to address this impasse and to push theoretical understandings of masochism beyond the formulations of orthodox psychoanalysis. Jessica Benjamin, for example, explores how erotic domination is related to socially conditioned and gendered dynamics of intersubjectivity;[8] Kaja Silverman asserts that male masochism may challenge the "dominant fictions" of masculinity;[9] Gilles Deleuze and Félix Guattari propose that masochistic practices can serve as a program of "desubjectivization," an ecstatic dismantling of self that offers an alternative to psychoanalytic accounts of identity as founded upon lack and frustration of desire,[10] and Leo Bersani has added a radically skeptical voice to liberative readings of masochism.[11] Feminism and queer theory have been particularly effective at reading masochism "against the grain" of the psychoanalytic model,[12] and critics such as Pat Califia and Gayle Rubin emphasize the importance of an awareness of actual practice to a nuanced reading of masochism.[13] *Ulysses* is more useful than the average case-study, for it illuminates the psychology, the ideology, *and* the practice of masochism.

On its most apparent level, Bloom's interest in sexual punishment is clearly a response to guilt. He blames himself for his son Rudy's death, since which he and his wife, Molly, have not had full intercourse (605). Both Molly and Bloom have extramarital affairs: she with the jingling Blazes Boylan and he principally through voyeurism and the sadomasochistic correspondence under the name of Henry Flower, Esq. (592) with respondents to an ad he places in the *Irish Times:* "Wanted: smart lady typist to aid gentleman in literary work" (131). In church, Bloom thinks about the *curative* powers of punishment, musing: "Punish me, please. Great weapon in their hands. More than doctor or solicitor . . . . Doctor Whack" (68–69). Martha Clifford's letters serve the same curative function as a "doctor whack," or, as Bloom explains elsewhere, as a kind of Swinburnian therapy: "Refined birching to stimulate the circulation" (382).

Nevertheless, Joyce gives us clues that Bloom's dreams of erotic domination are more than an expiation of guilt; they are *also* closely related to Bloom's identity as "the world's greatest reformer." He possesses "an inherited tenacity of heterodox resistance" and "professed [his] disbelief in many orthodox religious, national, social and ethical doctrines" (544). His commitment to "civic selfhelp" (399) surfaces everywhere in *Ulysses*, but particularly in relation to his sexual fantasies.

One of the first indications of Bloom's masochistic tendencies is his response to a novel Molly is reading called *Ruby: The Pride of the Ring:* "He turned over the smudged pages. *Ruby: The Pride of the Ring*. Hello. Illustration. Fierce Italian with carriagewhip. Must be Ruby pride of the on the floor naked. Sheet kindly lent. *The monster Maffei desisted and flung his victim from him with an oath*" (52). Molly Bloom is disappointed with the erotic content of *Ruby: The Pride of the Ring*, dismissively pronouncing that there's "nothing smutty in it." Bloom's imagination, however, is inflamed by the material, and thereafter, throughout his long, erotically challenging day, Bloom's fantasies of sexual domination revolve around this book and its beleaguered heroine, Ruby—whose name echoes that of Bloom and Molly's lost child, Rudy.

Like so many images in *Ulysses*, *Ruby: The Pride of the Ring* can be traced back to an actual book from which Joyce borrowed. The described illustration—a "fierce Italian with carriagewhip"—appears in a real turn-of-the-century novel that also features a heroine called Ruby but is significantly different from its *Ulysses* counterpart. Mary Power has identified Joyce's source for the fictional *Ruby: The Pride of the Ring* as Amye Reade's 1889 *Ruby: Founded on the Life of a Circus Girl*,[14] a novel that Power points out was "written in the Dickensian tradition of crusade and reform" (115). Joyce's—or, rather, Bloom's—transformation of Reade's novel of protest into *Ruby: The Pride of the Ring*, a steamy sadomasochistic tale, elucidates the associative operations of masochistic fantasy, and particularly those that link erotic domination to the discourse of social reform. *Ulysses* shows how easily a text of social reform is coopted by Bloom to "resignify" as soft-core sadomasochistic porn, and it also suggests that some fantasies of erotic subjugation are actually founded on, and constructed from, social and political concerns. Bloom's transformation of Amye Reade's moralistic tale into his own erotic crime and punishment underscores the masochist's often-noted impulse to *legislate* and *regulate* power, and connects it to an explicitly reformist agenda.

In Reade's novel, Ruby is born to unhappy parents. Her selfish mother, Cynthia—who is compared to "the flowers. . . . But the flowers cannot sin" (25)—resists marrying Ruby's virtuous father, Jack. He bemoans, "I wish she were willing to be legally made my wife. I can't force her, but she must be made a wife before she becomes a mother. . . . She must conform to the ceremony demanded by national custom" (123). Cynthia, however, is convinced by her maid that she should stall on Jack's proposal and preserve her freedom, because she is beautiful enough to marry a lord. In a chapter called "Cynthia Forces Jack's Hand," she tells him, "Don't forget, Mr. Haywood, there is a wide difference between mistress and wife. One is a toy; the other a slave" (174). This is the first of many invocations of slavery in Reade's novel; Cynthia never finds out what it means to be a "slave," for that fate is reserved for her daughter. Despite Cynthia's hesitations, the couple is united in a "Scotch" marriage, a provisional, not quite legal, arrangement. After Ruby is born, the couple separates; Cynthia sends Ruby to be raised elsewhere while she plots a marriage to an earl. Fearing her daughter will return and ruin her efforts to reinvent herself, Cynthia arranges to indenture Ruby to Signor Enrico, a trainer of female horseback riders for the circus. (Signor Enrico, as Mary Power indicates, becomes Signor Maffei of *Ulysses*. His name is also related to Bloom's pseudonym Henry Flower; Reade makes continual references to flowers in her novel, comparing them to characters and using them to represent the pure state from which Cynthia and Ruby have fallen.) She is assured that he will keep Ruby "until she is twenty-one—if she lives as long, for it's a pretty hard life" (230).

Signor Enrico is a very cruel but also handsome, intelligent, and compelling man: he has "a face that would command absolute obedience." His "cruel satire and stinging insults" make people fearful, but he is "worshipped" for his charismatic power. Reade writes that Enrico is so

Calm and dignified at times, passionate and cruel at others, it was no wonder that he gained absolute and entire control over those who called him master. . . . In his profession he was a monarch and wielded the power usurped by him with an iron rod. It was his pride to turn out the best lady riders in the world. (250)

Even as he insists that corporal punishment is the most effective means of disciplining his "lady riders" (his favorite mode of castigation is stripping the girls naked and whipping them) Signor Enrico appreciates Ruby's beauty and notes that she has "a face that's like the Venus of Medici" (257). Mary Power rightly notes that "What defies belief is that Signor Enrico sees Ruby and the other girls as workhorses and never as sexual beings," even as he "beats them in the nude" (118). This is especially true given the moments that Signor Enrico, cold-hearted but not without his charms, is obligated to marvel at Ruby as a woman rather than a horse — as if Reade expects her readers to consider her heroine as a desexualized being, and to assume that Signor Enrico does the same. From Enrico's brutish charms (surely a forerunner of the Harlequin Romance hero) to his fortuitous reference to Venus, the quintessential masochistic love object, the erotic potential of *Ruby: A Novel: Founded on the Life of a Circus Girl* is easily discernible, even if it takes a reader like Bloom to render it explicit. In fact, Mary Power notes that a *Pall Mall Gazette* review of *Ruby: A Novel: Founded on the Life of a Circus Girl* remarks that "in her zeal for verisimilitude, Miss Reade outdid herself and though she intended to show the abuses of circus life, she goes too far in incorporating the circus trainer's profanity and cruelty into the novel" and cautions that this could "unwittingly promote the very abuses it ought to have attacked" (cited in Power, 120).

Although Ruby clings to her modesty, pride, and virtue as long as she can, Enrico's brutal treatment leads to her early death. Ruby's father resurfaces too late to rescue his daughter, but he saves Ruby's best friend, another circus trainee, by buying back her contract from Signor Enrico and marrying her: "The next day the slave was loosed from her fetters. The lash would fall no more upon her quivering flesh — she was free from the task-master" (426). Thus, the contract enslaving Ruby to Signor Enrico is countered by a redemptive marriage contract.

Reade's novel is heavy-handed and didactic in promoting its social agenda. Chapter headings include "Shame! Shame!" and "Peace! Peace!"; characters are either unflaggingly righteous or relentlessly depraved. The good are rewarded, the bad are killed off (scheming Cynthia, who would rather marry for money than love, dies hallucinating about the devil), and the fortunes of virtue triumph over all. As clumsy as the novel seems today, it was taken quite seriously when it was published. It was part of Reade's mission to expose the exploitation of children working for traveling circuses; a catalogue by the publishers of *Ruby* describes the novel as "the foundation of an inquiry now being made by certain Members of Parliament as to the Methods of Training Circus Children, with a view to bringing the matter immediately before the House."[15] Reade's second novel, *Slaves of the Sawdust*, continues the fight to expose "the veritable horrors of the ring."[16]

Leopold Bloom's perverse translation of Reade's earnestly reformist novel into the erotic *Ruby: The Pride of the Ring* begins, as Power points out, when he glances at the illustration from Reade's *Ruby*. (See illustration 8.1, showing Signor Enrico with one of Ruby's fellow trainees.)[17] *"The monster Maffei desisted and flung his victim from him with an oath.* Cruelty behind it all. Doped animals. Trapeze at Hengler's. Had to look the other way" (52). Bloom responds to the illustration accompanying Reade's text in proper reformist spirit, but his moral outrage is directed not at the abuse of the circus girl, Ruby, but at the abuse of animals:[18] the first suggestion that his political engagement follows an idiosyncratic logic.

Bloom considers himself a voice of reason in Dublin affairs—"You must look at both sides of the issues," he insists—and he emphatically protests against force: "I resent violence and intolerance in any shape or form" (525). Nevertheless, he is fascinated by certain kinds of violence: specifically, that practiced by women upon men. Also, later in *Ulysses*, he announces his platform for his ideal society: "I stand for the reform of municipal morals and the plain ten commandments. New worlds for old," including "Free money, free rent, free love and a free lay church in a free lay state" (399). O'Madden Burke replies, "Free fox in a free henroost" (400), pointing out a persistent sexual theme in Bloom's political interests.

We know from Bloom's epistolary exchange with Martha Clifford, his prurient interest in nuns and barbed wire,[19] and his fantasies in Nighttown that he is excited by the idea of sexual domination at the hands of a burly woman—an arrangement that mirrors the tableau in Reade's illustration, with a crucial reversal of gender. Although Bloom's initial response to the illustration is high-minded self-justification (he

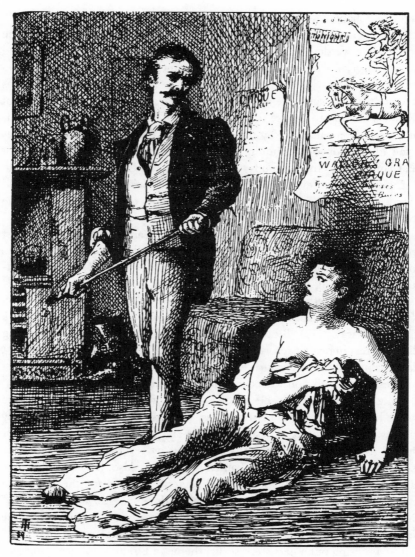

FIG. 8.1 Illustration by Talbot Hughes from Amye Reade's *Ruby: Founded on the Life of a Circus Girl.* By permission of The British Library.

sniffs that "all tales of circus life are highly demoralizing" [371], and recalls having to look away from such spectacles), it surfaces in his fantasies in a very different form. Despite Bloom's famous concern for animals—he brags about scolding a tramdriver for "illusing the poor horse with his harness scab" (371)—we only have to glance at the circus poster above the prone woman (in illustration 8.1) to see a scenario that appears repeatedly in *Ulysses*, much to Bloom's delight.

The heroine of Bloom's sexual fantasies is often an equestrian, such as The Honourable Mrs. Mervyn Talboys in Nighttown, "In amazon costume with hunting crop" or Bella Cohen—"Master! Mistress! Mantamer!"—astride a happy "bondslave."[20] (Amye Reade's Ruby is billed as "The Queen of the Equestrians," an imperial-sounding epithet that harkens to the titles of dominatrixes in sadomasochistic pornography.) Thus, Bloom's initial sympathy for the animals—like his response to Ruby—masks a more significant desire to be in their place. Laplanche and Pontalis, following Freud's "A Child Is Being Beaten," have suggested that fantasy is a "setting up" of a scenario, and that the creator of that fantasy may appear in any subject position—even as a verb—in that scenario.[21] We must be careful in determining which psychic position Bloom occupies in a fantasy, for multiple identifications are possible. Bloom sympathizes with the naked, oppressed girl (who he assumes is Ruby) but then *becomes* Ruby in the "Circe" chapter, and clearly enjoys the beating. Bloom *identifies* with Ruby and exploits the erotic possibilities of her predicament: cowering naked on the floor under a whip-wielding Italian master. He sympathizes with the downtrodden *and* experiences the exquisite pleasure of occupying that downtrodden position—trodden, that is, by a well-placed stiletto.

In one chapter of Amye Reade's novel, suggestively called "Ruby Receives Degrading Punishment," the chaste Ruby refuses to put on a skimpy costume. Signor Enrico is furious with her insubordination: "She was cold and haughty and seemed to accept him as an inferior instead of an authority. . . . He resolved to break her proud spirit and make her submit to his rule with the obedience of a slave" (296). He orders her to strip, ties her hands with a handkerchief, and beats her with a cane, "demand[ing] from her the obedience which slaves give to their owners." This scene is reworked in "Circe" when Bloom is introduced as "Mademoiselle Ruby, the pride of the ring." The newly masculine Bello Cohen commands Bloom: "you are unmanned and mine in earnest, a thing under the yoke. . . . You will shed your male garments, you understand, Ruby

Cohen?" While Bloom/Ruby promises "never to disobey," Bello threatens to inflict "correction . . . for your own good. . . . Like the Nubian slave of old" (434). Bello puts a ruby ring on Bloom's finger, declaring, "With this ring I thee own," and pronounces himself married to "Miss Ruby" (439).

While Reade valorizes marriage as the only safe moral and spiritual position for women, and clearly opposes it to the contractual slavery of circus training, Joyce associates the bonds of marriage with those of slavery through Bloom's fantasies of sexual bondage. Bloom's mock marriage refigures Ruby's contract with Signor Enrico, and Joyce draws a direct correspondence between Reade's disparate themes of indentured servitude—which she constantly describes in terms of slavery—and marriage. Bloom's fantasy scenario also uses the language of slavery, but for incongruously erotic ends: his "bondage" to Bello is the thrilling culmination of a fantasy of sexual subjugation. To determine just what this transformation means in terms of *Ulysses* and masochism requires further textual excavation.

Richard Ellmann, Mark Shechner, Frances L. Restuccia, and other Joyce critics have noted the numerous ways in which Bloom's masochism is based on the novels—especially *Venus in Furs* (1870)[22]—and the life of Austrian writer Leopold von Sacher-Masoch: particularly, how the rituals of *Venus in Furs* are reproduced in the "Circe" episode of *Ulysses*, and how Joyce borrows from Sacher-Masoch's real-life epistolary exchanges with fair flagellants to create Bloom's letters to and from Martha Clifford. Out of the piles of "fan mail" Sacher-Masoch received from his literary admirers, he replied to those letters that seemed to be written by potential dominatrixes,[23] and modeled his affairs on the relationship between Severin and Wanda in *Venus in Furs*. (See illustration 8.2, a caricature of Sacher-Masoch that appeared in a contemporary Austrian journal.) What has not been explored is how Sacher-Masoch's interest in social reform, and specifically women's rights, makes its way into his erotic stories, and how Joyce replicates this association in *Ulysses* and in his own Leopold.

Sacher-Masoch's work can be divided into two types. The first is the writing for which he is famous: tales of men in erotic subservience to voluptuous, imperious mistresses. *Venus in Furs* is the best example of this. However, his representations of masochism not only refer to, but in fact depend upon, a platform of political reform. Sacher-Masoch, whose father was a police chief, recalled that his most significant early memories were of witnessing the bloody 1848 uprisings in Austria and Galacia. The formative images of his childhood, he once said, were soldiers, policemen,

FIG. 8.2 "Leopold von Sacher-Masoch and some of his works," *Weiner-Figaro*, 1875.

chained criminals and conspirators, and barred jail windows.[24] Sacher-Masoch's political environment, with its struggles for national identity and religious freedom, bears clear parallels to Ireland's history of colonization. (Bloom himself is a hybrid of these cultures; in *Ulysses* there are numerous references to the Hungarian heritage of Bloom's father, Virag; Austrian-Hungarian coins and coupons are found in Bloom's top drawer [593].) Throughout his life, Sacher-Masoch worked on a massive project called *The Heritage of Cain*, a six-part cycle encompassing the themes of love, property, war, work, the state, and death: evidence that his imagination ranged far beyond whips and sable coats. Sacher-Masoch was a supporter of the panslavism movement, and was an outspoken critic of anti-Semitism. He was invited by Jewish groups to lecture in Hungary and Budapest about Jewish concerns, although he was not Jewish himself[25] (this suggests another way in which Joyce modelled Leopold Bloom on the "other" Leopold). Sacher-Masoch wrote many stories like those in *Tales of the Ghetto*, to which Joyce makes reference in *Ulysses*, which were, Gifford notes, "primarily concerned with anti-Semitic persecutions" (271).

Sacher-Masoch also experienced the rise of the women's movement in Austria. The first major Austrian women's organization, the Viennese Women's Employment Association, was founded in November 1866, four years before *Venus in Furs* was published. Historian Harriet Anderson notes that the projects of the Employment Association were "a direct response to the events of 1866, which had brought the defeat of Austria by the Prussians in the Six Weeks' War and financial ruin to many middle-class families" (25).[26] The women of these families were increasingly looking for jobs outside the home, and often met with difficulty. Along with promoting women's employment, the Austrian women's movement addressed educational opportunities and suffrage; although women gained the right to vote for the Lower Austrian Provincial Assembly in 1849, it was revoked in 1888 (Anderson, 39). In 1904, the General Austrian Women's Association's concerns included improving the legal status of women in civil marriage, establishing maternity insurance, and revising the Civil Code "to extend forms of sanctioned sexual cohabitation, to whittle away the control of men and patriarchal institutions such as the state and the Church over such cohabitation, and at the same time to protect women and their children and to extend their rights" (Anderson, 70).

Sacher-Masoch publicly supported the women's suffrage movement in

Austria,[27] and he critiqued conventions reinforcing women's second-class status, such as the Austrian educational system. He was particularly outspoken about marriage laws that deprived women of property rights and the Catholic ban on divorce and civil marriage.[28] Sacher-Masoch himself experimented with alternatives to legal marriage; for "progressive" social reasons, he lived with his first wife for a year under the terms of a "mock" marriage before they married legally. In his fiction, he created an alternative world where women ruled over men.

Sacher-Masoch's two main themes—polemical historical accounts and masochistic eroticism—are united throughout his work by the figure of the dominatrix: a voluptuous, proud, disdainful woman draped in fur, off whose tongue trip abusive monologues like, "I know you now, I know your doglike nature; you worship whoever tramples you underfoot, and the more you are abused the more slavish your devotion."[29] In *Venus in Furs*, Wanda rules over the supersensualist Severin: "I have a certain talent for playing despotic roles. . . . I also have the indispensable furs" (163). In Sacher-Masoch's historical work, the dominatrixes are "world historical" tyrannical female rulers like Maria of Hungary (about whom Sacher-Masoch wrote a scholarly biography in 1862, and whose name appears in *Ulysses*),[30] a "historical prototype" of his "preferred female type" (Koré, 74).

Czarina Catherine the Second, who appears in Sacher-Masoch's 1880 story "Cupid with the Corporal's Cane,"[31] epitomizes the historical dominatrix. The Czarina rules over a society in which women hold all positions of authority, including "a very learned and intellectual woman" who "gained the Presidential Chair of the Academy of Sciences." Sacher-Masoch's Catherine is domineering, alluring, and androgynous in terms of her strength: "Nobody would guess that the small, beautifully-shaped hand of the one who was toying so innocently with a fan, at the same time wielded the sceptre of the greatest empire in Europe with masculine energy." Bloom's accusers in "Circe" are patterned on Sacher-Masoch's politically and sexually tyrannical women: Bella Cohen, the "massive whoremistress" who runs the Nighttown brothel and abruptly changes sex, cools herself with a talking fan that declares "the missus is master. Petticoat government" (430).

But what looks like a proto-feminist scenario in "Cupid with a Corporal's Cane" is inevitably shot through with sadomasochistic dynamics. The Czarina is impetuously aggressive, performing such acts as signing a decree granting her friend legal possession of a man who makes the mistake of calling her a "subordinate creature" (107). This "punishment," however, is actually the masochist's ultimate dream: masochistic rituals, as many have pointed out (Stoller, Deleuze, Victor Smirnoff, etc.), almost always include a verbal "contract" in which the masochist pledges to relinquish himself to a dominatrix. The "love contract" of *Venus in Furs*— in which Severin signs himself over to Wanda's sovereignty—was copied from the real contracts Sacher-Masoch drew up with his dominatrixes.[32] Joyce, in turn, based the Bello and Bloom alliance in "Circe"[33] on this ritual. The "love contract," as will become apparent, is a key element of the masochist's reformist and judicial impulse.

Sacher-Masoch is clearly considering the question of female empowerment in his stories about sensual masochism, and his interest in sociopolitical reform is united with his erotic interest in relinquishing power to a woman. The social reformer and the masochist share a common goal of exposing and realigning distributions of power. This begins to explain how such a reformist tract as Reade's *Ruby: Founded on the Life of a Circus Girl* is susceptible to an erotic reading. Amye Reade's representations of extremely polarized power positions are appealing and thrilling to Leopold Bloom because they work on the same terrain as masochistic fantasy. Bloom can project himself into Reade's portraits of domination and subjugation and cast himself against (gender) type, into the role of the vanquished. But how can we account for the masochist's erasure of very concrete social oppression in the construction of his own fantasy?

An orthodox psychoanalytic interpretation of masochism emphasizes the superego, or the role of guilty repression: the turning back of aggression upon the self.[34] Freud describes this process in general terms as civilization's "mastery over the individual's dangerous desire for aggression by weakening and disarming it and by setting up an agency within him to watch over it, like a garrison in a conquered city."[35] However, the reversals and paradoxes of masochism are more effectively accounted for by Foucault's speculations in *The History of Sexuality* about the *pleasure* involved in *both* sides of civilization's regulating and "policing" of sexuality. This includes the pleasure of being mastered, disarmed, and *watched* as a helpless supplicant:

the fact is that they function as mechanisms with a double impetus: pleasure and power. The pleasure that comes of exercising a power that questions, monitors, watches, spies, searches out, palpates, brings to light, and on the other hand, the pleasure that kindles at having to evade this power, flee from it, fool it, or travesty it. The power that lets itself be invaded by the pleasure it is pursuing; and opposite it, power asserting itself in the pleasure of showing off, scandalizing, or resisting. Capture and seduction, confrontation and mutual reinforcement: parents and children, adults and adolescents, educator and students, doctors and patients, the psychiatrist with his hysteric and his perverts, all have played this game continually since the nineteenth century. These attractions, these evasions, these circular incitements have traced around bodies and sexes, not boundaries not to be crossed, but *perpetual spirals of power and pleasure.*[36]

Bloom's masochistic "incitement" is indeed "circular," not only in its literal form—the circus ring, the mock-marriage ring—but also in the "spirals" of its thematic content. Although Bloom—after Sacher-Masoch—protests the social contract that makes women subordinate subjects, he also imagines a compensatory sexual pleasure in being subject to that contract: a fantasy that he tries to realize through his erotic correspondence with Martha Clifford, and that is played out in the "Circe" episode of *Ulysses.*

Just as Sacher-Masoch's masochism is closely connected to the question of women's empowerment, throughout *Ulysses* Leopold Bloom's concern for women's rights is enmeshed with his masochistic fantasies. We know that Joyce shared many of Sacher-Masoch's sociopolitical concerns. The letters of Nora Barnacle to Joyce suggest she spent a considerable amount of time trying to convince Joyce to marry her legally. His letters demonstrate how his philosophical objections to the institution of marriage are involved in broader social issues: "My mind rejects the whole present social order and Christianity—home, the recognized virtues, classes of life, and religious doctrines."[37] Bonnie Kime Scott notes that Joyce "regretted the Irishwoman's supposed alliance with the Catholic Church" and "the control exercised over" women by father confessors, compounded by the "verbal and physical brutality" of some husbands toward their wives.[38] Versions of these concerns appear in *Ulysses* as Bloom's concerns.

Bloom ponders the Catholic church's treatment of women: its imperative to "be fruitful and multiply," and its condemnation of birth control. Bloom imagines Mrs. Purefoy's birthing pains and invents an economic program to benefit mothers:

Child's head too big: forceps. Doubled up inside her trying to butt its way out blindly, groping for the way out. Kill me that would. . . . They ought to invent something to stop that. Life with hard labour. . . . They could easily have big establishments whole thing quite painless out of all the taxes give every child born five quid at compound interest." (132)

He is preoccupied with women's bodies, and dreams up several public schemes for women's health.[39] He speculates about his daughter's, Martha's, Molly's, and Gerty's menstrual cycles—"the monotonous menstruation of simian and (particularly) human females extending from the age of puberty to the menopause" (572)—and observes the public urinals for men in Dublin, thinking that there "Ought to be places for women" (133). In the bookshop, Bloom examines *The Awful Disclosures of Maria Monk*, and then "Aristotle's *Masterpiece*. Crooked botched print. Plates: infants cuddled in a ball in bloodred wombs like livers of slaughtered cows. Lots of them like that at this moment all over the world. All butting with their skulls to get out of it" (193). Shuddering, Bloom thinks of Mrs. Purefoy in the hospital and reminds himself that he must visit her—but this charitable resolution is interrupted when he catches sight of some soft-core erotica on the shelf.

A similar associative slip between Bloom's concern for women's conditions and his sexual interests occurs when he is masturbating on the beach while watching Gerty MacDowell. Upon discovering she is lame he remarks "Poor girl! That's why she's left on the shelf. . . . A defect is ten times worse in a woman" (301), but rather than contemplate this state of affairs in which a woman's fate is determined by how closely she conforms to a standard of physical beauty, he thinks "Glad I didn't know it when she was on show" (301). We are also told that the "domestic problem" that most concerns Bloom is "What to do with our wives" (561),[40] emphasizing Bloom's continual legislative proposals for helping women, but also making an indirect reference to Bloom's own problem at home: what to do with *his* wife, who is cheating on him. This double investment appears again in Bloom's concern for his daughter's future. Just as Stephen Dedalus is anxious when he realizes how poorly his sister Dilly has been served by the Irish tradition of meager education for women, Bloom supports his daughter's work as a photographer's apprentice. Nevertheless, Bloom's thoughts about "those girl graduates" he sees in the library turn inevitably to their sexual appeal: "Happy chairs under them" (308). Similarly, the inventory of Bloom's top drawer in the "Ithaca" chapter includes a "press cutting from an English weekly periodical *Modern Society*" (392), confirming Bloom's engagement in social issues. However, the clipping (nestled in the drawer next to condoms, pornographic postcards, and a magnifying glass)—"subject corporal chastisement in girls' schools" (592)—turns out to be yet another means for Bloom to cloak his sexual fantasies in the guise of social enlightenment.[41]

Bloom's "desire to amend many social conditions" (572) is mocked in the surreal, dream-like "Circe" chapter, where the similarities of his reformist impulse and his masochistic fantasies are made explicit through a parody of progressive legislation and the staging of a trial. Bloom pontificates as ruler of the preposterously utopian "Bloomusalem" and women fawn over him—even feminists, albeit "masculinely" (393): "That's the famous Bloom now, the world's greatest reformer" (392). But the women turn on him, banding together to accuse him of writing lewd letters and making "improper overtures." Mrs. Bellingham, "in cap and seal coney mantle, wrapped up to the nose," with a "huge opossum muff" (380), testifies that Bloom "addressed me in several handwritings with fulsome compliments as a Venus in furs. . . . He urged me (stating that he felt it his mission in life to urge me) to defile the marriage bed, to commit adultery at the earliest possible opportunity" (380). The Honourable Mrs. Mervyn Talboys asserts: "This plebeian Don Juan . . . urged me to . . . misbehave, to sin with officers of the garrison . . . to chastise him as he richly deserves" (381). The women's accusations show the masochist's preposterous, often hilariously backhanded strategies. Bloom's "interest" in women's rights, like the masochists' in Sacher-Masoch's work, creates an opportunity to be beaten by those "empowered" women. In this wish-fulfilling trial, Bloom is abused and accused by not just one, but a group of dominatrixes. The scenario shows the futility of threatening someone who quivers in gleeful expectation of corporal punishment, whispering "I love the danger" (381).

Bloom—like Sacher-Masoch—imagines a world in which female power does not cancel out sexual pleasure. He seeks out the position culturally constructed as feminine, invests it with libidinal ecstasy, and is ostensibly happy to give up patriarchal power. Both Sacher-Masoch and Joyce appear to be reacting against "social purity" branches of the feminist movement that call for sexual restraint rather than increased sexual agency. Bonnie Kime Scott discusses those divisions of the Irish women's movement that advocated sexual abstinence for women, "a doctrine that 'nauseated' " Joyce (33). Harriet Anderson documents a similar sex-reform movement in turn-of-the-century Austrian feminism that inadvertently promoted the "marriage morality of the bourgeoisie" and condemned "the unmarried mother from the working class" (67).[42] Although masochism's "pro-sex" stance is clear—"Free fox in a free henroost" (400)—its "pro-woman" stance is hardly straightforward. Richard Brown observes that Joyce was "presenting a kind of feminism that was compatible with his interests in socialism and with the other kinds of sexual liberalism which informed his ideas" (117). However, if birth control is not available to women, or is banned by religious order, then recreational sex becomes an extremely fraught subject. This kind of double-edged issue indicates the complicated impulses at work in masochistic championing of women's rights.

Joyce and Sacher-Masoch demonstrate that the relationship between politics and fantasy is far from mimetic. The masochistic strategy *both* protests and recapitulates traditional power dynamics, for the "thrill" of female domination is predicated on the inversion of women's subordinate status in patriarchal society. Thus, claiming male masochism as a "revolutionary" feminist technique seems as erroneous as dismissing it as surreptitious misogyny. There are many indications that the masochist himself is aware of the conflicting relationship of his sexual desire to his reformist project and to the status quo.

Joyce points out the inevitable frustrations of masochism and its limited efficacy for effecting the social change it appears to support. In *Ulysses*, the contradictions involved in the realization of masochistic fantasy center on the dominatrix's role. Martha Clifford's reply to Bloom's advertisement in the *Irish Times*, which seems to be the most promising of the forty-four he receives, is later dismissed as a "*silly* I will punish you letter" (my emphasis, 301). Bloom is disappointed with Martha's aptitude for castigation. Her punitive prowess is undermined by her lack of facility with words: her sentence fragments, spelling mistakes, and errors in verb conjugation. These blunders are doubly glaring as the letter is ostensibly from a "smart lady typist" to a "literary gentleman." Clearly, Martha is no editor, and, it appears, an only marginally proficient typist: "I called you naughty boy because I do not like that other world," she slips (weary at her typewriter, as Shari Benstock has suggested),[43] "Please tell me what is the real meaning of that word?"

Joyce critics have been as disappointed with Martha as Bloom is: Suzette A. Henke agrees with Benstock that Martha is "a lonely and pathetic working-class girl who pines for release from the prison of dreary secretarial duties" (187). Claudine Raynaud, following Hélène Cixous, reads Martha's "lapsus"—her slip from "word" to "world"—as a symptom that "woman's desire remains unfulfilled."[44] These critics would have us believe that Martha is an automaton, garnering no pleasure from her position as dominatrix.

Bloom recalls another similarly disappointing masochistic scene:

Girl in Meath street that night. All the dirty things I made her say. All wrong of course. My arks she called it. It's so hard to find one who. Aho! If you don't answer when they solicit must be horrible for them till they harden. And kissed my hand when I gave her the extra two shillings. Parrots. Press the button and the bird will squeak. (303)

Even as Bloom "makes" the dominatrix "say dirty things"—that is, as he writes her script for her—he longs for her to be something other than a parrot repeating his words. Somehow he would like her to speak his desires without prompting—and yet he seems to doubt that any woman is capable of such erotic telepathy. Molly, Bloom believes, "understood little of political complications, internal, or balance of power, external" (562), which is precisely what an adept dominatrix must understand and manipulate to the satisfaction of the masochist.

It is significant that the dominatrixes' mistakes most upsetting to Bloom are linguistic errors such as Martha's faulty subject-verb agreement and the inelegant "arks." This brings to mind the concern raised at various points in *Ulysses* about Irish women's limited access to education, and Bloom's observation about "the deficient appreciation of literature possessed by females" (583). "Catholic women of Joyce's era," Bonnie Kime Scott writes, "stood at the end of the line for opportunities in university education" (39). One woman in *Ulysses* who does "appreciate literature" is the aspiring poet Lizzie Twigg, who responds to Bloom's advertisement with misguided earnestness. Believing it to be a legitimate request for assistance of a literary nature, she reels off her *c.v.*: "My literary efforts have had the good fortune to meet with the approval of the eminent poet A.E. (Mr Geo. Russell)" (131). When Bloom glimpses her later on the street with A.E., he observes: "Holding forth. She's taking it all in. Not saying a word. To aid gentleman in literary work . . . a listening woman at his side" (136). Even though she does not comprehend the ad, Lizzie Twigg is still assuming the parrot/dominatrix position, worshipfully listening to A.E.

The question of the dominatrix's agency in masochism is underscored by Joyce's "dirty letters" to Nora Barnacle that were considered too obscene to be included in the first edition of Joyce's collected letters.[45] It is difficult to get beyond the content of these letters, equal parts sadomasochism and scatology, for at first it seems that there isn't much beyond. However, an intriguing pattern appears throughout the letters. In almost every one of the explicitly sadomasochistic letters, Joyce calls attention to an aporia in his text—a place where he cannot speak a "certain word." In the first letter in the sequence, dated 22 August, 1909, Joyce writes to Nora from Dublin: "There is a letter which *I dare not be the first to write* and which yet I hope every day you may write to me. A letter for my eyes only. Perhaps you will write it to me and perhaps it will calm the anguish of my longing" (my emphasis, 163). We know from retrospective consideration that the letter Joyce imagines is a sadomas-ochistic masturbatory epistle. Like Leopold von Sacher-Masoch, Joyce seems to need the woman to initiate the sadomasochistic exchange, but he still cues her as to how to proceed.

Less than two weeks later (2 September 1909), Joyce writes explicitly of his desire to be flagellated by Nora:

Nora, my "true love," you must really take me in hand. Why have you allowed me to get into this state? . . . Tonight I have an idea madder than usual. I feel I would like to be flogged by you. I would like to see your eyes blazing with anger. . . . I wonder is there some madness in me. Or is love madness? (166)

Joyce worries about Nora's response, and he asks "What do you think of me at all? Are you disgusted with me?" However, it appears that he is not *too* concerned, for his eager follow-up recalls: "I remember the first night in Pola when in the tumult of our embraces you used a certain word. It was a word of provocation, of invitation and I can see your face over me (you were *over* me that night) as you murmured it" (166). The "certain word" is only identified in its context of Nora mounting him.

The letter that can't be written and the word that can't be cited are closely associated with sadomasochism. Specifically, they are related to Nora taking on a dominant sexual role. This is confirmed by the next aporia, which appears in Joyce's trembling reply to a satisfactorily stalwart letter from Nora. Joyce opens his November 18, 1909, letter without a salutation:

I dare not address you tonight by any familiar name. All day, since I read your letter this morning, I have felt like a mongrel dog that has received a lash across the eyes . . . like some filthy cur whose mistress had cut him with her whip and hunted him from her door. . . . You write like a queen. As long as I live I shall always remember the quiet dignity of that letter, its sadness and scorn, and the utter humiliation it caused me. (177)

Joyce takes this submissive posture even further in his letter of November 22, in which he abandons the conventional second-person address for the third person. Too "frightened" to address Nora, he writes to her like a cringing dog.

By December 2, he has recovered sufficiently to solicit her directly, writing

My darling. I ought to begin by begging your pardon, perhaps, for the extraordinary letter I wrote you last night. When I was writing it your letter was lying in front of me and my eyes were fixed, as they are even now, on *a certain word in it*. There is something obscene and lecherous in the very look of the letters. The sound of it too is like the act itself, brief, brutal, irresistible and devilish. (my emphasis, 180)

Over and over, Joyce suggests that there is a word (or words) that is so licentious that it cannot be articulated.[46] In his December 8 letter, Joyce concludes "there is one lovely word, darling, you have underlined to make me pull myself off better. Write me more about that and yourself, sweetly, dirtier, dirtier" (185). Joyce's insistence on "a certain word" that cannot be spoken is baffling, given the raunchy language that surrounds this taboo word (including a lengthy description of Nora defecating and masturbating in a closet). What, one wonders, could he have possibly left out? Just what is the significance of this evasive "certain word"? Obviously, Joyce is making reference to particular language in Nora's letters; they both knew what the "certain" words were, so there was no real mystery. Why, then, did Joyce persist in this mode, simultaneously reticent and flagrantly calling attention to the "unspeakable"?

I propose that these tantalizing "certain" words serve an important function in the construction of masochistic fantasy. Within the scene itself, the masochist needs to believe that he is not in control, that the "parrot" is not just repeating his words. Thus, Joyce's constant reference to words Nora has written, but he cannot, maintains the illusion that she is directing the scene, not parroting a script he wrote for her. Leopold Bloom's sentence, "it's so hard to find one who," could be completed as, one who can speak (to) the masochist's desires, command language convincingly, and, more importantly, *efface all manifestations of women's social inequality*. If Bloom the social reformer begins to think about the circumstances behind Martha's letter, or the girl in Meath street, he cannot enjoy the illusion that she is in control. (Henke, Raynaud, and Cixous have the same difficulty believing in Martha's pleasure in playing dominatrix.) Martha's errors make it impossible to forget that she has been poorly educated and types in an office all day.

Molly Bloom herself has something to say about the irony of women's ostensible power in the masochistic scenario. Thinking about the sadomasochistic novels Bloom brings her, she declares:

I hate that pretending of all things. . . . anybody can see its not true and that Ruby
and Fair Tyrants. . . . I remember when I came to page 50 the part about where
she hangs him up out of a hook with a cord flagellate sure theres nothing for a
woman in that all invention (619)

Raynaud points out that Molly is aware of the self-effacing mechanism in
masochism; "she can write to the male addressee the words he likes to see
and hear" (317). But Raynaud's pessimistic conclusion that language cannot "ever speak woman's desire," or the hopelessness of a woman ever
learning to "write letters that have not been taught to her by a writing
master" (319), needs to be qualified. What is Molly's investment in acting
as dominatrix?[47] What was Nora's?

The notion that the masochist is "really" in control of the dominatrix
(or "top") has become a truism among most theorists of sadomasochism.[48]
But this notion of one-way "control" is as reductive as a reading of
"power" as an absolute, uninflected force. The dynamics of sadomasochism are a complex dialectic of control between the partners that operates
differently according to its context. The dominatrix does not have to be
simply an "instrument" of the masochist's desires, as Theodor Reik calls
her,[49] or a disembodied "element," as Gilles Deleuze asserts ("Coldness,"
42). Pat Califia, a self-proclaimed sadist, and others who have written
about their experiences as "tops," have convincingly demonstrated that a
woman *can* take pleasure in her role as dominatrix.[50] To conclude that the
dominatrix finds no pleasure in her role is to fail, as Carol Siegel puts it,
to "distinguish the figure of the desiring dominant woman, veiled as she
is, from the ground of her man's and her culture's desires" (133). Surely
it is conceivable that a woman like Martha, whose abjection has been
emphasized by so many critics, might enjoy the idea of exercising authority, however limited, over a man, and controlling his subjugation from the
safe distance of her typewriter.

Molly's skepticism about the dominatrix's desire brings us to the sentiments of another wife of a famous literary masochist: Wanda von Sacher-
Masoch, the first wife of Leopold von Sacher-Masoch. "Wanda," née
Aurore Rumelin, met Leopold von Sacher-Masoch through an epistolary
exchange very much like Bloom's with Martha Clifford, and they were
married in 1873. She was publicly acknowledged as the dominatrix to her
famous husband, and she published "cruel stories" uncannily similar to
his under the name of his most famous dominatrix, Wanda in *Venus in
Furs*. They were bitterly divorced in 1888, each accusing the other of

adultery. In order to shore up her case and counter accusations put forward by Leopold von Sacher-Masoch's secretary,[51] Baron Carl Felix von Schlichtegroll, that she was a "sadist"—that she married Sacher-Masoch only for his notoriety and wealth, made his life miserable, and was now asking for alimony she did not deserve—Wanda von Sacher-Masoch published an autobiography, *The Confessions of Wanda von Sacher-Masoch*, in which she asserts that she was *coerced* into playing the role of the dominatrix in Leopold von Sacher-Masoch's "diabolical" lifestyle. She details his crescendo of harsh demands on her, coupled by threats that he would leave her or take mistresses if she did not obey his wishes.

Her melodramatic style in *The Confessions* lends itself to charges of hyperbolic embellishment: she proclaims that she is out to expose "Leopold's true deviant nature"[52] by describing the "hideous, insane experiences" and "mental torture" (92) she had "endured" (45). "He constantly tried to suck out my soul—to appropriate it" (100), she writes; "he drew me down to the mire where his passions crawled" (103). Critics seized on Wanda's alarmist tone to establish her as a scheming gold-digger who refused to understand her sensitive, artistic husband. However, in trying to prove her malicious motives, such critics as Schlichtegroll and James Cleugh overlooked the elements of Wanda's account that illuminate the complicated reworkings of social dynamics in the masochistic scenario, and that hinge on the dominatrix's role.

The authenticity of Wanda von Sacher-Masoch's stories is routinely questioned. Cleugh accuses her of plagiarizing Leopold von Sacher-Masoch's work. Bernard Michel, who seems a more careful chronicler, with less interest in establishing Wanda's moral bankruptcy, notes that her first book, *Novel of a Virtuous Woman*, is "a replica" of Sacher-Masoch's *The Separated Wife*. Indeed, the stories in Wanda von Sacher-Masoch's 1881 collection, *Ladies in Furs* (all translations are mine), are thematically identical to her husband's: both are set in the aristocratic kingdoms and rustic landscapes of middle to late nineteenth-century Eastern European countries, usually in the winter months (the better for the dominatrixes to don their furs). In *Ladies in Furs*, the heroines are gorgeous and disdainfully virtuous, torturing their admirers "like an unintelligible riddle."[53] Men are inevitably tricked and mastered by these haughty women who always come out on top.

Most of *Ladies in Furs*, however, is rather formulaic and plodding: the expression repetitive and uninflected, and the characters one-dimensional and predictable. Scenes, usually no more than a paragraph long, follow one another abruptly, with a minimum of writerly embellishment. The plots are simple and mechanical: secretive liaisons, sleighrides, and fur, fur, fur. *Ladies in Furs* lacks the fetishistic and psychological detail of Leopold von Sacher-Masoch's well-known works, such as *Venus in Furs*. The foreword to Wanda von Sacher-Masoch's collection and her husband's aforementioned story "Cupid with a Corporal's Cane,"[54] however, bear a remarkable resemblance. Wanda's piece is in the form and tone of a sociopolitical manifesto. She begins by citing Alexandre Dumas on the importance of women's suffrage but observes that such a likelihood seems far off. She points to "the rule of Czarina Katherine II of Russia" as an example of a realm ruled by women, "an inverted world, a complete regiment of women," including "the princess of Daschkoff . . . President of the Academy of Sciences" (vii).

Leopold von Sacher-Masoch's story is not curtly descriptive, like Wanda's, but instead connects the political to the sensual. While Wanda von Sacher-Masoch proceeds to launch into a summary about the "efforts and struggle which take aim at gaining and securing equal rights for women in all areas as men," Leopold von Sacher-Masoch puts this sentiment in the mouth of a cruel female beauty, who remarks when jilted, "I hate men more than ever, and I despise them so utterly that I cannot understand how these weak creatures, who have no will of their own, can have ruled for so long! . . . We must not rest until we rule, and men are altogether subject to us!" (164). In Leopold von Sacher-Masoch's story, Czarina Catherine II is not just "highly gifted," as in Wanda's account, but manifests a complex psyche. She is seen to "exclaim . . . angrily, pulling out the wings of a butterfly that she had just caught, throwing it on the ground" (165).

Certainly, these are grounds on which to declare that Leopold von Sacher-Masoch is simply a more interesting and better writer than Wanda; there remains the possibility that he did indeed hurriedly pen these stories, inferior to his major works, and publish them under her name. The limited pool of vocabulary upon which the author of *Ladies in Furs* draws, and the dully mechanical quality of these stories, is not reflected in the later autobiographical works of Wanda von SacherMasoch (the *Confessions* and the *New Confessions*).[55] *Ladies in Furs* and Wanda's late work almost seem to be written by two different authors.

Wanda's own account of the conditions under which she wrote does not necessarily contradict accusations of plagiarism:

as I had to stay close to Leopold when he worked, it was better that I also write and earn some money. Each week I wrote a piece for the *Pester Journal,* for a newspaper in Berlin or Hamburg, so that I earned 40 to 60 florins per month.

I did this willingly and would have done it more willingly still if I had been able to write to please myself, but alas—I could not do it. My work also had to please my husband—therefore I had to write "cruel" stories. In order to put myself in an appropriate frame of mind, I had to wear a fur and place a huge dog whip on the table before me. Swelteringly hot in my fur, I would wrack my brain to invent cruel dilemmas. Forced work such as this could be worth nothing—and *was* worth nothing. I was ashamed of writing it and am still ashamed today: the public has the right to judge me unsparingly. (*Confessions,* 87)

Her story confirms the classic masochistic arrangement, as exemplified by Nora's letters to Joyce and Bloom's arrangement with Martha Clifford and the girl in Meath Street. Wanda von Sacher-Masoch suggests that in writing her stories, she was merely going through the motions that her husband prescribed, like the "parrot" in *Ulysses.* "Press the button and the bird will squeak"—or publish.

But to read Wanda von Sacher-Masoch as locked into a marriage from which she gained nothing is to turn the tables and read her as a "masochist"—in the psychoanalytic sense, in which masochism is simply a synonym for femininity. According to the analysis I have suggested of *Ulysses,* there must be some personal gain for the dominatrix in the masochistic scenario. Martha Clifford seems to relish the novelty of exercising power over a man. The "parrot"—the prostitute in Meath Street—was rewarded for her efforts, however disappointing, with an "extra two shillings": an amount, according to Jennifer Levine, that would finance an entire family's rent for two weeks in Dublin in 1904.[56] And as for Wanda von Sacher-Masoch?

Bernard Michel suggests that Wanda von Sacher-Masoch's goal was "to pass from poverty into the petite-bourgeois" by marrying Leopold von Sacher-Masoch, and her own version of her poverty-stricken childhood certainly supports this. Wanda's father abandoned her and her glovemaker mother, leaving them in extreme poverty. When she met Sacher-Masoch, he shepherded her writing into print, provided her with money, and when they began living together, she was able to escape the constant cold and hunger of her childhood. Financially, her relationship with Sacher-Masoch was an immense improvement on her previous lifestyle.

According to Wanda, her first "love contract" with Leopold von Sacher-Masoch, modelled on the contract in *Venus in Furs,*[57] granted her control over their finances, a step which would appear to move toward inversion of traditional gender privileges: "he did not like to take care of money matters, and besides, he found it truly charming to be dependent entirely on me. He wanted to have a signed contract giving me the right to dispose of all his income" (32). The contract, placing the masochistic male protagonist in a "legally" subservient position to the dominatrix, apparently reverses the socially determined roles of men and women as they were defined by nineteenth-century Austrian law and in social practice. Thus it seems that the masochistic contract might, within a limited scope, provide a space that sanctions unconventional behavior for women (and men). This scenario appears to be subversive in imbuing a woman with such sovereignty at a time she was legally and financially disempowered.

The controversy over the nature of the Sacher-Masochs' first contract exemplifies the problems in determining just what powers Wanda actually gained. Wanda's editors maintain that the first contract was a general "love contract" written by Wanda "under Sacher-Masoch's direction" (*Confessions*, 3). Both biographers of Leopold von Sacher-Masoch, Cleugh and Michel, however, maintain that the first contract was drawn up at Wanda's initiative and according to her motives: to secure a husband and financial stability.

Cleugh states that "like the majority of women who marry above their original social level, she [Wanda] desperately feared abandonment and divorce. She resolved to indulge his sexual caprices" (115–16). Cleugh confidently adds that Leopold von Sacher-Masoch's effort to play Pygmalion to Wanda were doomed because "the limits [of] Wanda's intelligence were closed with the rigidity of iron" (186). Clearly, upward mobility and financial security were part of Wanda's interest in securing a relationship to Leopold von Sacher-Masoch. As Aurore Rumelin, she did initiate a correspondence with Sacher-Masoch, about whom she had heard long before, when a friend told her about "the escapades of Sacher-Masoch . . . : 'He needs a woman who will drag him under the yoke— who will chain him up like a dog and kick him when he growls' " (*Confessions*, 10–11). By writing to Sacher-Masoch with this knowledge, and by signing her name after the dominatrix of *Venus in Furs*, Wanda intimated that she shared his enthusiasm for the relationship described in the novel. However, Cleugh's explanation neglects a more obvious motivation for the dominatrix in this scheme in which a man worships a woman and submits fully to her will and desires: the desire for agency and control over her life, however circumscribed. Cleugh and Schlichtegroll both fail to notice that Wanda von Sacher-Masoch went to such great lengths to obtain such limited control because she had so little of it.

Throughout *The Confessions*, Wanda constantly fears Sacher-Masoch will leave her, and he does not hesitate to take advantage of this fear. When she balks at whipping him, he tells her:

If you persist in being stubborn about not satisfying my fantasy, I will not insist, but on the first occasion that arises I will address myself to *another* woman about it, and you can be sure I will meet no resistance. Needless to say, this may eventually result in undesirable consequences for you. (93)

The threats achieve their ends: "This was very shrewd and did not fail in its effect," Wanda recalls. "I had not a shadow of a doubt what would happen if he put himself in the hands of a woman of the character whom he sought. I could count on his putting his threat into action if I continued to avoid my 'duty' " (*Confessions*, 93).

Wanda constantly invokes her subordinate status as a woman under Austrian law to explain her difficulties. She resists fulfilling her husband's plot for her to have an affair with another man because, she says, "the first infidelity that I commit is *legally* a crime against you. You can divorce me, and take my children from me" (*Confessions*, 44). And when she first wants to leave Sacher-Masoch, she is unsure if she has any representation at all under the current laws: "I could perhaps have gone to a court and asked for legal protection against this man; perhaps there was such a law" (*Confessions*, 99). Whether it was originally drafted by Wanda or Leopold, their "love contract" suggests how the masochistic alliance offered to alleviate Wanda's worst fears and fulfill her desire for increased control: "I shall be allowed to exercise the greatest cruelty. . . . You shall kiss the foot that tramples you without a murmur. I shall have the right to dismiss you at any time, but you shall not be allowed to leave me against my will" (*Confessions*, 279).

Given Wanda's account of her life, the clause in the "love contract"— "you shall not be allowed to leave me against my will"—begins to seem more than rhetoric for the benefit of the male masochist. Wanda's *Confessions* casts a new light on Deleuze's observation that "In all Masoch's novels, the woman, although persuaded, is still basically doubting, *as though she were afraid:* she is forced to commit herself to a role to which she may prove inadequate, either by overplaying or by falling short of expectations" (my emphasis, "Coldness and Cruelty," 20). Wanda is afraid, but not because she fears she is not a skilled thespian, but rather because she is afraid of losing the precarious power she has secured through the masochistic contract—a contract, most importantly, that would not hold up in a court of law. The parodic masochistic contract may indeed have offered Wanda a certain degree of freedom and pleasure which was revoked when they entered into the "old rotten institution of marriage," as she puts it. "In uniting myself to him of my own free will a year previously, my heart had felt joyous and easy.... [But now] my life was no longer my own. All that I had been freely willing to give was no longer a present, it was a duty" (*Confessions*, 23). Part of the reason Leopold von Sacher-Masoch found the contracts so "charming" was that they described a whimsical arrangement without any real social repercussions. Relinquishing power, it seems, is the luxury of one who is in no real danger of losing it.

Here it is interesting to consider one of the more complex stories in Wanda's *Ladies in Furs*, "The Animal Tamer" ("Die Tierbändigerin")—a story that doubles back to Amye Reade's *Ruby: Founded on the Life of a Circus Girl* and *Ruby: The Pride of the Ring*. In fact, "The Animal Tamer" seems to *be* what Reade's *Ruby* becomes to Leopold Bloom and to *Ulysses*. This story is, on the surface, the masochist's fantasy par excellence, a dominatrix-authored *Ruby: The Pride of the Ring*—as opposed to Martha Clifford's feeble efforts at epistolary punishment.

Set in Bucharest of 1859, "The Animal Tamer" begins with the arrival of the famous Habsberg Menagerie. Word of mouth soon spreads about the incredible female animal tamer, Herma Dalstrem, "a young Swede, beautiful, noble, daring—and unapproachable" (3). Wanda von Sacher-Masoch's "pride of the ring" possesses a "vestal-like severity and reserve" that "excited the senses of amorous men and the curiosity of everyone." Dashing Prince Maniasko of Bucharest falls in love with Herma from the moment he sees her exercising the lions in their cage:

She cast off the great velvet fur in which she was wrapped with an inimitable, haughty gesture, and, dressed wholly in white satin and red ermine-trimmed velvet, she strode effortlessly and smiling into the cage, a wire whip in her hand. ... The Prince, following her every movement with mounting excitement, was instantly captivated. His heart pounded as she put her beautiful head in the lion's ferocious mouth, and a sweet shudder came over him as she harangued the disobedient beasts with wild shouts, and began to treat them roughly, with kicks and lashes of her whip. (5)

The Prince introduces himself to Herma and she responds to him "not proudly and coldly, as usual, but, on the contrary, self-consciously and with an indescribably winsome smile." He attends her performances every night and they exchange meaningful glances as she steps into the cage to flog the beasts.[58]

Although Herma allows the Prince to hold her furs, "this was all he ever attained . . . and his desire to possess this woman became frenzied" (5). Finally she asks him about the rumors of his engagement, and he admits "it is true, but as soon as you want, that tedious story will end and I will lie at your feet as your slave" (6). They begin to meet in the menagerie at night; here Wanda von Sacher-Masoch's prose trails off euphemistically.

One night the Prince fails to meet Herma or attend her performance, and she does not see him for four days. Edgar, the son of the menagerie owner, tells her that the Prince is preparing to marry in two days. She is furious, and terrifies Edgar with her Medusa-like rage, "with dread in her demonical gaze, surrounded by her red tresses, like fiery snakes, flashing and angry" (8)—a state not unlike the Honourable Mrs. Mervyn Talboys in *Ulysses*, telling Bloom, "You have lashed the dormant tigress in my nature into fury" (382).

Coincidentally, that night the Prince's fiancée demands to be taken to the menagerie to see the famous lion tamer. While Herma is executing a particularly perilous feat, the Prince's fiancée, staring at Herma through her lorgnette, cheers and hurls a gold-filled purse into the cage. A "resentful murmur" goes through the crowd and Herma loses "her control over herself and the beasts." A confused lion suddenly seizes her arm, but Herma recovers: "A stare, a commanding word, and the lion let her arm fall. She sprang up, dragged him by the mane, planted her foot on him, and struck him with her whip; he fell, perfectly subdued, at her feet. Storms of applause and shouts rewarded the courageous woman" (10). Furious at the Prince and his stupid fiancée, Herma sends a letter to him through Edgar. She asks the Prince to meet her at night one last time. When he appears, she leads him through the darkness into the lion cage, where she looses the beasts on him. They tear him to pieces "while she, leaning against the cold bars, feasted her eyes on his terror and agony" (12) (illustration 8:3). Sure enough, as soon as this "tedious story" ends, the Prince is, as he predicted, lying at Herma's feet as the lions "lick and retract their bloody claws" (13). The Prince's death is eerily vivid,

FIG. 8.3 Illustration from Aurora Rümelin [Wanda] von Scher-Mosoch's *Die Damen im Pelz: Geschichten und Novellen.* By permission of Houghton Library, Harvard University.

given the affectless tone of the rest of Wanda von Sacher-Masoch's stories.

Like the circus girl Ruby, Herma is situated in a carnivalesque setting, rather than the palatial or domestic settings of most of the other stories in *Ladies in Furs*, and she performs her routine in the prison-like enclosure of a cage. The narrative itself emphasizes Herma's crossings in and out of the cage ("Kaum hatte die Schwedin den Käfig verlassen," "sobald sie in den Käfig trat"), insisting on the fact that she is performing these tricks in a restricted site, for an audience looking on from outside, scrutinizing her through eyepieces. The end of "The Animal Tamer" is thus particularly striking in that Herma is in an unusual place of spectatorship, outside the cage.

A comparison of two drawings (see illustrations 8.1 and 8.2), the caricature published in the Austrian magazine *Wiener-Figaro* of 1875,[59] and the sketch that accompanies "The Animal Tamer" underscores the differences between Wanda von Sacher-Masoch's role as dominatrix in her marriage and the bloody denouement of "The Animal Tamer." Both portray a tableau of a woman standing, in the upper left-hand corner, over a man, with a whip in her hand. In the former, the man is kneeling on his hands and knees, and in the latter, he is lying down, torn to pieces by lions. Both drawings clearly demarcate two spaces: an "inside," where the male masochist is beaten, and an "outside," from which spectators look on. In the former, the inside tableau is the study of Sacher-Masoch, as evidenced by books and manuscripts titled after his work scattered around. Two men, mustachioed and well dressed, look on through a window in the upper-right hand corner. The cartoon reflects how the Sacher-Masochs' relationship was "observed" and analyzed by the public, readers, and sexologists alike. The dominatrix here is seen as all-powerful, gritting her teeth and lording over the weak, subservient male masochist. In the illustration for Wanda von Sacher-Masoch's story, the main tableau is inside the cage, but unlike the cartoon, the lions are positioned in the place of the dominatrix, while Herma stands outside the cage, looking in — in virtually the same place as the male onlookers in the cartoon.

The illustrations also trace how the gaze — and specifically, the gaze of the reader — functions in the masochistic tableau. The reader appears to be implicated as a voyeuristic spectator in both illustrations 8.2 and 8.3, as a mirror image of the critics and the dominatrix, respectively. However, upon further examination, it appears that the reader is actually positioned in the space of the tableau itself, enclosed within the Sacher-Masochs' study and in the cage with the lions and the Prince. This raises the question of the relationship of the reader to erotic literature, and the nature of "readerly" masochistic pleasure. Recall that although Bloom brings the sadomasochistic books home for Molly,[60] they seem to interest him more than her: an effacement that corresponds to the masochist's classic position of mock-subordination to the dominatrix. Furthermore, Bloom's identification with Ruby—placing himself, through identification, in her place—suggests that "readerly" masochistic pleasure operates through a paradoxical, disavowed identification.

Both drawings reproduce Amye Reade's melodramatic tableau of male domination over a woman but reverse the sex of the participants. "The Animal Tamer" adds a further element. The end of the story and the accompanying drawing suggest the constructed nature of "domination" and "submission" in masochism—that is, their radical contingency on context—and underscore the fact that although the *fantasy* is constructed out of far-reaching sociopolitical concerns, the *performance* itself has a very limited scope. It is no coincidence that the setting of both *Ruby* and "The Animal Tamer" is the circumscribed ring of the circus. The dominatrix may appear to usurp control from the masochist, but this is not necessarily the case if self-effacement is the masochist's ultimate desire.

This reading is emphasized by the polemical preface to *Ladies in Furs*. Wanda von Sacher-Masoch calls for complete legal equality for women, but curiously concludes that

in fact and in secret, women already rule now, and thus there should really be less talk of women's emancipation, and more of men's emancipation.

The woman, who is legally excluded from all rights of men . . . has to avenge herself through cunning and the art of disguise. . . . She easily becomes the tyrant of man . . . making him subservient to her own egoism, abusing him . . . and destroying him. . . . Only the woman who is equal to man in every respect and whose education equals his, will be his loyal, honest and brave comrade.[61]

Wanda von Sacher-Masoch shows the substance and the tenuousness of the link between masochistic fantasy and social reform. She suggests that the power women do possess needs to be reinforced by the legal system, so that it is not a reactive position limited to the realm of the bedroom.

Molly Bloom articulates and interrogates the connection between social reform and masochism in a similarly legislative mode:

I dont care what anybody says itd be much better for the world to be governed by the women in it you wouldnt see women going and killing one another and slaughtering when do you ever see women rolling around drunk like they do or gambling every penny they have and losing it on horses yes because a woman whatever she does she knows where to stop sure they wouldnt be in the world at all only for us. (640)

Thinking about the sadomasochistic novels Bloom is convinced she savors, such as *Ruby: The Pride of the Ring, Fair Tyrants*, and *The Sweets of Sin*, she remarks: "Oh Jamesy let me up out of this pooh sweets of sin whoever suggested that business for women what between clothes and cooking and children this damned old bed" (633). Calling to no less than her very creator, "Jamesy," implicating the author of the masochistic fantasy as well as the reader, Molly is not, however, a helpless Ruby. She introduces her own version of the "reality principle"—menstruation and domestic labor—to the image of the dominatrix, insisting on those persistent corporeal, economic, and quotidian conditions masochistic fantasy seeks to erase.

Ultimately, Bloom also seems to abandon the masochistic pursuit. "Nothing new under the sun. Care of P.O. Dolphin's Barn," he thinks, reciting Martha Clifford's post office box address: "Are you not happy in your? Naughty darling. At Dolphin's barn charades in Luke Doyle's house. . . . So it returns. Think you're escaping and run into yourself. Longest way round is the shortest way home. And just when he and she. Circus horse walking in a ring" (309). Dolphin's Barn is not only Martha's address: it is also where Bloom and Molly first met. Hence, just when you "think you're escaping" you "run into yourself," by way of a repetition compulsion underpinning predictable fetishistic patterns. Bloom's correspondence with Martha now reminds him of the monotony of the bored circus horse (echoing the frightening story of Johnny the mill-horse in Joyce's short story "The Dead"):[62] hardly the spirited "pride of the ring." Bloom himself articulates the shortcomings of masochism in terms of containment, as his vision of the sexualized circus ring is transformed back into the limited, circumscribed ring that Reade originally presented.

Despite this acknowledgement of masochism's limits, at the end of *Ulysses*, after Stephen and Bloom have found each other and have found atonement, they turn to the sadomasochistic novel that Bloom fetches for Molly, *The Sweets of Sin*:

On the penultimate blank page of a book of inferior literary style, entitled *Sweets of Sin* (produced by Bloom and so manipulated that its front cover came in contact with the surface of the table) with a pencil (supplied by Stephen) Stephen wrote . . . Irish characters . . . and Bloom in turn wrote . . . Hebrew characters. (563)

Molly's dismissal of the appeal of masochism for women resonates as two men achieve connection across this pornographic novel, which, like *Ruby: The Pride of the Ring*, Bloom ostensibly obtained to please Molly. (Moreover, "metempsychosis," another term of great resonance in *Ulysses*, appears in "the book about Ruby" [52, 534].) This triangulated desire that strives to write out, and yet depends upon, female agency, functions as masochism does in *Ulysses*, supposedly supporting female autonomy, yet revealing in its own operations just how ephemeral that arrangement is.

More than the static stereotypical masochistic tableau, the ring—a symbolic figure that binds the body to social codes and institutions—is an apt model for thinking about masochism. Just as the circus ring is valorized as a contained or isolated arena for masochistic practices, its contractually drawn boundaries and regulations are inevitably shown to be provisional. Joyce's and Sacher-Masoch's representations of masochistic fantasy protest the restriction of women's rights, only to eroticize and in some senses perpetuate that restriction by effacing the very real inequalities that exist outside the ring. By presenting Ruby the circus girl and Ruby the pride of the ring, Bloom the crusader for women and Bloom the coach of amateur dominatrixes, and Martha Clifford the frustrated secretary and Martha the martinet at the keyboard, Joyce indicates the extent to which even the most personal of pleasures are shaped by political and social consciousness. Even so, the cast of characters in *Ulysses* demonstrates that masochism is ultimately subject to the most ideologically unruly force of all—fantasy.

NOTES

A version of this chapter was presented at the James Joyce and Modern Culture Conference at Brown University (June 15, 1995).

I would like to thank the many readers who generously responded to this paper in its various permutations: D. A. Miller, David Damrosch, Sylvère Lotringer, Michael Seidel, Victoria Rosner, Teri Reynolds, Miranda Sherwin, Anna Brickhouse, and Tim Griffin.

1. *Ulysses: The Corrected Text*, ed. Hans Walter Gabler with Wolfhard Steppe and Claus Melchior (New York: Vintage Books/Random House, 1986), 63. All subsequent references to this work will be included parenthetically in the text.

2. "Coldness and Cruelty" in *Masochism*, tr. Jean McNeil (New York: Zone Books, 1989).

3. Bloom shares the masochistic spotlight with Stephen Dedalus, whose psychology is quite different. Joyce's delineation of two separate masochistic person-

alities conforms to Michelle A. Masse's suggestion in *In the Name of Love: Women, Masochism, and the Gothic* that masochism can have "widely differing functions" (Ithaca: Cornell University Press, 1992), 2. I have chosen to limit my analysis here to Bloom—who is clearly patterned after his namesake, Leopold von Sacher-Masoch—and refer the reader to Carol Seigel's excellent discussion of Stephen, "The Masochist as Exile between Two Goddesses," in *Male Masochism: Modern Revisions of the Story of Love* (Bloomington: Indiana University Press, 1995), 48–76.

4. Mark Schechner's *Joyce in Nighttown: A Psychoanalytic Inquiry into Ulysses* (Berkeley: University of California Press, 1974) is the classic psychoanalytic account of Bloom's masochism, and has been followed by readings like Frances L. Restuccia's "Molly in Furs: Deleuzean/Masochian Masochism in the Writing of James Joyce," which begins from the assumption that masochism was a "weakness that possessed" James Joyce (*Novel: A Forum on Fiction*, vol. 18, no. 2. [Winter 1985]: 101–16). While feminist Joyce critic Suzette Henke, in *James Joyce and the Politics of Desire* (New York: Routledge, 1990), takes issue with the biologistic and cultural assumptions in Freud's work, she also invokes the psychoanalytic model to read *Ulysses*. An important exception is Richard Brown's *James Joyce and Sexuality*, which insists on "the importance of subject-matter in Joyce's fiction" (Cambridge: Cambridge University Press, 1985), 9. Brown also elaborates on how Joyce bases Bloom's masochism on, and parodies, the scientific language of psychoanalysis and sexology. Most recently, Carol Seigel's *Male Masochism* has suggested that what has been called "masochism" for over a century is really a continuation of the tradition of courtly love and male submission to the loved one.

5. Stephen Dedalus's comments in *A Portrait of the Artist as a Young Man* (New York: Penguin Books, 1986), 215, are reinforced by Joyce's own sentiments about the relationship between his art and his politics: most notoriously, "don't talk to me about politics, I'm only interested in style" (Cited in Helene Cixous's *The Exile of James Joyce* [New York: David Lewis, 1972], 203).

6. See, for example, the medical evaluations of Bloom in Nighttown by Dr. Malachi Mulligan, "sex specialist," Dr. Madden, Dr. Crotthers, and Dr. Punch Costello (402, 403), and Richard Brown's commentary.

7. The difficulty of evaluating unconscious impulses contradicting political ideology has always been a problem for feminist theories of sexuality. This question received considerable attention in the late 1970s and early 1980s "pornography debates" and discussions of feminist appropriations of psychoanalysis. See, for example, *Pleasure and Danger*, ed. Carole S. Vance (New York: Pandora/HarperCollins, 1992) and Lis Duggan and Nan D. Hunter's *Sex Wars: Sexual Dissent and Political Culture* (New York: Routledge, 1995).

8. *The Bonds of Love: Psychoanalysis, Feminism, and the Problem of Domination* (New York: Pantheon, 1988).

9. *Male Subjectivity at the Margins* (New York: Routledge, 1992).

10. "How Do You Make Yourself a Body Without Organs?" in *A Thousand Plateaus: Capitalism and Schizophrenia*, tr. Brian Massumi (Minneapolis: University of Minnesota Press, 1987), 149–166.

11. See Bersani's discussion of sadomasochism in *Homos* (Cambridge: Harvard University Press, 1995).

12. Mandy Merck's essay on "The feminist ethics of lesbian S/M" is a useful survey of the progress and problems with feminist work on "the sex wars" (*Perversions* [New York and London: Routledge, 1993], 236–66). Also see Parveen Adams's "Of Female Bondage" in *Between Feminism and Psychoanalysis*, ed. Teresa Brennan (New York: Routledge, 1989), and Julia Creet's "Daughter of the Movement: The Psychodynamics of Lesbian S/M Fantasy" in *differences: A Journal of Feminist Cultural Studies* 3.2 (1991): 135–59.

13. See Pat Califia's "A Secret Side of Lesbian Sexuality" in *Public Sex: The Culture of Radical Sex* (Pittsburgh and San Francisco: Cleis Press, 1994), *Coming to Power* (Boston: Alyson Publications, 1981), "Dialogue with a Dominatrix" by Howard Smith and Cathy Cox in *S and M: Studies in Sadomasochism*, ed. Thomas Weinberg and G. W. Levi Kamel (Buffalo: Prometheus Books, 1983), Bob Flanagan's *Supermasochist* (San Francisco: Re/Search Publication, 1993), essays by Michel de M'Uzan, Francois Peraldi, John Preston, and Jason Klein in *Polysexuality*, ed. Francois Peraldi (New York: Semiotext[e], 1981), and the issue of *Social Text* examining the sex trade, edited by Anne McClintock (no. 37, Winter 1993).

14. Mary Power, "The Discovery of Ruby," *James Joyce Quarterly*, vol. 13, no. 2 (Winter 1981): 115–21. All citations here are taken from the second edition of Reade's novel, *Ruby: Or, How Girls Are Trained for a Circus Life, Founded on Fact* (London: Trischler, 1890).

15. This catalogue follows the text of the 1890 editor of *Ruby*.

16. *Slaves of the Sawdust* features another foreign circus master, Signor Emilio Castelli, whose cruelty is more overt than Signor Enrico. The novel begins with a preface in which Reade counters criticisms of her first book. Interestingly, Reade herself inadvertently introduces a comparison of her book to pornography, asking, "Is it not hypocritical to cry down that which is true, whilst erotic novels with profligate heroes abound in fashionable libraries and adorn the drawing-room, in order that fair and thoughtless women may while away the languid hours?" (London: F. V. White and Co., 1893), vi. In *Slaves of the Sawdust*, the connection between indentured servitude of circus children and race-based slavery is more explicit than in *Ruby*: the second half of the novel is set in South Africa, where the main character's brother is a trader.

17. This illustration appears only in the first edition of *Ruby: A Novel: Founded on the Life of a Circus Girl* (London: Authors' Co-Operative Publishing Company, 1889).

18. Bloom's/Joyce's revision of Reade's Ruby fits into a tradition of such S/M eroticization of the circus, including Djuna Barnes's *Nightwood*, Rachilde's *The Juggler*, Max Ophuls's 1955 film *Lola Montes*, and Angela Carter's novel *Nights at the Circus*.

19. "It was a nun they say invented barbed wire" (127), Bloom ponders. Later his thoughts slip from "Girl friends at school, arms round each other's necks or with ten fingers locked, kissing and whispering secrets about nothing in the convent garden," to "Nuns with whitewashed faces, cool coifs and their rosaries going up and down, vindictive too for what they can't get. Barbed wire," to a

recollection of Martha's last letter, asking him to write (302). Bloom's nun fixation is an interesting conflation of two masochistic themes: erotic pain inflicted by strict women, and imitation of the techniques of the torture of martyrdom. See Silverman's *Male Subjectivity at the Margins* and Theodor Reik's *Masochism in Modern Man*, tr. Margaret H. Beigel and Gertrud M. Kurth (New York: Grove Press, 1962).

20. Reade's Ruby is billed as "the queen of the Equestrian world" (344).

21. Jean Laplanche and Jean-Bertrand Pontalis, "Fantasy and the Origins of Sexuality" in *Formations of Fantasy*, ed. Victor Burgin, James Donald, and Cora Kaplan (London: Routledge, 1986), 3–34.

22. See Richard Ellmann's *James Joyce* (New York: Oxford University Press, 1982) and *Ulysses on the Liffey* (New York: Oxford University Press, 1972) and Don Gifford and Robert J. Seidman's *Ulysses Annotated: Notes of James Joyce's Ulysses*, second edition (Berkeley: University of California Press, 1988).

23. Sources of biographical information on Leopold von Sacher-Masoch include: Cleo Elfi Kore's *Decadence and the Feminine: The Case of Leopold von Sacher-Masoch* (dissertation abstract, Stanford: June 1983), Bernard Michel's *SacherMasoch* (Paris: Editions Robert Laffont, 1989), Wanda von Sacher-Masoch's *Confessions of Wanda Von Sacher-Masoch*, tr. Marian Phillips, Caroline Hebert, and V. Vale (San Francisco: Re/Search Publications, 1990), Carl Felix de Schlichtegroll's *Wanda sans masque et sans fourrure*, ed. Claude Tchou (Paris: Tchou, 1968), and James Cleugh's *The First Masochist: A Biography of Leopold von Sacher-Masoch* (London: Anthony Blond Ltd., 1967).

24. Michel, 31.

25. Cleugh, 158–68.

26. *Utopian Feminism: Women's Movements in Fin-de-Siecle Vienna* (New Haven: Yale University Press, 1992).

27. Although Sacher-Masoch's first wife, Wanda von Sacher-Masoch, accuses her husband of forcing her to play an oppressive role in their marriage, she does mention his public support of women's issues—support she ultimately dismisses as hypocritical (*The Confessions of Wanda von Sacher-Masoch*).

28. Proposals to introduce civil marriage and divorce for Catholics were rejected, and others met with little success. By 1914, Anderson notes, "The only change of consequence was that the illegitimate child was given the same inheritance rights as the legitimate child to its mother's and her relatives' estate" (70).

29. Wanda in *Venus in Furs* (in *Masochism* [New York: Zone Books, 1989], 202).

30. Bloom's first memory of his father, Rudolph Virag, who changed his name to Bloom, was being told about "a retrospective arrangement of migrations and settlements in and between Dublin, London, Florence, Milan, Vienna, Budapest, Szombathely with statements of satisfaction (his grandfather having seen Maria Theresa, empress of Austria, queen of Hungary)" (595). Molly's name—Marion—may also be related to this famous woman who so captured the imagination of Sacher-Masoch.

31. "Amor mit dem Korporalstock" (188) in *Venus and Adonis*, tr. unknown ("Privately printed," 193–?).

32. Sacher-Masoch's "love contracts" are printed in *Masochism* (New York: Zone Books, 1989).

33. Don Gifford's *Ulysses Annotated* remarks on the references to masochistic contracts in the Circe episode: e.g., Bello calls Bloom "bondslave" and demands that he "sign a will and leave us any coin you have" (443); Bloom promises (in a verbal contract) "never to disobey" (433).

34. Freud's formulations of masochism changed considerably over time. In "Three Contributions to the Theory of Sex," Freud proposes that there is no primary masochism, but that it is, rather, "nothing but a continuation of sadism against one's own person" (*The Basic Writings of Sigmund Freud*, tr. and ed. A. Brill [New York: Modern Library, 1938], 553–629). In "A Child is Being Beaten: A Contribution to the Study of the Origins of Sexual Perversions" (1919), Freud outlines the sequence of a beating fantasy in which masochism "is not the manifestation of a primary instinct, but originates from sadism which has been turned around and directed upon the self" (in *Sexuality and the Psychology of Love*, ed. Philip Rieff [New York: Collier Books, 1963], 107–32). In *Beyond the Pleasure Principle* (1920), masochism is presented as a compulsive repetition of a destructive drive corresponding with the death instinct (tr. and ed. James Strachey [New York: W. W. Norton and Company, 1961]). This changes in "The Economic Problem in Masochism" (1924), in which a primary erotogenic masochism is proposed, as well as a later reflexive sadism, which becomes a kind of secondary masochism (*General Psychological Theory: Papers on Metapsychology*, ed. Philip Rieff [New York: Collier Books, 1963], 190–201).

35. *Civilization and Its Discontents*, Standard edition, tr. and ed. James Strachey (New York and London: W. W. Norton and Company, 1989), 84.

36. *The History of Sexuality*, vol. 1, tr. Robert Hurley (New York: Vintage Books, 1980), 45.

37. Letter of August 29, 1904 in *The Letters of James Joyce*, vol. 2, ed. Richard Ellmann (New York: Viking Press, 1966), 48.

38. *Joyce and Feminism* (Bloomington: Indiana University Press, 1984), 62. Scott discusses Joyce's relationship to the Irish Suffragist movement, including Joyce's attitude toward women of Sinn Fein and the Gaelic League, such as Hanna Sheehy-Skeffington, and relates this to Bloom's attitudes about figures like Maud Gonne.

39. Suzette A. Henke suggests that "Bloom, despite a professed interest in social justice, attributes [women's] depression and physical discomfort to menstrual malady rather than a situation of angst" (108).

40. Like Leopold von Sacher-Masoch, Bloom is not just concerned with women's issues; his argument with the Citizen suggests that he sees the world in terms of larger patterns of domination and subjugation. Before he is hit with an airborne biscuit box, Bloom tells Alf: "Force, hatred, history, all that. That's not life for men and women, insult and hatred. And everybody knows that it's the very opposite of that that is really life. . . . Love. I mean the opposite of hatred" (273).

41. Ian Gibson's *The English Vice: Beating, Sex, and Shame in Victorian England and After* discusses a remarkable conjunction of judicial reform and erotic interest in newspaper columns and letters to the editor concerning the practice of corporal

punishment in nineteenth-century England. "One of the more extraordinary features of the English flagellant phenomenon," Gibson writes, "is the extent to which the corporal punishment of children was discussed in the respectable press of the nineteenth century, and the degree to which (while much of the discussion was clearly pornographic) almost all overt reference to the possible sexual implications of the practice was excluded from debate. At the same time the semi-pornographic scandal papers churned out masses of flagellant material which differed only in a slightly greater explicitness from that appearing in 'polite' publications" (London: Duckworth, 1978), 194.

42. These feminists claimed that "only love could make a sexual union moral and condemned a union formed for any other reason" (Anderson, 68).

43. "The Printed Letter in *Ulysses*," *James Joyce Quarterly*, vol. 12, no. 4 (Summer 1982): 415–27.

44. "Woman, the Letter Writer; Man, the Writing Master," *James Joyce Quarterly*, vol. 23, no. 3 (Spring 1986): 299–324, 313.

45. See Richard Ellmann's foreword to *The Selected Letters of James Joyce* (New York: Viking Press, 1975). Further references to Joyce's letters are from this collection.

46. A similar pattern appears in Molly's soliloquy in the final chapter of *Ulysses*. She remarks: "I couldn't think of the word" (624); "a letter with all those words in it" (615); "always the worst word" (613).

47. Henke points out that Molly puts up with, but does not personally share an interest in, Bloom's sexual masochism. She does, however, "secretly take pride" in understanding him so well (145): "course hed never find another woman like me to put up with himt he way I do know" (613). Molly's own fantasy of cruising the docks—"Lord God I was thinking would I go around by the quays there some dark evening where nobodyd know me and pick up a sailor off the sea thatd be hot on for it and not care a pin whose I was only do it off up in a gate somewhere"—has sadomasochistic overtones, as she recalls—"that black-guardlooking fellow with the fine eyes peeling a switch attack me in the dark and ride me up against the wall without a word" (639).

48. See Deleuze, Peraldi, Reik, M'Uzan, and Robert J. Stoller's *Pain and Passion: A Psychoanalyst Explores the World of S & M* (New York: Plenum Press, 1991).

49. Reik's treatment of the dominatrix is typical; she haunts his text *Masochism in Modern Man* in vague allusion—"the figure of the woman on the stage," "a partner who eventually will be sought out in real life" (80), "the spectator or witness" (83), "another person [asked] to bring pain or shame on him" (85), "an instrument on which to play or rather which is supposed to play on the masochist" (252).

50. See "A Secret Side of Lesbian Sexuality" (cited above), as well as interviews in *Skin Two*, ed. Tim Woodward (New York: Masquerade Books, 1993). These are among many, many recently published testimonials about women's involvement in S/M.

51. See Schlichtergroll's *Sacher-Masoch und der Masochismus* (Dresden: 1901) and *Wanda ohne Pelz und Maske* (Leipzig: Leipziger Verlag, G.m.b.H., 1906).

52. *Confessions of Wanda Von Sacher-Masoch*, tr. Marian Philips, Caroline He-bert, and V. Vale (San Francisco: Re/Search Publications, 1990), 102.

53. "Eine Kongressdame," *Die Damen im Pelz: Geschicten und Novellen* (Berlin: Schreiteriche Verlagsbuchbandlung, n.d.), 103. My thanks to Jonathan Skolnik for checking my German translations.

54. "Amor mit dem Korporalstock" in *Venus and Adonis*.

55. All translations from *Nouvelles confessions de Wanda de Sacher-Masoch*, in Carl Felix von Schlichtegroll's *Wanda sans masque et sans fourrure*, ed. Claude Tchou, tr. from German not given (Paris: Tchou, 1968).

56. Address at The James Joyce and Modern Culture Conference, Brown University, June 16, 1995.

57. In *Venus in Furs*, Wanda and Severin draw up a contract that commits him to be her slave, unconditionally, for any period of time she desires: "I want your power over me to become law; then my life will rest in your hands and I shall have no protection whatsoever against you. Ah, what delight to depend entirely on your whims, to be constantly at your beck and call!" Severin enthuses (*Masochism*, 195).

58. Homer's Circe was also a tamer of wild animals, and especially lions. Numerous wild animals appear in the "Circe" episode of *Ulysses*, including a lion. Bloom is associated throughout *Ulysses* with the name "Leo," and Signor Maffei appears in "liontamer's costume and carriagewhip," proclaiming: "bring your lion to heel, no matter how fractious" (371).

59. Frontispiece to Cleugh's biography.

60. Molly sends Bloom out for "smutty" books: "Get another of Paul de Kock's. Nice name he has" (53). He evaluates the choices at the bookstore according to his perception of his wife's literary and erotic taste. He decides that "*Sweets of Sin*" is "More in her [Molly's] line" (194) when he sees it includes a woman in furs who spends her husband's money on her opulent wardrobe (194).

61. "Vorwort," *Die Damen im Pelz*, vii-xi. Once again, the authenticity of Wanda's writing is called into question. The close reader of *Venus in Furs* will recognize this line from Severin's bitter concluding words after Wanda has humil-iated him by bringing in "the Greek" to flog him: "The moral is that woman, as Nature created her and as man up to now has found her attractive, is man's enemy; she can be his slave or his mistress but never his companion. This she can only be when she has the same rights as he and is his equal in education and work" (in *Masochism*, 271).

62. "The Dead" in *Dubliners* (New York: Penguin Books, 1987), 175–223.

Contributors

GAURAV DESAI is Assistant Professor of English at Tulane University. His research interests include twentieth-century African studies, cultural and gender Studies, literary theory, and colonial and postcolonial studies. His articles have appeared in *Research in African Literatures, English Today, African Studies Review*, and *Cultural Critique*, among other places.

LAURA FROST is a Ph.D. candidate in the department of English literature at Columbia University. She is currently working on representations of eroticized fascism in British and French literature.

SANDER L. GILMAN is the Henry R. Luce Professor of the Liberal Arts in Human Biology at the University of Chicago. He holds positions there as Professor of Germanic Studies and Professor of Psychiatry and is a member of the Fishbein Center for the History of Science and the Committee on Jewish Studies. He is a cultural and literary historian and the author of *Picturing Health and Illness* and *Franz Kafka: The Jewish Patient*, among many other books. He is the immediate past president of the Modern Language Association.

NAOMI MORGENSTERN is a lecturer in the department of English at Cornell University where she received her doctorate in American literature. She is currently working on a book-length study of trauma theory and twentieth-century Gothic fiction.

NICOLA PITCHFORD is Assistant Professor of English at Fordham University. She is currently working on a manuscript, *Redefining Postmodernism*, that addresses the potentially fruitful intersections of feminism and postmodernism in Britain and the United States, focusing on strategies of reading in the novels of Kathy Acker and Angela Carter.

ELISSA J. RASHKIN is a doctoral candidate in communication studies at the University of Iowa. She has published essays on gender and national ideology in Latin American, Chinese, and U.S. cinemas, and is presently writing a dissertation on women filmmakers in Mexico.

JAMES SMALLS is Assistant Professor of Art at Rutgers University where he teaches nineteenth-century modern art and twentieth-century African American art. His research focuses on the interrelatedness of race, gender, and sexualities in and on visual representation. He has just completed a book entitled *Esclave, Negre, Noir: The Black Presence in French Art, 1700–1900.*

VICTORIA L. SMITH is Assistant Professor of English at Miami University. She is currently completing a book entitled *Nothing to Lose: Narration as Recuperation in Modern Women's Fiction and Feminist Theory.*

Guidelines for Prospective Contributors

Genders welcomes essays on art, literature, media, photography, film, and social theory. We are especially interested in essays that address theoretical issues relating sexuality and gender to social, political, racial, economic, or stylistic concerns.

All essays that are considered for publication are sent to board members for review. Your name is not included on the manuscript in this process. A decision on the essay is usually reached in about four months. Essays are grouped for publication only after the manuscript has been accepted.

We require that we have first right to any manuscript that we consider and that we have first publication of any manuscript that we accept. We will not consider any manuscript that is already under consideration with another publication or that has already been published.

The recommended length for essays is twenty-five pages of double-spaced text. Essays must be printed in letter-quality type. Quotations in languages other than English must be accompanied by translations. Photocopies of illustrations are sufficient for initial review, but authors should be prepared to supply originals upon request.

Place the title of the essay and your name, address, and telephone number on a separate sheet at the front of the essay. You are welcome to include relevant information about yourself or the essay in a letter to the editor, but please be advised that institutional affiliation does not affect editorial policy. Since the majority of the manuscripts that we receive are photocopies, we do not routinely return submissions. However, if you would like your copy returned, please enclose a self-addressed, stamped envelope.

To submit an essay for consideration, send *three* legible copies to:

Thomas Foster
Genders
Department of English
Ballantine Hall 442
Indiana University
Bloomington, IN 47405

Subscribe to *Genders!*

For nearly a decade, *Genders* has presented innovative theories of gender and sexuality in art, literature, history, music, photography, TV, and film.

Today, *Genders* continues to publish both new and known authors whose work reflects an international movement to redefine the boundaries of traditional doctrines and disciplines.

Since 1994, *Genders* has been published as a biannual anthology, each volume focusing on a particular gender-related issue and offering original essays on the specific theme.

Don't miss the next edition of *Genders*. Subscribe today!

Please enter my subscription for the 1997 issues of *Genders* (2 issues, about 300 pages each) at the cost of $40.50 (shipping and handling are included in the subscription price):

Name _____

Address _____

City _____

State _____ **Zip** _____

I enclose   ❑ check,   ❑ money order (in U.S. dollars),
or please charge by bank card,   ❑ MasterCard   ❑ Visa

Account # _____

Expiration Date _____

Phone _____

Signature _____

Mail to:
New York University Press
70 Washington Square South
New York, NY 10012

Or call:
1-800-996-NYUP (6987)

Or fax:
212-995-3833

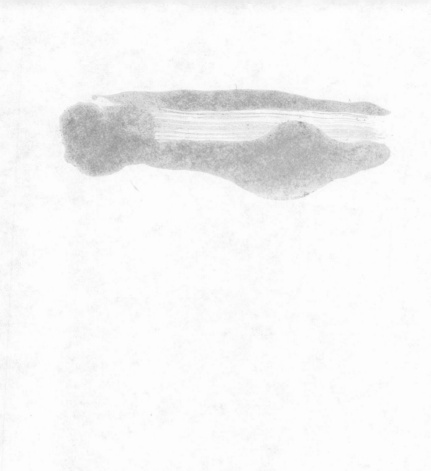